WHAT MAKES

GREAT
LEADERS
GREAT

WHAT MAKES
GREAT
LEADERS
GREAT

MANAGEMENT LESSONS FROM
ICONS WHO CHANGED THE WORLD

FRANK ARNOLD

NEW YORK   CHICAGO   SAN FRANCISCO
LISBON   LONDON   MADRID   MEXICO CITY   MILAN
NEW DELHI   SAN JUAN   SEOUL   SINGAPORE
SYDNEY   TORONTO

Originally published as *Management: Von den Besten lernen,* © 2010 Carl Hanser Verlag Munich, Germany, www.hanser.de. Updated and revised English version: *What Makes Great Leaders Great: Management Lessons from Icons Who Changed the World.* Translation: Rob Gartenberg, Linguanet sprl, Brussels, Belgium, www.linguanet.be, and Frank Arnold, ARNOLD Management GmbH, Zurich, Switzerland, www.arnoldmanagement.com.

Illustrations: Silke Bachmann, illustratoren.de/Silke Bachmann

1 2 3 4 5 6 7 8 9 0   QFR/QFR   1 6 5 4 3 2 1

ISBN: 978-0-07-177051-4
MHID: 0-07-177051-8

e-ISBN: 978-0-07-177211-2
e-MHID: 0-07-177211-1

In memoriam

Peter F. Drucker

(1909–2005)

CONTENTS

PART 2 MANAGING INNOVATION

PART 3 MANAGING PEOPLE

PREFACE

Management is one of the most fascinating—and useful—disciplines there is. In fact, the success of *people, organizations,* and *societies* crucially hinges on effective management, and knowledge and skills in this area directly impact on performance and results. The achievements of great icons in all domains of society show just how strong the influence exerted by management knowledge can be. Such individuals can teach us a great deal about how to apply management skills to our own lives. Regardless of the domain in which *you* wish to achieve your goals, one thing is certain: management know-how will be an essential prerequisite for attaining them. As the many different examples set out in this book show, management know-how is *not* just applicable and essential to business. Human beings who are successful in a huge range of domains have used such knowledge, often unknowingly. This book tells you which areas need your attention if you are interested in *being effective* and *achieving lasting success.*

What Makes Great Leaders Great: Management Lessons from Icons Who Changed the World sets out to convey *effective* management in a simple and entertaining manner. It makes fairly complex material not only readily understandable but, more importantly, easy to apply in your own life. In this respect, it is a *practice-based manual* that is itself *designed to be put to practical use.* Reading it will enable you to successfully apply management skills and attain your goals.

The numerous examples provided in the book will help you remember what you need to bear in mind when applying management know-how. At the same time they also illustrate how creatively and effectively management skills can be applied. If you adopt the mind-set advocated in this book, you will very quickly find many more examples of the practical application of insights into management. Management skills are applied in all social domains, including art, music, culture, sport, medicine, the military, science, politics, and of course business. Indeed, management know-how is invaluable whenever people are intent on performing well and achieving results. And while different disciplines require distinct *expertise*, the *management know-how* applying to all of them remains universally applicable.

This compact, entertaining, and practical book both presents the key elements needed for organizations to be managed effectively and provides a wealth of tips on the practical application of *effective management*. Offering an overview of prominent issues covering the entire spectrum of management, it breaks them down into three core areas, namely:

- Managing organizations
- Managing innovation
- Managing people

In many instances it would have been easier to write far more extensively rather than to focus on limited aspects, but certain choices had to be made to enable the book to cover the widest possible range of examples and topics in a way that is both absorbingly instructive and geared toward practical application. In this respect, the many facets of management covered in the book's individual chapters combine like the pieces of a mosaic to form an overall picture of what effective management entails and what you need to bear in mind when applying its methods.

If this book kindles your interest in finding out more about effective management, it will probably end up doing more for you than you can presently imagine. If you consistently apply the management insights discussed on these pages, you will become exceedingly *effective* and highly *efficient*—and probably extremely *successful* as well.

I would like to thank everyone who directly or indirectly contributed to this book, but first and foremost my three most important teachers:

- Professor Hermann Simon, who taught at the university I attended, for it was he who aroused in me a strong desire to gain a profound understanding of management.
- Professor Fredmund Malik, who provided me with countless valuable insights. During the five years and more in his employ, including two years as head of one of his company's divisions, I gained invaluable experience in the practice of management.
- Professor Peter F. Drucker, whose ideas and works truly unlocked the fascinating world of management to me.

My views on effective management are based primarily on their works and on those of others management thinkers listed in the bibliography.

I also owe a huge debt of gratitude to the many managers with whom I have had the privilege of talking and working; they have taught me a tremendous amount.

Particular thanks are due to Helmut Hilgers for his invaluable advice, help, and support in so many ways.

Furthermore, I would like to thank the following for their invaluable advice and support: Professor Klaus Evard, Dr. Helmut Maucher, Fred B. Irwin, Dr. Josef Ackerman, Dr. Friedhelm Plogmann, Claus Seibel, Professor Wolfgang Mewes, Dr. Kerstin Friedrich, Professor Lothar Seiwert, Professor Herbert Kargl, Professor Klaus Breuer, Willy Pfister,

Dr. Gunter Nittbaur, Klauspeter Nüesch, Silke Bachmann, Martin Janik, Dr. Hermann Riedel, Jim and Kathy Aceto, John Harris, Mark Walker, and Christoph Evard.

I would also like to thank Britta Kroker for our precious discussions on the original concept for the book and Evelyn Boos for her inestimable assistance in critically reviewing the German manuscript and suggesting numerous improvements.

In addition, I am most grateful to Rob Gartenberg for cooperating so diligently and constantly aspiring to excellence in the translation of this book.

Thanks, too, to Philip R. Ruppel and Knox Huston at McGraw-Hill Professional for their support and unfailing cooperation.

Extra-special thanks are owed to my family, especially my wife Isabel, who with our two children Julius and Valérie, makes family life a source of great strength and joy. Without her unwavering support this book, *What Makes Great Leaders Great*, would quite simply never have seen the light of day. Last, but not least, I am deeply indebted to my father Klaus and mother Gunhild for their tremendous support.

Frank Arnold
New York, N.Y.
July 4, 2011

INTRODUCTION

When I was writing this book, I wanted it to appeal not only to experienced managers but also to many people who would normally never consider picking up a book on management.

Once you delve deeper into management and start taking a serious interest in it, it becomes one of the most fascinating subjects there is. The many useful and directly applicable tips and suggestions contained in this book, if diligently applied, should *ease or speed up your path to success*. So if the successes you go on to achieve inspire you to take a keener interest in effective management, this book will have fulfilled one of its main objectives.

Management know-how is the key to success. Having it means *knowing how to succeed*. This tried-and-tested body of knowledge is what all human beings—not just managers—need in order to perform well, achieve results, win acclaim, and in rare instances actually attain greatness.

People who read this book will gain a fuller appreciation of individual icons' impact on their organization or society. In so doing, they will have appropriated its core message: that *management know-how is the key to success for individuals, organizations, and societies.*

Success can be learned
Success comes to those who set and attain goals. Whoever commands

management know-how can succeed, in any discipline, by combining their *skills, expertise,* and *specialist knowledge* to perform effectively and achieve their goals.

This is good news because it means that *success can be learned. Anyone* who works for an organization needs at least *some* management know-how, as this is what determines individual effectiveness and efficiency and therefore determines the success of organizations and societies, too.

This is particularly apparent from the achievements of great icons, because it was their effective application of such know-how that enabled them to make a powerful impact on their area of activity, projects, or organizations. *Organizations* that make sure their staff members have management know-how have a clear competitive edge over others that fail to harness such knowledge. Such organizations not only boost their level of performance but at the same time minimize their risks. Bearing in mind these times of constant, rapid change, the value of both these advantages simply cannot be overestimated.

Management know-how not only makes *individuals and organizations* more effective and efficient, but it also helps to stabilize *society.* In a modern society, practically all social tasks are fulfilled within and by organizations, making modern society *a society of organizations.* Organizations are not ends in themselves, but they fulfill certain social tasks in a bid to make a tangible contribution that benefits individuals and society as a whole. Effective, efficient, and responsible management produces strong and healthy organizations whose achievements help to underpin society's stability. Accordingly, modern society needs to take the greatest possible interest in competent management.

Success can be learned, because anyone can learn how to set and attain goals. Management know-how is the body of knowledge required to do this, providing the means to harness your *skills* and the *expertise* required to achieve specific results. This know-how is something you can fall back on anytime, anywhere, when working alone or in a team, for a small organization or a huge conglomerate. Moreover, it is well-founded, substantiated, tried and tested, and—most importantly of all—effective. Management know-how and its skillful application can prove effective in a far wider range of situations than most people imagine. I reiterate: *Management know-how is the key to success for individuals, organizations, and societies.*

What makes great leaders great

Spotlighting key aspects of the achievements of icons from all kinds of social domains clearly shows just how widely and effectively management know-how can be used to attain specific objectives. The examples presented in this book underpin this assertion by demonstrating that management know-how is not only rife—or indeed useful or essential—in a *business* context. Many icons active in very different walks of life have utilized such knowledge, in some cases instinctively, unaware that in doing so, they were actually applying management know-how. Accordingly, icons can teach us a great deal about how we, too, can effectively apply management know-how, even though they would never describe themselves as managers.

Even as a youngster, I was always interested in biographies, fascinated by how people came to achieve what they did, how they became successful, what lessons could be learned from their choices, and how some of those lessons could be applied in my own life. Then at some stage it dawned on me that what linked my interests in management and the lives and achievements of famous people—what biographies revealed about how individuals had achieved greatness—largely concerned the effective application of management know-how.

This made everything fall into place: while management know-how may most clearly come into its own in running an organization, the knowledge underlying it is actually applied *everywhere*, whenever people perform, achieve results, or attain goals. This is why having management know-how means knowing how to succeed.

Anyone, then, who tries to pin down what *effective management* entails will stand a better chance of succeeding, not only in his career, but far beyond his professional life as well.

Management know-how versus expertise and specialist knowledge

That said, far too few people are aware of the vital distinction between *management know-how,* on the one hand, and *expertise and specialist knowledge,* on the other.

Every discipline has its specific expertise and specialist knowledge. Art, music, culture, sports, medicine, military activities, science, administration, education and training, politics, and naturally business, too, all require totally different types of proficiency and skills if the people active in these domains are to *gain expertise and display specialist knowledge.* Even within these various disciplines, the degree of expertise and specialist knowledge required for the execution of different tasks can vary tremendously. This is worth underlining because of the distinction between such expertise and specialist knowledge on the one hand and management know-how on the other. Moreover, while there is a healthy widespread tendency to spotlight the importance of expertise and specialist knowledge, the importance of management know-how is often grossly underestimated. Both are important, of course, but management know-how is the *engine that drives the application of expertise and specialist knowledge* and directs individuals, organizations, and societies to attain their goals and enjoy success.

What relatively few people realize is that whereas expertise and specialist knowledge *differ* substantially from one discipline to another, the *same* management know-how is needed to perform well and achieve results in *all* areas. So required *expertise and specialist knowledge* differ, but *management know-how* does not.

This distinction is of quite fundamental importance because it tells us that people never achieve success *solely* on the basis of expertise and specialist knowledge. Rather, they must also know how to translate that expertise and specialist knowledge into *performance* and *tangible results*. This entails knowing how to attain *goals* and achieve success. And doing this requires *management know-how*.

By the same token, excellent *management know-how* alone is not enough, and the relevant expertise and specialist knowledge is a prerequisite for success. In other words, truly competent, effective managers will always have profound management know-how as well as extensive expertise and specialist knowledge because both are needed to *perform effectively* and *achieve results*. In fact, they are two sides of the same coin, necessarily complementing each other.

There are three main areas of *effective management*:

- Managing organizations
- Managing innovation
- Managing people

Naturally, not everyone working for an organization who wants to be effective in it will need the same degree or depth of management know-how, so suitable judgment and a sense of proportion are called for. Indeed, depending on the tasks, duties, and responsibilities assigned to people, they will need differing degrees of both management know-how and expertise and specialist knowledge. Yet this much is clear: if they lack *management know-how*, they will not perform well or achieve results, just as success will elude them if they lack *expertise and specialist knowledge in their respective domains*. Figure I-1 illustrates this interdependence.

■　　■　　■

	DOMAIN OF EXPERTISE OR SPECIALIST KNOWLEDGE									
		ART	MUSIC	CULTURE	SPORTS	MEDICINE	MILITARY	SCIENCE	EDUCATION & TRAINING	POLITICS	ECONOMICS
MANAGEMENT KNOW-HOW	**MANAGING ORGANIZATIONS**										
	MANAGING INNOVATIONS										
	MANAGING PEOPLE										

FIGURE I-1: The relationship between management know-how and expertise or specialist knowledge

How to read this book

Feel free to use this book in whatever way gives you pleasure and arouses your interest. You can either start at the beginning and work your way through it or jump in wherever your fancy takes you, starting with a person or topic of particular interest to you. Each chapter forms a self-contained unit imparting key lessons and tips about effective management. If you systematically take up the questions and points raised at the end of each chapter, you will very soon start to achieve tangible results, improving your effectiveness and efficiency as a manager.

The book is divided into three parts, each covering an area to be mastered by anyone managing an organization.

First, *managing organizations*, covering aspects of management of central importance to the functioning of organizations.

Second, *managing innovation*, which to a certain extent, intersects with both the other parts: managing organizations and managing people. In other words, rather than being a separate factor, innovation comes into play when managing both organizations and people. The ability to innovate is a core skill needed by any organization.

Third, *managing people*, which entails both *managing others* and *managing oneself*.

Measures taken to make people more effective also have an impact on the other two areas, in the same way that how an organization is managed will affect the management of innovation and people. This is only logical, since managing an organization actually entails *managing a group of people*, and people management is actually all about *managing people within an organization*.

The advantage of this situation is this: if you systematically establish effective management in one area, there will be a positive effect on both the other areas. The disadvantage is that neglecting one area will have undesirable consequences in the others.

So neglecting to manage effectively poses a major risk, while diligently practicing effective management will open up extensive new vistas.

Let me now conclude by making a few remarks about the people featured in this book.

The featured icons were deliberately chosen for being famous and for covering a wide range of different social domains. Where there were alternatives, I always opted for the individual who seemed to provide the clearest, most memorable example.

It is also important to stress that no individual ever "represents" a single topic. Throughout the book I present situations that highlight a certain aspect of management particularly clearly, in many cases precisely the aspect that significantly shaped the life of the individual in question. However, this does not mean that the respective person *always* behaved that way. Many great icons have (or had) equally pronounced weaknesses—extreme individuals often display character traits at both ends of the spectrum. But I deliberately decided not to present any such shortcomings because it is very easy to list people's *in*capabilities. However, it is far more important to *recognize* their strengths and then make proper *use* of them. So this book consciously focuses on people's strengths and shows what we can all *learn* from them. This not only gives the book a positive slant but also focuses the reader on essentials, like *opportunities* and *effectiveness*. After all, if people are properly deployed, their weaknesses will never come to the fore anyway.

I hope that the book's subject matter and the many examples make for a fascinating and entertaining voyage into the world of management—and provide you with many practical pointers for your *effective* implementation of the insights showcased on these pages.

PART 1

MANAGING
Organizations

CHAPTER **1**

Harness the Power

of a Business

Mission

LEARNING FROM

Bill Gates

"Our Mission: At Microsoft, our mission and values are to help people and businesses throughout the world realize their full potential. . . .

Our Values: As a company, and as individuals, we value integrity, honesty, openness, personal excellence, constructive self-criticism, continual self-improvement, and mutual respect. We are committed to our customers and partners and have a passion for technology. We take on big challenges, and pride ourselves on seeing them through. We hold ourselves accountable to our customers, shareholders, partners, and employees by honoring our commitments, providing results, and striving for the highest quality."[1]

These are Microsoft's business mission and values today. When Microsoft was founded in 1975, it also had a business mission that took the company pretty far: "*A computer on every desk and in every home. . . .*"[2] The foundations for Microsoft's meteoric rise were laid in 1981,

3

when *Bill Gates* (born in 1955) licensed IBM to use his MS-DOS operating system. A decisive element for Microsoft's future success was the contractual clause stating that only Microsoft was entitled to license third parties wishing to use the operating system. It is definitely no exaggeration to describe that decision by Bill Gates as one of the best management decisions ever made. Even the attempt to pull it off was a bold and truly brilliant gambit because at the time Microsoft was a relatively small, unknown software company from Seattle, whereas its partner, IBM, was the most powerful giant in the computer sector. The audacity shown by Bill Gates and his then business partner, Paul Allen, to secure for themselves exclusive rights to re-award licenses for their software, indicates just how farsighted their approach was.

They saw clearly something that IBM had evidently overlooked, namely that the computer sector was about to undergo a fundamental change. And in that change, software, rather than hardware as in the past, would become decisive from the *consumers'* point of view. By winning IBM as a partner, Gates succeeded in imposing a universally applicable standard for software applications. MS-DOS was duly installed on every PC supplied by IBM, giving Microsoft a huge market share within a very short space of time. And the introduction of Windows 3 merely added to that momentum. As more and more suppliers of hardware forced their way into the PC market, they too used Microsoft's operating system. In other words, for Bill Gates harnessing the might of IBM was the most direct way of realizing his dream and fulfilling Microsoft's business mission.

An effective *business mission*[3] undoubtedly indicates that the organization in question has very clearly understood what its business is all about. To achieve that, it must acquire a profound understanding in three areas—*needs*, *strengths*, and *convictions*—and base its actions on certain assumptions.

Taking *needs* first of all, an *understanding* of the respective *needs* and *context* can be gained by asking the following questions: *Who is our customer? Who should be our customer? What does our customer pay us for? What does the customer gain from us?* But also: *Who is not a customer of ours and why not?* Of course, answering these questions is anything but easy. More to the point, the answers themselves are far from obvious. In fact, it is only by discussing *differences of opinion* about those answers that an understanding can be reached and which people in an organization can then duly share and sustain.

The second essential building block of a business mission entails *understanding your own strengths and core skills.* The questions to be answered here are: *What can we do better than anyone else? Where do we outperform others by at least a little bit? In which domain might we even be a market leader?* The answers point to strengths the company can build on and also identify domains in which positive results can be achieved. At the same time, though, they indicate which strengths need to be consolidated to attain—or retain—a leading position and also highlight any areas where there is need for improvement. Moreover, these same answers spotlight any weaknesses that may currently be preventing the organization from fulfilling its potential.

The third component of a business mission is about *understanding people's convictions and recognizing what the organization deems to make sense.* The questions to address here are: *Why is it important for the market that we do this? To which cause or task do we want to commit? Why does what we do make sense? What makes it worthwhile? Which values do we wish to embrace as guiding principles?*

Systematically deliberating and working through the three building blocks presented above can help to prevent an organization from defining its business mission only superficially or inaccurately. Whether the outcome of those deliberations can be neatly summed up in an elegant slogan is of secondary importance. If it can, great, though this is by no means essential. Instead, the main aim should be to gain a clear view of what the organization in question is all about. For this reason, you will be better off carefully formulating a few clear sentences that prove to be effective and of practical use rather than using an impressive, but ineffectual slogan. In other words, what counts is *craftsmanship*, not *showmanship*.

On closer inspection, the version of Microsoft's old business mission from 1975 cited above is not even complete, because in full it read: "*A computer on every desk and in every home, running Microsoft software.*" Adding that brief final phrase makes a big difference, and even Bill Gates himself could have had no inkling that one day his dream would be fulfilled and lead his company to success. We can only wish him similar success in his current work in the *Bill & Melinda Gates Foundation*, which helps people lead healthy, productive lives.

ACTION POINTS AND FOOD FOR THOUGHT

- Does your organization have a clear business mission? Is everyone aware of it? Does everyone practice it? If not, what can you do to prompt serious, extensive discussion of the three building blocks of an effective business mission?
- What can you do to ensure that your organization's business mission is actually implemented? What results do you plan to achieve within the next six months? Who can help you achieve them?

CHAPTER **2**

Create Customer Value

LEARNING FROM

Lou Gerstner

Former IBM CEO *Lou Gerstner* (born in 1942) is said to have been one of the best managers of his generation. Many people rank him alongside Jack Welch, Bill Gates, or Andy Grove. And a look at what Gerstner achieved at IBM, where he masterfully engineered one of the most stunning turnarounds in business history, more than justifies the claim that he genuinely earned his place in such illustrious company. The major lesson to learn from him is how important it is to focus a business totally on generating *customer value.*

In 1993, IBM was in a bad way—such a bad way, in fact, that Intel CEO Andy Grove struggled to find words to sum it up: *"It's hard to describe how beaten down that company was."*[1] The computer giant, leader in its industry at the time, had previously reported what was at the time the biggest-ever annual loss posted by a company: $8.1 billion. Then, in April 1993, Lou Gerstner was appointed CEO of IBM. One of his first— and most important—decisions was not to implement the plan drawn up by his predecessor John Akers, which would have carved up IBM into smaller units. Instead, Gerstner opted to keep the giant intact and derive the greatest possible competitive advantage from the company's wide range of products, services, and know-how. One of the biggest changes made by Gerstner at IBM was that from that time on, the company *uncompromisingly focused on customers and customer value:* As Gerstner himself explained: *"In the spring of 1993, a big part of what I had to do was get the company refocused on the marketplace as the only valid measure of success. I started telling virtually every audience . . . that there was a customer running IBM, and that we were going to rebuild the company from the customer back."*[2]

Lou Gerstner's decision to reintroduce such *an uncompromising focus on customer orientation* and make IBM once again concentrate on generating *customer value* proved vital to the company's successful comeback. His extensive rationalization program, which initially entailed cutting costs, banked on a fundamental strategic change of tack, shifting the emphasis primarily onto service provision and concentrating on the Internet. His massive *investments in research and development* sent out an unmistakable message that IBM was really serious about meeting customers' requirements. The path he chose to take to put the spotlight firmly back on *customer value* and *meeting customers' needs and requirements* applied a principle that Thomas Watson, Sr., who for decades called the shots at IBM, would have been proud of. Watson had always made generating customer value his top priority. Consequently, Lou Gerstner's biggest achievement may well have been that he reminded IBM that it was IBM, reiterating the true essence of what the company was actually all about. Gerstner's highly readable book *Who Says Elephants Can't Dance?* gloriously illustrates that some elephants *can* indeed dance.

As the highly influential management thinker Peter F. Drucker put it in his seminal 1954 book *The Practice of Management:* *"There is only one valid definition of business purpose: to create a customer."*[3] Ever since, this valuable nugget of knowledge has been available to everyone, yet most people are either unaware of it or simply allow it to slip their mind. Customers are the foundations on which everything has to be built because they secure the company's existence and safeguard jobs. German billionaire manufacturer Reinhold Würth perfectly summed this up by saying: *"It's my customers, not me, who employ my staff."*[4] If only more company bosses adopted this attitude toward their customers! And Würth speaks from experience, having turned the Würth Group into a global market leader with some 60,000 employees on its payroll.

So the question you need to begin with is this: *What does your customer regard as value?* This question is far too seldom asked, often because top executives believe the answer is clear, whereas in actual fact the conclusion reached *inside* a company is more often wrong than right. Instead of trying to *guess* the correct answer, managers should instead *work out* a viable response by regularly *talking* with their customers and at the same time *closely monitoring* what they actually buy. After all, customers will often *say* one thing, but actually go on to *do* something completely different. Lou Gerstner and other leading CEOs used to regularly spend substantial amounts of their time interacting directly with their customers. Gerstner led by example, which is why he chose not to delegate this task.

The only way Gerstner could see of fulfilling his aim of creating a company obsessed with generating customer value was, as he put it, to *"look at technology through the eyes of the customer."*[5] Doing that necessitates maintaining highly intensive relations with customers and dealing with their problems and wishes in the greatest possible depth. It was for this same reason that Alfred P. Sloan, the legendary CEO and chairman of the board of General Motors, used to serve as a lowly car salesman several times a year.

The above-mentioned Würth Group, too, sets standards around the world for its intensive contacts with customers and systematic dialogue with its target group. Essentially, customers never buy products or services, but rather the *value* they derive from them. It is crucial to understand this value, not only to target marketing effectively and systematically innovate, but also to decide which activities and product features can be dispensed with. *Customers see no loss in doing without something that does not create value for them.* It is important to understand this because saving these costs frees up resources that can then be deployed to deliver genuine value to customers.

In addition, it is becoming increasingly important to understand what *noncustomers* deem to be of value. Even when companies enjoy such a dominant position in their market, as IBM did in the mainframe and PC sectors, there are still vast swaths of the market that elude them (and let us not forget that the towering dominance of IBM was actually something pretty exceptional). For a company to acquire a 30 percent market share is a major entrepreneurial achievement, but it also means that 70 percent of customers are buying elsewhere. Why? *What do noncustomers regard as value?* You need to understand these noncustomers, because it is always changes starting with *them* that have a lasting impact on your sector.

Lou Gerstner once brilliantly summed up the required approach by saying: *"IBM is a solutions company. We start with a customer's business problem, and work back to the right combination of technologies and expertise."*[6] Is there any better way of living up to Peter F. Drucker's definition of business purpose, as cited earlier in this chapter?

ACTION POINTS AND FOOD FOR THOUGHT

- What does your customer regard as value? What can you do to gain a closer understanding of your customers and their views on perceived benefits?

- What do noncustomers regard as value? What will you do to ensure that you understand your noncustomers better in the future?

- What will you do to launch an intensive debate about these issues within your organization? And which results are to be achieved within the next three months?

CHAPTER **3**

Make Effective
Decisions

L E A R N I N G   F R O M

Alfred P. Sloan Jr.

Alfred P. Sloan Jr. (1875–1966) is one of those managers who can be said, with certainty, to have transformed the world of management. From 1923 to 1946 Sloan was CEO of General Motors, and from 1937 to 1956 he chaired the company's board. Under his 33-year stewardship, GM managed to expand massively, and it steadily built up its market share. In Sloan's day his analytical powers, his grasp of the problems of running a business, his farsightedness, and his exceptional judgment were all viewed as key contributors to the success and growth of GM and were considered largely responsible for the headway the automotive giant made under his leadership. That appraisal still stands today. From Sloan we can learn how to make effective decisions.

Fundamental decisions by the top management at General Motors were invariably preceded by extensive discussions. One time, however, a particular motion had been so well prepared that everybody in the room supported it. Sloan was also expected to back it, but instead he said: *"Gentlemen, I take it we are all in complete agreement on the decision here."* Everybody sitting around the table nodded their assent. *"Then I propose we postpone further discussion of this matter until our next meeting to give ourselves time to develop disagreement and perhaps gain some understanding of what the decision is all about."*[1]

You do *not* make the right decisions by reaching a *consensus* as swiftly as possible. Rather, you arrive at correct, effective decisions by deliberately creating *differences of opinion* and using *dissent* to the company's advantage. This is precisely what Alfred P. Sloan did—systematically. *Organizing dissent and reaching a consensus by talking through the various pros and cons* is the ground rule for making correct, effective decisions. Preconditions for this include adopting differing viewpoints, weighing things up differently, and then engaging in an intensive dialogue. This lays the foundations for finding better alternatives as well as for establishing a consensus that is solid enough to withstand any problems arising during the practical implementation phase.

Of course, there is a great deal more to learn about making effective decisions, which is a key task for managers. It is not their *sole* task, but it is a specific one that *only* managers perform. In other words, anyone who makes decisions *is*, by definition, a manager.

Effective managers expect any decisions they make to be good and to achieve the desired result. To this end, they discipline themselves to adhere to a fixed decision-making procedure comprising the following clearly defined steps[2]:

1. Recognize and define the problem.
2. Set the specifications that the decision must meet.
3. Define what is right.
4. Work out alternatives, use dissent, and exploit the insights gained from differences of opinion.
5. Decide to build actual implementation into the decision.
6. Gather feedback and follow up systematically.

1. Recognize and define the problem

This first step entails carefully thinking through the following question: *What is the actual issue here?* If this question is just superficially glossed over, mistakes are bound to follow. There is only one way of making sure that a problem has been properly defined: *Constantly test the definition of the problem against all available facts.* (For more on this topic, see Chapter 4 on M.C. Escher.)

When defining the problem, the main issue to clarify is what type of problem you are facing. Is it a generic event or a unique event? *Generic events* require *decisions of principle.* In other words, a rule, principle, or corporate policy guideline needs to be defined that stipulates the procedure to follow when faced with the generic event in question. By contrast, *unique events* call for *tailor-made solutions,* because the problem in question will probably never reoccur. Since decisions of principle are more momentous than responses to unique problems, correspondingly greater care and more time should be spent on making them. Yet when unique events occur, pragmatic (and often improvised) solutions can usually be applied. If no such distinction between generic and unique problems is drawn, the approach taken in attempting to resolve the difficulty will be wrong, with all the corresponding negative consequences.

2. Set the specifications that the decision must meet

This second step entails asking the following questions:

- What objectives does the decision have to attain?
- What are the minimum objectives to be achieved?
- Which specifications need to be fulfilled?
- What is the very least that is required to solve this particular problem?

Accordingly, setting specifications does *not* entail stating a desired *maximum,* but rather stipulating the *required minimum.* This minimum must be attained if the decision is to be effective. Otherwise the decision will not fulfill its purpose.

3. Define what is right

The basis for any decision must be the question: *What would be right?* Until that has been clarified, you cannot distinguish between a *right* and a *wrong* compromise. Starting off by asking this question may not guarantee that correct decisions will follow, but if you do *not* begin with it, you can be almost certain that your decision will be wrong.

It goes without saying that the issue of *what is right* is distinct from the question of *who is in the right*.

4. Work out alternatives, use dissent, and exploit the insights from differences of opinion

Seeing alternatives is a prerequisite for making any decision. If a single solution is all there is, instead of actually deciding anything, you will merely be confirming a single, given option, not making an active choice. So insist on exploring alternatives in any scenario in which a decision is required, regardless of how plausible, worthy of support, or promising these alternatives may appear. Constantly force yourself and your colleagues to work on decent alternatives because there are always more alternatives than appear at first sight. Remember, too, that one alternative is to leave things as they are, so do not let yourself be coerced into changing something if, after careful consideration, maintaining the status quo seems to be the best decision at the time.

This step also necessitates thoroughly thinking through the *risks and consequences* of each alternative, which entails a lot of work but is absolutely essential. Try asking yourself these questions:

- For how long will this alternative tie us down?
- To what extent is it reversible and how easy is it to correct?
- What risks are associated with it?
- If a potential threat becomes a reality, what kind of situation will we be facing?
- Can we afford to run the risk of this happening in the first place, even if you believe it is highly unlikely?
- On which assumptions and premises is our thinking based?
- What would have to happen to make us accept that this line of

thinking had been wrong and that the decision needs fundamental reconsideration?

Write down those assumptions and premises—some people call them *boundary conditions*—so that you can see when they have been disproved and then review the decision in light of fresh circumstances.

5. Decide to build actual implementation into the decision

Who does what by when? A decision can truly be said to have been made only when essential measures have been identified, once responsibility for their implementation has been assigned, and after deadlines have been set. Any decision that lacks a concrete *action plan* is effectively nothing more than a hope. Consequently, a decision will have no impact until its implementation has been set out in a plan of action. Most action plans will comprise just a handful of key measures. These measures, which are all the more essential for being few in number, should be directly and fundamentally relevant to the issue at the core of the decision, as determined by the decision maker.

The details will then be filled in by the designated manager and the associated team. So usually the people who actually make the decisions will not be responsible for implementing them in detail. As a result, if you are a decision maker who *is* interested in the practical implementation of your decisions and want them to achieve the desired results, you should specify the relevant key measures required to make this happen. Clarity about what the designated manager needs to know and be capable of achieving and about what authority that individual will need to effectively implement a decision is also vital.

Other essential questions about implementation are: *Whom do we need to involve in the implementation of our decision? Who needs to be told about it? What needs to be done to guarantee support for the decision's implementation and to ensure proper understanding of it? And* finally, *how can we control and guide the implementation of our decision?*

6. Gather feedback and follow up systematically

The sixth step involves monitoring the decision's implementation until the desired outcome has been achieved. Decision makers should always make sure that they receive regular, in-depth reports. If at all possible, go and see for yourself what progress is being made in the implementation of your decisions, what impact they have had, and which difficulties have been encountered.

Specific deadlines of action plans should be reimposed until your decision has been effectively implemented. So regularly follow up on measures and make sure there is enough time for implementation to be successful. Effective managers will also regularly inform all those who are affected by, or who contribute to, a decision's implementation about the current situation and any headway made. Any successful progress you can report will not only motivate everyone involved, but will also generate confidence in management's professionalism.

If, after what you have read above about Alfred P. Sloan, you would like to know more, you may be interested to hear what Bill Gates wrote about Sloan's book: *"I think Alfred Sloan's* My Years with General Motors *is probably the best book to read if you want to read only one book about business. The issues [Sloan] dealt with in organizing and measuring, in keeping [other executives] happy, dealing with risk, understanding model years and the effect of used vehicles, and modeling his competition all in a very rational, positive way is inspiring."*[3]

ACTION POINTS AND FOOD FOR THOUGHT
- Follow the six steps given above when making key decisions.
- Use dissent and different viewpoints to help you reach a viable consensus.

CHAPTER 4

Recognize the True Nature of the Problem

LEARNING FROM
M. C. Escher

The works created by *M. C. Escher* (1898–1972) fascinate art lovers around the world. On close inspection, images that at first glance seem natural appear full of contradictions, with water flowing up- and downhill at the same time, stairs simultaneously leading up and down without any actual progress possible, and impossible rooms that could never exist in reality. Other images created by Escher depend on the eye of the beholder, with what is inside or outside, concave or convex, up or down eluding *objective* definition. These images irritate the viewer and often cannot be *rightly* resolved. Above all, the various possibilities they present cannot be viewed simultaneously. The management insights we can derive from the works of M. C. Escher likewise have to do with *perception*.

One of the most frequent errors managers make when they're trying to make effective decisions is rashly assuming that the problem has been correctly defined. Make a habit of assuming that the problem is not clear. Defining the problem is probably the most important step in effective decision making. There is a very simple reason for this. Generally speaking, a *wrong* answer to the *right* question is easy to put right. But the *right* answer to the *wrong* question is usually hard to rectify, if only because it is so hard to recognize the wrongness of the question. When defining a problem, effective managers ask the following fundamental question: *What is the real issue here?* And they then give themselves enough time, if at all possible, to come up with an answer.

Only when the problem has been viewed from all angles will the opportunity present itself to genuinely grasp the situation and accurately pinpoint the problem. For this reason, the identified problem must constantly be verified against all the available observable facts. Until the definition of the problem covers and can satisfactorily explain all the observable facts, it will be incomplete and quite often altogether wrong. In this connection it is worth reminding yourself that in many cases you will only *seem* to be dealing with *actual facts*: all too often they will, at best, turn out to be *opinions about facts*. So take your time and be thorough when defining problems. Otherwise omissions, shortcuts, and inaccuracies will sooner or later come back to haunt you.

Do you now see the parallels with Escher's confusing or sometimes utterly impenetrable drawings and lithographs? Learn from them by making a habit of questioning what you see before making any decisions. Assume that the seemingly obvious problem facing you—if indeed it genuinely *is* the problem—is probably not as clear-cut as it appears to be.

ACTION POINTS AND FOOD FOR THOUGHT

- Before you make a decision, doggedly try to gain the deepest possible understanding of your problem. Make a general point of questioning everything.
- Consider one of the main problems facing your organization: What is *really* at issue?

CHAPTER 5

Make the Right Compromise

LEARNING FROM

King Solomon

To give you a clear idea of what this chapter is about, let us start off by reading the famous Old Testament story of King Solomon's judgment[1]:

"Then two women who were harlots came to the king and stood before him. The one woman said, 'Oh, my lord, this woman and I live in the same house; and I gave birth to a child while she was in the house. It happened on the third day after I gave birth, that this woman also gave birth to a child, and we were together. There was no stranger with us in the house, only the two of us in the house. This woman's son died in the night, because she lay on it. "So she arose in the middle of the night and took my son from beside me while your maidservant slept, and laid him in her bosom, and laid her dead son in my bosom. When I rose in the morning to nurse my son, behold, he was dead; but when I looked at him carefully in the morning, behold, he was not my son, whom I had borne.' Then the other woman said, 'No! For the living one is my son, and the dead one is your son.' But the first woman said, 'No! For the

dead one is your son, and the living one is my son.' Thus they spoke
before the king. Then the king said, 'The one says, "This is my son
who is living, and your son is the dead one"; and the other says,
"No! For your son is the dead one, and my son is the living one."'
The king said, 'Get me a sword.' So they brought a sword before
the king. The king said, 'Divide the living child in two, and give
half to the one and half to the other.' Then the woman whose child
was the living one spoke to the king, for she was deeply stirred over
her son and said, 'Oh, my lord, give her the living child, and by no
means kill him.' But the other said, 'He shall be neither mine nor
yours; divide him!' Then the king said, 'Give the first woman the
living child, and by no means kill him. She is his mother.' When
all Israel heard of the judgment which the king had handed down,
they feared the king, for they saw that the wisdom of God was in
him to administer justice."

As you and all managers know, (virtually) all decisions entail some degree of compromise. But do you nevertheless always start out by asking, *"What would be right?"* rather than merely, *"What is acceptable?"*
Until you identify the right outcome, you will have no way of differen-
tiating between a right and wrong compromise. And a surfeit of wrong
compromises leads to what are commonly qualified in rather veiled
terms as *"circumstantial constraints."*

The old German proverb that, *"Half a bread is better than no bread*
at all" is right insofar as bread is still food, making the choice of half a
loaf the *right* kind of compromise. Not so the bluff by King Solomon.
His deliberately absurd suggestion that the baby be cut in two would
have been a clear example of the *wrong* kind of compromise because it
would not have produced an acceptable *minimum* outcome: leaving at
least one of the women with a living child.

Let us now return for a moment to *Alfred P. Sloan Jr.* Soon after
Peter F. Drucker started his first big consulting assignment at General

Motors to conduct a study on the company's management structure and management policies, Sloan called Drucker into his office and said to him:

> *"I shall not tell you what to study, what to write, or what conclusions to come to. This is your task. My only instruction to you is to put down what you think is right as you see it. Don't you worry about our reaction. Don't you worry about whether we will like this or dislike that. And don't you, above all, concern yourself with the compromises that might be needed to make your recommendations acceptable. There is not one executive in this company who does not know how to make every single conceivable compromise without any help from you. But he can't make the* right *compromise unless you first tell him what 'right' is."*[2]

Managerial competence is reflected in the ability to distinguish between right and wrong compromises. A precondition for drawing such distinctions is the meticulous and unequivocal stipulation of a minimum acceptable outcome.

ACTION POINTS AND FOOD FOR THOUGHT

- Think about a decision you need to make at the moment: what would be right?
- The next time you have to make a key decision, scrupulously define the minimum acceptable outcome.

CHAPTER **6**

Just Do It!
Keep Fine-Tuning
the Right Strategy

LEARNING FROM

Phil Knight

Fundamental changes always start *outside* your own organization. If you fail to systematically collect, organize, and process relevant information about your business environment, your chances of success will be slim. The strategy pursued by an organization must be based on information about its context: *only then* can you set the direction to be taken by the organization and match its specialized *know-how* to a *need*.

Most people regard the need to be informed about customers, markets, and technologies in their own sector of activity as obvious. It is essential, however, not to overlook the fact that in the past most new technologies that fundamentally altered an entire sector stemmed *not from within that sector, but from elsewhere.* This makes it indispensable to monitor other branches of industry very closely indeed. Since many organizations do *not* systematically do this, those that *do* also stand to gain a considerable, and easily leveraged, competitive advantage.

The same applies to customers. Most managers will immediately say that it is strategically important to understand their *own* customers.

22

Far less widespread, though, is the realization of how crucial it is to adopt the mind-set of *non*customers. For a company to command a 30 percent market share is a tremendous feat, yet this also means that 70 percent of the market remains to be conquered. Practically all organizations (there are very few exceptions, regardless of the degree of success achieved) have far more *non*customers than customers. For this reason, fundamental change almost invariably stems from noncustomers before affecting the sector as a whole.

Let us consider the above against the backdrop of the runaway success of sporting goods manufacturer Nike: *Phil Knight* (born in 1938) turned what had previously been a simple accessory, the sports shoe, into a high-tech products, and converted a small company into a group that dominates its sector. Nobody has revolutionized sports marketing more than Knight, and over the past 40 years few people have made such a lasting impression on the world of sports as he has done. Knight, like no other, has been both praised and vilified for his business practices, but whichever view one adopts, there is no denying that he played a major part in creating an entirely new lifestyle industry that developed from the production of a humble sports shoe.

Knight can certainly teach us all a thing or two about strategy, because it is flagrantly obvious that he not only understood and drew conclusions about his market, customers, noncustomers, technological possibilities, the development of his and other sectors of industry, and changes in both the global economy and society, but did so *differently* and *better* than anyone else in his field at the time.

The list of things he did differently thanks to his alternative outlook is long, extending from the use of new materials to the adoption of more efficient manufacturing processes and of a radically different approach to marketing. For example, long before sports shoes became fashion items, he had the idea of linking the Nike brand with leading sports stars. The greatest success in this respect was undoubtedly

Nike's collaboration in the 1980s with basketball superstar Michael Jordan, who played for the Chicago Bulls. The *Air Jordan* sport shoe, named after the iconic hero, proved a phenomenal success, generating unbelievable sales for Nike.

Then, in the early 1990s, Nike's growth, which had previously been driven by the popularity of basketball in the United States and the boom in jogging, began to falter. Once again, however, Knight exhibited an ability to spot the next big trend and strategically reoriented the company accordingly. He turned Nike into a manufacturer not just of sports shoes in particular, but also of other sports articles and clothing as well. At the same time, though, the company stuck with its stalwart stars, concluding contracts with top sportsmen like Andre Agassi, Kobe Bryant, Cristiano Ronaldo, Tiger Woods, and Roger Federer.

Knight's recognition of successive trends was definitely no coincidence. No human being or company can remain successful for 40 years by chance or through luck alone. The key is to view strategy as a continuous, adaptive process. To this end, an organization's management team must set targets in the following eight areas: *market standing; innovation; productivity; physical and financial resources; profitability; managers' performance, development, and attitude; employees' performance, development, and attitude; and corporate social responsibility.* These are key areas on which a strategy should be based. (Chapter 13 on IBM CEO Andy Grove takes a deeper look at these key areas.) The important thing is to regard strategy as an *evolutionary process.* Many organizations review their strategy only at lengthy intervals instead of *constantly* developing it. Yet *continuously* adapting the potentially shifting *content* and *limits* in the eight key areas listed above is far more effective, because it substantially tightens the focus of the organization's strategy, thus enhancing its general orientation. When doing this, it is also important not to ignore the *links* between the eight aforementioned key areas; after all, they influence each other and are interdependent. Analyzing them in isolation or taking action in just one area would result in a strategy that was anything but balanced and holistic in its outlook.

Time and time again, Nike's adaptability and the unerring correctness of many of its strategic decisions underscored the need to adopt a holistic, evolutionary view in that domain. Closely in keeping with the spirit of the age, Nike switched its focus from sports shoes to sports clothing and equipment as well as lifestyle products.

Another lesson on strategy to be learned from Phil Knight is this: *Just do it!* Even the very best strategies and plans are worthless unless they are actually implemented. One decisive feature of a strategy that genuinely achieves tangible results is that it assigns the best people in the organization to fulfill key tasks. Strategies that fail to clarify *who* needs to do *what* by *when* will remain ineffective, de facto leaving the organization in question without any strategy at all! At best, such woolly strategies can be described as no more than "good intentions," whereas good *strategies* are geared toward practical implementation and result in the right people doing the right work at the right time, thereby achieving the desired results.

Saint Augustine (354–430 AD), the bishop of Hippo Regius, once said: *"One prays for miracles but works for results."*[1] Herb Kelleher, the unconventional former CEO and founder of Southwest Airlines, who like Phil Knight pretty much overhauled an entire sector, said much the same thing, just worded more pragmatically: *"We have a very special plan, it's called doing things."*[2]

So far Nike has been portrayed in a very positive light. But there can be no denying that the company has also made some big mistakes. In the late 1990s, Nike slipped into a grave crisis in light of persistent reproaches that it was both exploiting workers in the low-wage countries where its products were being manufactured and still using child labor. Only when public pressure really mounted and the company's image had sustained considerable damage did Phil Knight make a public pledge to improve working conditions in factories turning out Nike products. What the company achieved over the ensuing decade is exemplary and earned it widespread recognition. In 2008, Nike climbed to third place in the annual rankings of the "100 Best Corporate Citizens" compiled by *Corporate Responsibility Officer Magazine* to map companies' commitments in the social domain. And in the 2011 list, Nike still figured in the top ten.

At the same time, this example also shows just how important it is not to ignore *any* of the eight key areas listed above. Nike's failure to tackle *corporate social responsibility* temporarily caused it serious damage and plunged it into a deep crisis. Since, as stated above, these key areas combine to constitute an interlinked whole, decisions made and results achieved in one area will always have an impact on one or more others. Any decisions that ignore this fact are likely to fall short of achieving the desired outcome.

ACTION POINTS AND FOOD FOR THOUGHT

- What can you do tomorrow to improve your own personal understanding and your company's perception of the context in which you operate? Make sure that you keep customers, noncustomers, markets, the technologies of your and other sectors, and social and macroeconomic changes on your radar and expand this list of relevant factors as the need arises.
- Put your strategy to the test. Where do you stand in relation to the targets you set for yourself with respect to the eight key areas?

CHAPTER 7

Structure Your Organization Around the Customer

LEARNING FROM

Michael Dell

"From the start, our entire business—from design to manufacturing to sales—was oriented around listening to the customer, responding to the customer, and delivering what the customer wanted. Our direct relationship—first through telephone calls, then through face-to-face interactions, and now through the Internet—has enabled us to benefit from real-time input from real customers regarding product and service requirements, products on the market, and future products they would like to see developed."[1]

MICHAEL DELL (BORN IN 1965),
THE FOUNDER AND CEO OF THE DELL COMPUTER CORPORATION.

Michael Dell questioned existing models of business organization more than almost anyone before him. By realizing his idea of combining direct sales with highly customer-oriented production, he revolutionized the computer sector. The changes he made, whenever necessary, to his company's interaction with customers and suppliers were just as radical as those made to the company's internal organization. And all the time his eyes were firmly set on one, clear objective: generating customer value.

At the tender age of 12, Michael Dell set up his own stamp-dealing business, producing his first product catalog titled *Dell's stamps*. Even today, he describes the $2,000 he netted over a four-year period as the sweetest profits he ever earned. The importance of direct contact with his customers was something he learned to appreciate very early on. At the age of 16, he began running direct marketing campaigns to sell subscriptions to newspapers to people who had just moved to a new area. It proved to be a highly lucrative business, earning him $18,000. When he was 19, however, he ended what could otherwise be described as a "normal" career, because that was when he set up the *Dell Computer Corporation*, which proceeded to grow at an astounding rate. Just four years later the company was already listed on the stock exchange, and a few years after that, at the age of 27, Michael Dell was the youngest chairman of the board of a company listed in the Fortune 500.

There is one particular aspect of Michael Dell's success that merits close attention. Clearly, there are no "golden rules" for building a company of your own that ranks thirty-third in the Fortune 500 and owns one of the most valuable brands in the world, but we can draw some valuable conclusions from Michael Dell's achievements about structuring an organization effectively—conclusions that you may well be able to apply to your own activities.

The basic purpose of any organization is to make strengths productive and weaknesses irrelevant. Doing this should enable normal individuals to achieve excellence. Even the best of structures cannot guarantee results or performance, but a badly structured organization will be doomed to failure because bad structures intensify the tensions that inevitably arise wherever people work together. A bad structure diverts attention to the wrong things, accentuating people's weaknesses instead of making the most of their strengths. So structuring an organization the right way is essential for its success.

The development of the right kind of organizational structure requires extensive reflection: the business needs to be thoroughly *thought through*. It also requires accurate analysis and the adoption of a systematic approach. A company's strategy will determine how its business is organized, because the structure of the organization is what enables it to deploy its strategy effectively in the first place. The well-known adage that, "Structure follows strategy" may be correct, but it is far too weak. A far more accurate statement is that, "*Structure enables strategy*," as this reflects the equal value of both elements: strategy and structure. The starting point must be the purpose of the business, its strategy, and the goals associated with it. That said, unless similarly generous attention is lavished on an organization's structure, even the best strategy will not fulfill its optimal potential. Many organizations let major opportunities in the structural domain pass them by. If a company is to be successful, its organization *must* be optimally fit for the task it sets out to fulfill. Consequently, the company's management needs to constantly keep on learning, adapting, and trying out new things.

Put more concretely, any company must answer the three fundamental questions about organization, regardless of its size[2]:

1. How must we organize our business to focus—and remain focused—on whatever customers pay for?
2. How must we organize our business so that our employees can actually do what we pay them for?
3. How must we organize our business so that our top executives can actually do what we pay them for?

1. How must we organize our business to focus—and remain focused—on whatever customers pay for?

Michael Dell developed his company while maintaining a very close dialogue with his customers. The original reason for this was not so much that he had spotted a future trend toward having small series of products come as close as possible to meeting customers' needs, but that he purely and simply lacked the capital to engage in mass production, as he has freely admitted. The success of his approach quickly made him realize, however, that the path he had chosen enabled his company to find out what customers genuinely wanted and what they were prepared to pay for. It is anything but easy to find out what customers *really* pay for. And it may be a good idea to take a fresh look at how your organization habitually answers this question.

Even if the answer it provides is right, there is still no guarantee that the organization will not lose sight of whatever it is that its customers are actually paying for. Indeed even the mighty Dell itself provides several examples of how easily a company can lose its focus. In 1989, the new *Olympic* product range Dell introduced at great expense turned out to be one of the biggest flops in the company's history. For despite the product's impressive technology, there was a problem: Customers did not need or want such a complex product. Michael Dell commented as follows: "*We had gone ahead and created a product that was, for all intents and purposes, technology for technology's sake, rather than technology for the customer's sake. If we had consulted our customers first about what* they *needed—as we had been accustomed to doing—we could have saved ourselves a lot of time and aggravation.*"[3]

In the 1990s, Dell then proceeded to miss out on the trend toward laptops and cheaper chips from AMD, and then, after 2000, also failed to spot the trend toward cheap netbooks. These errors were subsequently corrected, but they cost the company a great deal of time and money. So even when you know what customers are willing to pay for, it takes some effort to organize your business in such a way that customers remain the focus of its attention.

2. How must we organize our business so that our employees can actually do what we pay them for?

A company must be organized in such a way that its employees can effectively and efficiently contribute to its success. The way things are organized must make it easy for them to achieve positive results. Returning to Dell, after the Olympic fiasco, Michael Dell started talking about *"relevant technology,"* meaning technology that generated benefits to the customer. The conclusion he reached was that the technical people were not to blame. Rather, there were organizational reasons why sales faltered. The technicians simply did not know what customers deemed useful. They endeavored to deliver the latest technical developments instead of satisfying customers' needs. As a result, Dell stepped up *cooperation between its various departments* in a bid to foster a deeper understanding of what customers perceived as value. For example, the company's technicians were actively encouraged to work more closely together with the company's sales and product development departments. In short, you would be well advised to regularly ensure that your employees *really* know what is expected of them, instead of assuming that this is always clear.

In addition to enabling employees to do their job by enhancing their know-how and understanding, companies should also quite pragmatically check whether the way in which their procedures are organized actually *enables* employees to do their job. For instance, if nurses or external sales representatives find themselves having to spend most of their time fulfilling administrative requirements instead of attending to their patients or customers, they will *not* be doing what they are actually paid for.

3. How must we organize our business so that our top executives can actually do what we pay them for?

The company management must have the time to deal with those issues that can be spotted and resolved only by people with an overview of the business[4]:

1. Defining the business purpose and business mission; developing the corporate strategy.
2. Setting values, standards, benchmarks, and examples.
3. Building up and developing the company's structure.
4. Building up and retaining human resources.
5. Building up and cultivating key business relationships.
6. Representing the company.
7. Being prepared to act very swiftly to exploit opportunities or overcome crises.

Check whether the setup of your organization is really geared toward handling these issues appropriately, and if you are in a position of influence, make great efforts to ensure that your company's top executives have the time to deal with them properly. These are some of the most important tasks for any organization, and if its top managers fail to get a grip on them, it is highly likely that they will not discharge their duties in this connection at all, or not do so in a manner that serves the organization's best interests in the long run.

Whenever Michael Dell steers his company in a completely new direction, it provides us with living proof that he still takes organizational development extremely seriously, just as he did back in the company's good old days. For some time now, like Hewlett-Packard, Dell has favored a dense dealer network. Dell is also considering the production of mass-produced goods in a manner similar to Acer, and is making intense efforts to reach small customers all over the world, just as Lenovo, for example, is trying to do.

ACTION POINTS AND FOOD FOR THOUGHT

- Discuss the three fundamental questions about organization.
- If you hold responsibility in the upper echelon of your organization, discuss with your colleagues where specific measures could improve how the top management discharges its seven key duties and how you intend to implement those measures.

CHAPTER 8

Be Productive

LEARNING FROM

Frederick Winslow Taylor

There was a time when the findings and conclusions of the *"father of scientific management"* Frederick Winslow Taylor (1856–1915) were hotly debated in countries throughout the industrialized world. Taylor set out his views in a book published in 1911 titled *The Principles of Scientific Management*. Those views not only helped to shape mass production, but also for a long time they exerted extensive influence over the organization of labor in the twentieth century. Taylor's main concern was always how to boost labor productivity. By using time-and-motion studies, he ascertained the most effective deployment of a worker, while at the same time examining the tools that worker used, which were sometimes subsequently redesigned to help boost efficiency. His suggestion that the labor process be broken down into small steps of set duration entailing precise movements created the conditions required for rationalization and assembly line work.

The successes achieved by applying his findings and their continued development by Henry Ford into so-called *Fordism* in the auto industry brought Taylor to the notice of many labor practitioners. He was both a pioneer in labor organization and at the same time a radical advocate of a management approach based on enforced methods and checks. According to his "scientific management" (dubbed *Taylorism*), a production process required no initiative whatsoever on the part of the workers involved. The instructions issued by management were stipulated in almost painful detail and had to be followed to the letter. In other words, people had to go about their work like machines, without thinking.

The worldwide debate about Taylorism ranged from uncritical imitation and great admiration to indignant rejection.

Many entrepreneurs, as well as political leaders like Lenin or Mussolini, believed that in Taylorism they had found the ideal way to boost productivity. Others maintained that what they regarded as an inhumane method merely led to the ruthless exploitation of the workforce. Charlie Chaplin clearly agreed more with the latter, lampooning assembly line work in his movie *Modern Times*. But when Taylor died in 1915, many companies were busily implementing the measures he had advocated.

Taylor's convictions can be properly understood only against the backdrop of the age in which he lived. Nowadays his radical views on labor productivity tend to be condemned for obvious reasons. Nonetheless, Taylor is to be credited with being among the first people to think about how labor can be *productively* organized. Today our answers to that question differ from the conclusions he reached, but the question about how to optimize productivity is more important than ever. *Every organization and every individual human being can constantly improve productivity.* To ensure that this happens in the twenty-first century, which points need to be borne in mind?

Today the focus needs to be on boosting the *productivity of the knowledge worker* and the *productivity of knowledge*. Therein lies major potential; the question is how to tap into it. In the rest of this chapter we concentrate on these issues, whereby *productivity* should be understood in the sense of *Total Factor Productivity (TFP)*, the variables of which include not only the above-mentioned productivity of knowledge, but also the productivity of *labor*, of *time*, and of *capital*. The points set out below could facilitate the initiation of a debate on this topic within your organization.

1. Become more productive by boosting the productivity of knowledge

In this day and age, most major productivity gains should be sought in the productivity of knowledge workers, not in manual labor or so much in the other factors contributing to productivity. The first consequence of this is that existing *knowledge* needs to be harnessed to enhance *the productivity of knowledge*. Doing this in practice requires an organization to systematically ask itself *how the productivity of knowledge can be increased* and *what kind of fresh know-how should be accumulated* and in what way. Incidentally, deciding where knowledge needs to be accumulated will also determine where *innovations* are ultimately achieved. So it is well worth investing sufficient time in such decisions. Never lose sight of the productivity of knowledge *workers*, though; after all, it is they who bring knowledge into your organization and apply it there.

2. Individual productivity

All knowledge workers have specialized knowledge, and it is the specific combination of their skills and knowledge that distinguishes them, even if they are active in the same domain. Knowledge workers should know more about their individual specialist area than others in their organization. After all, this is what they are paid for. In this respect, knowledge workers are above all *responsible for the state of their knowledge* and must therefore keep *learning all the time* and also assume *responsibility for their productivity*.

While in the industrial age a job's title, by virtue of the available technologies and products associated with it, dictated *what* the respective worker was required to do and also *how* to go about the tasks, in today's society precisely the opposite applies: Job incumbents have to organize large parts of their work themselves, since it is *they* who determine what to do and how to do it. In short, they largely manage themselves.

Even though there are probably as many ways of working as there are people, there is nonetheless one generally applicable "secret" for ensuring that work is productive and effective: *concentration on a single task*. People interested in optimizing productivity must organize their activities around a few key tasks and set aside lengthy, consecutive blocks of time to work on them undisturbed. However, it is important not to overlook the fact that knowledge work can also entail manual tasks, as is the case when knowledge workers use tools and implements, for example. True professionals practice applying tools and equipment so that they can put their training to good use whenever called upon and work effectively even under stressful conditions or severe time constraints. For doctors, pilots, soldiers, athletes, and musicians the need for such training is self-evident. It is always worth reconsidering where in your organization *manual labor* is essential and which *skills, tools, equipment,* and *aids* could help to boost productivity.

3. The productivity of an organization

As explained above, it is knowledge workers who offer the main potential for boosting productivity, and they essentially manage themselves. This is why the skill needed by knowledge workers to boost their own productivity is *management* knowledge, first and foremost *self-management* knowledge. Organizations that value *good knowledge of and adeptness in self-management* will have a pronounced edge in terms of productivity. In fact, let us take this a step further. In an organization that builds up management knowledge at all levels in its hierarchy and accumulates a suitable level of management knowledge at each level, with respect to *managing the organization, managing innovations,* and *managing people,* people will prove more productive and will at the same time more effectively contribute toward the attainment of the organization's shared objectives.

Costs arising from systematically training staff in management knowledge very soon pay for themselves through the edge they generate in terms of productivity, the more effective deployment of employees, and the resulting greater overall efficiency of the organization as a whole. These things in turn create, almost as a by-product, a *corporate culture of effectiveness and professionalism*, which makes work not only efficient and more functionally reliable, but also more pleasant. And those who have worked with real professionals within or outside their organization will know how gratifying true professionalism can be.

Productivity gains will not always be strictly *measurable*, but they should be readily *assessable*. If productivity can be measured, however, it is best to use *value creation* as your parameter. Labor productivity will be the value created per employee, capital productivity will be the value created per invested monetary unit, and time productivity will be the value created per unit of time.

Always be on the lookout for ways of further boosting productivity, even if the results of doing so are less directly visible. Make it possible for all employees to contribute to your organization's knowledge base. Exploit all the possibilities offered by modern technology, but also create opportunities for face-to-face discussions, especially regarding issues affecting multiple divisions or departments. Holding interdisciplinary closed-door meetings that focus on your greatest challenges can be an exceptionally fruitful way of harnessing knowledge.

Everyone *talks* about "knowledge organizations," but very few people *systematically apply* the latest findings. Someone who has thought very extensively about how knowledge can be productively harnessed in his own organization is Bill Gates. He and his fellow Microsoft executives invested a great deal of time and energy in creating an organization in which *all* employees could contribute to the company's knowledge base. Of course, countless companies *say* this is their objective, but at Microsoft it genuinely *is*. Gates has long held the view that: *"Smart people anywhere in the company should have the power to drive an initiative."*[1] Back in the early 1990s, the Internet had not yet become Microsoft's top priority, but when a Microsoft worker visited Cornell University and noticed that the Internet was being used for far more than computer applications, as soon as he returned to the company he wrote a dramatic e-mail stating that if nobody heeded him and unless Microsoft immediately shifted its strategy with respect to the Internet, the company would be driven straight into bankruptcy. That e-mail ultimately reached Bill Gates, prompting a complete U-turn in Microsoft's approach. Gates subsequently attributed the company's drastic strategic change of direction to the author of the e-mail and other Microsoft employees. Just how long term and far reaching the resulting turnaround really was is clear from something Gates said only a few years later: *"If we go out of business, it won't be because we're not focused on the Internet. It'll be because we're too focused on the Internet."*[2]

It is clearly worthwhile to seek ways of harnessing the knowledge of a company's employees. Making the available knowledge productive will be one of the decisive factors that determines the success of your business and the success of its managers.

ACTION POINTS AND FOOD FOR THOUGHT

- What do you need to do to become more productive? By when do you plan to achieve this?
- Which specific steps can you take within your organization to make knowledge more productive?
- Discuss with your colleagues where you see opportunities for making your organization more productive.

CHAPTER **9**

Demand

Effective

Management

LEARNING FROM

Warren Buffett

What *is* effective management? One thing is certain: It is more than just a set of tools and techniques, necessary and useful though both of these things may be. Looking back at past management successes and management problems, we see that the crucial ingredient is a sprinkling of essential principles. And those who understand and use these principles to guide their behavior will perform better and achieve more[1]:

1. Management is all about human beings. The task of managers is to enable people to achieve something by working together. In the process, available resources (especially knowledge) are converted into benefits for customers. One of the main aims here is to ensure that the way human beings are involved in the process makes full use of their strengths, while their weaknesses become irrelevant.

2. Every organization needs a commitment to shared values and objectives. An organization's business mission must convey a clear picture of what it stands for. The objectives set for the fulfillment

40

of its business mission must be clear, simple, and binding. The job of the management will then entail not only carefully formulating and setting values and objectives, but also leading by example in applying them.

3. Wherever effective management is practiced around the world, managers do pretty much the same things. More specifically, *what* they do is the same, but *how* they do it can differ tremendously. Accordingly, the task of management, if human beings are to be effectively integrated into the organization that brings them together, entails making the specific culture of the country in question work *for* the organization. That said, it would be a mistake to try and reinvent management in every country.

4. The management must enable the organization as a whole and every individual employee to learn and continue to develop. Learning and further development must take place *constantly* and at *every* level, for they constitute an ongoing, never-ending process.

5. The knowledge and abilities of the human beings working for an organization are just as diverse and different as the activities they carry out. As a result, *communication* and *personal responsibility* are cornerstones of the dependable functioning of any organization. Employees ought to think hard about their personal contributions and objectives. At the same time, they should make sure their colleagues are both familiar with these objectives and know what they must do to help attain them. Similarly, employees should ask themselves what contribution they need to make to help colleagues attain *their* objectives.

6. The management has to look much further than just the organization's balance sheet, considering truly essential factors like its market standing, its capability for innovation, its productivity, the quality of its employees, and of course its financial figures, whereby financial variables should tend to be considered last, not first. Many of these factors cannot be measured or expressed in

absolute figures, but it is vital that people learn to weigh them accurately.

7. Last, and most important, the overriding objective is—and must always be—a satisfied customer. Worded deliberately provocatively, results could be said to exist only *outside* an organization, while costs only exist *inside* it.

One man who has emphatically shown the world how fully he understands what management is all about is *Warren Buffett*. Buffett was born in 1930 and went on to become one of the most successful investors of our age. The quality of the management of the companies in which he has invested has always been an important factor in his investment decisions. For instance, he was particularly favorably impressed by the management team when he bought a rather large stake in McDonald's, acquired GEICO (one of the biggest car insurers in the United States), and purchased interests in Coca-Cola, American Express, Gillette, and NetJets. He publicly and repeatedly praises the quality of his managers and actively encourages them to think and act as if they *owned* the company. In the 2008 annual report of his company Berkshire Hathaway, he wrote that he and his partner Charlie Munger *"subcontract all of the heavy lifting"* and *"delegate almost to the point of abdication."* So while Berkshire employed around 246,000 staff at the time, just 19 of these employees were at the company's headquarters.[2] It comes as no surprise, then, to learn that Buffett views his own task and that of his partners as covering two main areas: first capital allocation; and second, looking after key managers and engaging in intensive communications with them.

The most striking example of Warren Buffett's unwavering focus on the quality of managers came in spring 2006 when he announced that he would gradually be donating most of his fortune, a staggering $30 billion, no less, to the *Bill & Melinda Gates Foundation*. When asked in an interview with *Fortune* magazine why the second richest man in the world (at the time) was giving away so many billions to the man who was richest of all, Buffett said: *"When you put it that way, it sounds pretty funny. But in truth, I'm giving it through him—and, importantly, Melinda as well—not to him."*[3]

By entrusting his fortune to one of the most successful people of our time, Buffett's aim was to achieve an optimally effective result. Thus a superficially surprising decision by Buffett was actually another example of characteristic behavior on his part: selecting a great manager and focusing on effective management.

ACTION POINTS AND FOOD FOR THOUGHT

- What can you do tomorrow to achieve better results with respect to one of the seven principles presented above?
- Which specific steps taken in your organization would make the quality of management a higher priority?
- Use your position to improve the management know-how and management skills of those people for whom you are responsible.

CHAPTER **10**

Understand Profit; Strive for Independence

LEARNING FROM

Coco Chanel

Gabrielle Bonheur "Coco" Chanel (1883–1971) maintained that fashion ought to be comfortable and chic. She espoused this guiding principle at a time when the notion was totally alien to the fashion world. Accordingly, in 1916 she made the first ever proper clothes out of jersey, a material that had previously been deemed good enough only for men's underwear. In 1918 she went on to create the first women's pajamas, a previously inconceivable notion because during the first part of the twentieth century it was still self-evident that men's and women's clothing should be as different as night and day. Coco Chanel certainly challenged that convention, borrowing elements of men's apparel to incorporate in her fashion for women. In so doing she gave women unprecedented freedom of movement as well as clothes that were no less elegant than what women had been accustomed to. The unprecedented inclusion of trousers in her collection for women sent shockwaves through the society of her day, yet women loved the clothes she made.

In the 1920s, Coco Chanel's designs were the driving force behind French fashion. Their simple, understated elegance represented a break with tradition, their clear lines being not just innovative but almost revolutionary at the time. Furthermore, her ideas were totally in tune with the spirit of the age, because in the early twentieth century the role of women was changing radically. And her collections characterized the style of modern, emancipated women.

In business terms, however, Chanel is remarkable not just for her innovative, female customer-oriented approach, but also for her strong awareness of the need for financial independence.

To gain a better understanding of what drove her to pursue such autonomy, we first need to look at her childhood. The stories Coco Chanel spread about her upbringing were so often contradictory that it is extremely difficult to untangle myths and fiction from the truth. We know for certain that she was the illegitimate daughter of two market traders and that her mother died when she was just 12 years old. Since her father did not look after her, she was raised in an orphanage run by a Catholic order of nuns. Three of her five siblings died at a young age, and Coco later gave her two brothers financial support, demanding in return that they keep quiet about their childhood and stay out of her life in the loftier, more prosperous echelons of Parisian society. She is thought to have been ashamed of her family, and it is suspected that it was this feeling which very early on fueled her resolve never to become financially dependent on anyone. Consequently, as an entrepreneur she felt it was very important to repay her business debts immediately. And although Chanel had liaisons with some very wealthy men, who provided the capital she needed when she was starting out, she repaid them all in full. Clearly, she wanted to remain independent of men, and in addition to single-handedly financing her entire life, she also bankrolled the development of her company. Both of these accomplishments were unusual for women in Chanel's day.

Chanel opened her first shop at the age of 27 in Rue Cambon, near the exclusive Place Vendôme in Paris, where women from all over the world still come to buy Chanel clothes today. The hats she herself designed and then sold there from 1910 onward proved so popular with sophisticated Parisian ladies that she soon expanded her collection. By 1916 she already had boutiques in Paris, Deauville, and Biarritz and had around 300 employees. In 1920 she created her soon legendary perfume *Chanel No. 5*, and that same year she reported taxable income of over 10 million French francs. By the end of the 1920s her company employed over 3,000 people.

During that period, she made an indelible mark on the fashion world by coming up with innovations like the now proverbial "little black dress," which can be traced back to her design for a plain black dress in 1926, a reaction to a visit to the opera where she had been horrified and dismayed by the gaudy evening attire of her fellow opera goers. Alongside Chanel's elegant black number, every other dress looked too glitzy. Yet such brilliant understatement was not the only thing Chanel did to change the image of the emancipated woman. She steadily hacked away at old traditions, sometimes quite literally, for example switching to a short hairstyle allegedly after singeing her long hair when a gas heater caught fire. Short hair then became the trademark of the flapper, the emancipated young woman of the 1920s.

Another of Chanel's innovations was her introduction of costume jewelry, which she saw not as a cheap imitation of real gems, but as proudly worn artificial fashion accessories. Whereas jewelry had previously served, among other things, to indicate the social and professional status of the men behind women, self-confident women could now follow Coco Chanel in wearing what they pleased. And Chanel's innovations included not only sophisticated combinations of real and false gems, but also the use of both precious *and* cheap materials. The long string of pearls became just as classic a look as the soft Chanel tweed suit, which she unveiled in 1954.

Even more important than Coco Chanel's innovative and elegant fashion designs, though, were the modern look and lifestyle that she gave her contemporaries, setting an example for them as a professional woman of independent means. Nowadays it is virtually impossible to appreciate how much strength of will, character, and resolve this must have required in her day, when men not only dominated society and business, but also gave free rein to their prejudices and misogynistic mind-set.

Like many true greats, Chanel carried on working until the last day of her life. She died in 1971, rich and famous, at the ripe old age of 87, working on yet another new collection in Paris.

Chanel's life history and creative output provide countless examples of entrepreneurial originality, and it would take a whole separate chapter to do justice to the individual aspects of her professional management of innovation. Here, however, I would like to highlight two other aspects of her management: *profit* and her aspiration toward *financial independence*.

Let us start out from the basic notion that Chanel's *financial success* was a *consequence* of the fact that she understood *the needs of her female clientele* better and did more to fulfill those needs than any of her contemporaries. Most important of all, then, she delivered *customer value*. That may sound trivial, but at the time the concept was nowhere near as self-evident as it is today, because no fashion designer questioned everything as radically as Coco Chanel did. "*The cut of a dress should enable its wearer to sit on a horse as well,*"[1] she said, at a time when for many of her contemporaries there seemed to be no alternative to the tightly laced corset. Massive opportunities have always awaited anyone or those organizations bold enough to *radically question everything* and try to *gain a better understanding of their customers* than their competitors.

Those unknown market leaders or "*hidden champions*" demonstrate a particularly impressive and profound understanding of their customers' needs. Such world-beating companies are characterized, among other things, by their pronounced *proximity to customers*, which almost automatically yields competitive advantages. Yet at the same time they have other things in common with Coco Chanel, like placing the emphasis on *innovation*, knowingly *focusing their resources*, exploiting the positive aspects of *globalization*, deploying unusually capable and effective employees, and exhibiting a strong *will to succeed*.

The market leaders in question tend to hold *innovation* in very high regard, because in their eyes it is the most effective way to stave off the competition. Chanel would have seen things exactly the same way. Hidden champions focus *their resources* and concentrate on clearly defined markets and target groups, but they are also very clear about what they do *not* want. They exploit opportunities arising from the fact that they are in a position to offer their wares worldwide—just as Chanel did. For instance, Jackie Kennedy chose to wear Chanel outfits, landing the French style icon a perfect representative to showcase her designs in the United States.

Chanel always hired *excellent staff,* a tradition that her company's management continued to cultivate after her death, bringing in Karl Lagerfeld, to name but one example. Chanel's dogged determination to succeed sometimes gave her contemporaries the impression that she was inexorably tough, not only when it came to looking after her own interests, but above all being hard on herself—another factor she has in common with many great individuals.

But let us now return to Chanel's desire for financial independence, because here too there is a parallel, albeit a less obvious one, with the aforementioned hidden champions. Scrutinize the finances of these low-profile world-beaters, and the one factor that sticks out is their unusually *high equity ratio,* meaning the remarkably high relative proportion of equity used to finance a company's assets. Studies suggest that the actual figure lies somewhere between 36 and 42 percent, more than one-third of hidden champions even have equity ratios above 50 percent! These figures are multiples of the average for small and medium-sized German companies. So either the craving for *financial independence* is indeed very strong, or the correlation is purely coincidental—which would be very strange, to say the least.

One thing is certain: striving for financial independence almost inevitably entails the adoption of a different mind-set regarding *profits.* This is because the question asked by independent-minded entrepreneurs is not what their desirable *maximum* profit would be, but rather what *minimum* profit they need to generate to remain *financially independent* after deducting all their costs, taxes, and dividend payments.

In virtually all cases, that minimum profit will be considerably higher than the maximum profit that most entrepreneurs would have been willing to accept at the outset. Indeed, this is one reason to take a very critical view of discussions about excessive profits by companies, for the decisive issue about profits is not so much how high, but how *sustainable* they are. High profits can be achieved relatively easily in the short term by making savings, though this will almost always be at the cost of the organization's future well-being. However, the aim must be to ensure that the business remains strong and healthy in the *long* term, capable of withstanding even relatively major crises. Hidden champions have provided ample proof that such a company can also generate sustainable profits. The key is to do things in the right order: *first* build up strength, *then* generate profits on the basis of that strength.

In addition to viewing profit in a different light, striving for financial independence also induces a different way of dealing with *customers.* Come what may, customers must take center stage, for it is they who pay for a business's products or services, enabling the generation of profits which, in turn, secure the company's financial freedom. So in simple terms Chanel's success can be summed up as having been based not on *products* (after all, her rivals also produced great clothes), but on understanding contemporary women's *needs* for elegance, simplicity, clarity, and comfort.

Ultimately, where financial independence is concerned, profit should be seen for what it essentially is: proof of a correctly chosen and competently implemented business mission.

The discussion about aspiring to generate profits in an effort to secure financial independence should not lead us to conclude that this was Coco Chanel's overriding or, indeed, sole driving force. Nobody knows what ultimately prompts individual entrepreneurs to act as they do. Some want to become rich; some want to leave a legacy; others want to become powerful or famous. We know for certain that Chanel's financial independence was very important to her *and* that she herself attributed a large part of her success to coincidence. Almost too modestly she said of her career:

> "What did I know back then about my profession? Nothing. Was I aware of the revolution I would start? Not in the least. One world was dying and another had to be born. I merely happened to be there, when an opportunity came my way, which I duly seized. I was as old as the century. Somehow it became my destiny to develop a new style of attire. Women wanted simplicity, comfort, and clarity. I had always made those things my priority, without having an agenda. True success stories always contain an element of chance."[2]

While the tremendous success story of Coco Chanel may in retrospect seem to have been self-evident, natural, and easy, she nonetheless had to steer the company through successive difficulties, especially in the 1930s and 1940s. And later on, when she was 70, the press greeted her announced intention to launch a new women's suit with nothing but hurtful derision. Undeterred, she continued working on it, with the impressive outcome that the suit in question became a classic, the Chanel suit. In 1955, *Life* magazine devoted a full double spread to the "Chanel look," heaping praise on its simple elegance. If Chanel were still alive today, would she be surprised that the current crop of superstars still wears her clothes?

ACTION POINTS AND FOOD FOR THOUGHT

- Carefully consider whether you have set your minimum profit correctly. Discuss this with your colleagues.
- On which activities should you focus your resources in order to make progress for which customers will be willing to pay? Which activities should you drop?
- If you generate healthy profits, ask yourself the probing question of whether you are investing enough in the future.

CHAPTER **11**

Harness
Information

LEARNING FROM
Paul Julius
Reuter

In 1850, the European telegraphic network still had a yawning 75-mile gap between its Belgian terminus in Brussels and the first German telegraph station in Aachen. *Paul Julius Reuter* (1816–1899) saw all too clearly how this gap prevented the rapid transmission of information and, convinced that customers would be willing to pay for swifter information, took the bold step of setting up his own messaging service. To bridge the gap between Brussels and Aachen, he hit upon the clever idea of using carrier pigeons. The birds delivered information about the latest stock market and commodities prices so quickly that anyone receiving and making immediate use of that information could make a fortune in Europe's stock markets. In other words, this faster access to knowledge was worth a great deal of money, and Reuter's business flourished to such an extent that he was soon "employing" one breeder's entire team of homing pigeons, bringing his fleet of "messengers" to more than 200 birds. Every day, the pigeons were brought by train from Aachen to Brussels. From there, each message was carried by three birds, to make sure that its contents arrived safely. As soon as the pigeons arrived in Aachen, staff at Reuter's office telegraphed the information throughout Germany.

During 1851, as the size of the gap in the telegraph network steadily diminished, Reuter used horses and riders to carry the information over the ever shorter distance until the network was finally completed on April 16, 1851, bringing his monopoly to an end.

Reuter then moved to London to build up a company that would transmit news reliably and, above all, more rapidly than anyone else. In that endeavor he succeeded, creating a news service that provided British newspapers with up-to-date information from across Europe. In fact he even managed to ensure that "Reuters" was cited as the source of information at the bottom of every transmission, paving the way for Reuters to become a brand synonymous with information services.

A further breakthrough for Reuter came in April 1865 when, using the best available technology at the time and a sophisticated information relay system, he was the first to break the news of the assassination of Abraham Lincoln to newspapers and the business community. Clearly, Reuter had recognized the tremendous value of information. And to this day his name remains inextricably associated with breaking news.

Let us now consider the role played by information in management. In principle, managers need to be informed about goings-on, both inside and outside their organization. It is also essential to have a steady, guaranteed flow and exchange of information between individual parts of their organization and between that organization and its partners. In this chapter we focus on how to work effectively with information inside an organization and in exchanges with partners. Information on the environment and on other external aspects is primarily covered in the following chapter, about James Wilson.

Information makes knowledge workers effective and is the lifeblood of any organization. Consequently, the relevant questions to ask in this connection are: *"What information does the knowledge worker need to make a contribution?"* and *"What information does the organization need from the knowledge worker to enable others to make contributions?"*

Starting with the first question, we note that only the knowledge workers can decide what needs to be known in order to carry out their duties effectively. Data must always be provided in consultation with the user, who is best placed to decide which information out of the vast quantity of available data is actually useful, how that information needs to be organized, and what action subsequently needs to be taken based on that information, to achieve the desired results. As a rule, everyone knows the guidelines for doing this, yet by no means do all organizations regularly question the content, scope, and frequency of distributed information. As a result, many reports are drawn up "purely out of habit." Organizations that *do* regularly ask questions about the form and content of reports, correspondence, meetings, off-site sessions, and other methods of transferring information not only massively boost their *productivity*, but at the same time enhance their *effectiveness* by making sure that the right information is available.

The second of the two questions asked above, about what information the organization needs from an individual knowledge worker to function effectively, spotlights the *task* and *common goals* of people working there and enables the effective organization of communication. In this context, consideration needs to be given to the frequency with which information is to be provided, the *form* it assumes when conveyed, and the *list of recipients*. At the same time there is a need to stipulate who will *compile* the body of information and to specify which individuals need to make a contribution.

Organizations can function properly only when all the relevant people contribute to the continuous flow of information. For this reason, it is important for each individual to be aware of his or her personal *responsibility* for collecting and conveying information. Furthermore, these individuals must *discipline themselves* to fulfill that responsibility. Organizations that do this not only end up making better decisions, but do so considerably faster. This gives them something truly essential: *functional reliability*. And while this will not actually eliminate the risk of decisions being based on missing or incorrect information, it will substantially reduce that risk.

There is a very simple way of ensuring that those dispatching information pass on the *right information at the right time* and in a *suitable form*: Make sure that people talk with each other. If you are a manager, go to those people with whom you work and ask them this seemingly simple question: *"What information do you need from me to do your job effectively?"* Then state what information you require to do your job, specifying how often you would like to receive it and how much detail you require. This same conversation should be repeated at regular intervals, at least every 12 to 18 months or whenever the organization as a whole, a specific job, or key duties of the people involved undergo some major change. When deliberating all this, remember that most of the information that managers need to do their job can only be obtained from *outside* their organization. This aspect of management is covered in greater detail in the next chapter, on James Wilson.

ACTION POINTS AND FOOD FOR THOUGHT

- ■ Think about how you deal with information and how it flows within your organization. Where do you see room for improvements?
- ■ What information do you need so that you can contribute effectively, and what information does the organization need from you?
- ■ Question how you need to organize your work to leave enough time to devote to relevant information. What do you need to do to ensure that you can exploit and apply relevant information?

CHAPTER **12**

Understand Your Sphere of Action

LEARNING FROM

James Wilson

The Economist was first published in September 1843, "to *take part in 'a severe contest between intelligence, which presses forward, and an unworthy, timid ignorance obstructing our progress.'"*[1] The newspaper was founded by *James Wilson* (1805–1860), a hat maker from Hawick in Scotland, who held an unswerving belief in global free trade with the least possible government intervention. The protectionist Corn Laws, which imposed special taxes and constraints on imports were the decisive factor in the establishment of *The Economist*, because bread prices skyrocketed, causing the population of England to suffer great hunger. Wilson's view was that free trade is good for everybody, and although the Corn Laws were repealed in 1846, *The Economist* continued, remaining committed to cultivating and promoting the liberal ideas of its founder. Today, it is no exaggeration to state that *The Economist*, now published in magazine format, is viewed as mandatory reading by many top managers and leaders in all sectors of society all over the world. For many leading executives it is one source of information that helps them gain a better understanding of their overall sphere of action.

The original objective of *The Economist* was not exactly modest and remains unchanged today. For example, Rupert Pennant-Rea, its editor in chief from 1986 to 1993, who was appointed non-executive chairman of The Economist Group in July 2009, described *The Econo-mist* as "*a Friday viewspaper, where the readers, with higher than aver-age incomes, better than average minds but with less than average time, can test their opinions against ours. We try to tell the world about the world, to persuade the expert and reach the amateur, with an injection of opinion and argument.*"[2]

Instead of saying he *read The Economist*, Peter F. Drucker, the father of management known for his unerring estimations of future trends, is reputed to have said: "*I have learned to study* The Economist." What a difference!

As stated at the end of the previous chapter, much of the information that managers need can only be found *outside* their organization. According-ly, any organization needs to adopt a systematic procedure determining how it *gathers* and *organizes* information from the sphere in which it is active. In addition, it has to specify how that information will be *made available and integrated into the decision-making process.* Since the vast majority of trends and technologies that change an organization's own sector stem from other domains or areas of activity, developments over a broad area will need to be monitored. Every organization has assump-tions underlying its business purpose and strategy, as well as about their fulfillment and implementation. So the information it gathers from its sphere of action must serve to help it both *query these assumptions* and repeatedly test them. This same information must also help the organi-zation to spot *opportunities and potential dangers* in good time.

A broadly based search for information will, of course, focus on an organization's own market, current rivals, and the technology in use at the time. This is fine, but it is harder to obtain information about noncustomers—that is, people who *could* be customers of your organi-zation but instead buy from your competitors—or to procure informa-tion about seemingly imminent fundamental changes. Where should we look for information on potential new customers and markets, pos-sible competitors, or technologies that could be useful or pose a threat?

And how should we interpret and organize information on current and basic social issues with a view to using it in the right way?

These are just some of the general questions that have to be asked. Naturally they will need to be carefully honed according to the specific situation of your organization. Not all contextual information is readily available, but when organizations systematically seek it out, they usually unearth far more than they deemed possible. Developed information systems steadily improve over time, and the steady fall in the number of *surprises* is proof of their effectiveness. This happens because managers who use their information-gathering system will already have identified what is most important to them and long ago paved the way for any ensuing decisions. If you stop to think about how dependent managers' decision making is on such contextual information, it soon becomes clear that obtaining such data must be made an absolute top priority. Many organizations are too focused on *their own organization and the present* and pay far too little attention to *their sphere of action and the future.*

As one of Peter F. Drucker's superiors said to him when he was a young man: *"Make your nose twitch, when you read the daily paper. If there is something you don't understand, look it up. Don't just read on—try to understand."*[3]

ACTION POINTS AND FOOD FOR THOUGHT

- Which previously unused sources of information could help you enhance your understanding of your organization's sphere of action?
- Which domains and key factors do you need to monitor particularly closely to minimize risks or exploit opportunities?
- What do you need to do in your organization to ensure that relevant contextual information (e.g., about your organization's customers, noncustomers, markets, competitors, technology, social developments, and other similar factors) is available and can be put to better use?

CHAPTER 13

Recognize Inflection Points and Utilize Performance Indicators

L E A R N I N G   F R O M

Andy Grove

Former Intel CEO *Andy Grove* was actually born András István Gróf in Budapest in 1936. The son of a Jewish merchant family, he had to live under a false identity and escaped Nazi persecution only after finding shelter with friends. In 1957 he decided to flee to the United States after the Soviet armed forces' suppression of the popular uprising in Hungary in October 1956. Once in America, he changed his name to *Andrew Stephen Grove* but became known as Andy Grove. He assiduously taught himself English and enrolled at Berkeley, emerging with a Ph.D. in 1963. After his studies he took a job at Fairchild Semiconductor, where he got to know Gordon Moore and Bob Noyce, with whom he teamed up in 1968 to found Intel.

The three men made a remarkable team. When they met, Grove was just 27, while Moore and Noyce were in their mid-thirties. The trio provides us with one of many examples highlighting the fact that it is never too early to look out for top talent. Before working for Fairchild, Noyce and Moore had been employed by William Shockley, who had won the 1956 Nobel Prize for Physics for developing the transistor and published the first academic book on semiconductor electronics. In 1975, Moore formulated a hypothesis that would later become known as *Moore's law*, predicting that the number of transistors on a computer chip would double about every 24 months. This prediction turned out to be astonishingly accurate and bears witness to Moore's excellent foresight. Grove, on the other hand, brought not only his management skills to Intel's founding team, but also a healthy understanding of human nature, which was crucial for ensuring that everything the company developed stayed firmly in touch with reality and had a practical application. The following quotation really sums up his pragmatic approach: *"I have a rule in my business: To see what can happen in the next ten years, look at what has happened in the last ten years."*[1]

How Grove managed to overcome successive major crises when building Intel makes for fascinating—and valuable—reading. One of the worst dilemmas arose in the early 1980s when Japanese manufacturers succeeded in producing memory chips that were not only superior in quality to those turned out by Intel, but also cheaper. As a result, Grove's company lost its dominance of the market, and in 1985 the situation became so serious that Intel's survival hung in the balance. One day, when it became clear that all efforts to resolve the company's problems were in vain, Grove asked Moore what a new CEO would probably do. Without hesitating Moore replied: *"He would get us out of memories."*[2] Grove was shocked, though it was patently clear to him that doing so would mean changing the entire company from the bottom upward. After all, Intel had effectively lost its core market and would have to turn to a new one—a long and painful process.

As Grove would say later, it was one of the toughest decisions he and his management team ever had to make. They duly made a clean break with the company's past to embark on something completely new, ultimately creating a totally new business. The change took three years and involved closures due to redundancies in around one-third of all the company's areas of activity. Intel had finally decided to invest very deeply in microprocessor technology with a view to tapping into what at the time was an emerging mass market.

What lessons can be learned from this? First, true to one of Grove's guiding principles—*"Only the paranoid survive"*—a certain degree of paranoia or, more specifically, "healthy skepticism" is good, indeed essential, for anyone intent on being a successful entrepreneur. Intel almost waited too long before reading the writing on the wall and recognizing that its Japanese rivals were on the verge of forcing it out of a market it had previously dominated. With refreshingly down-to-earth clarity Grove said: *"Complacency often afflicts precisely those who have been the most successful."*[3] In over 40 years of Intel's existence, Grove has never allowed himself the luxury of complacency.

The second lesson to learn is how essential it is to always look at a business from the outside and ask: *"What would a new CEO do?"* By consciously looking at the company *from the outside*, Grove and Moore succeeded in reaching *totally new conclusions* and also used what Joseph Alois Schumpeter called *"creative destruction"* in a positive way, namely to create a new business that was stronger than its predecessor had ever been.

In 1994, Andy Grove found himself facing a second relatively major crisis with Intel. The company was just launching its latest generation of microprocessors, the Intel Pentium processor, when news reached Grove in December that IBM was immediately ceasing its deliveries of all Pentium-based computers. The reason cited for IBM's decision was a "minor design flaw" that had been reported to Grove a few weeks before but that was supposedly under control.

In fact, that "minor" flaw ended up plunging the company into one of the deepest crises in its history. The computer giant's refusal not to deliver some of its computers because they contained the Pentium chips in question not only damaged the reputation of Intel's product, but threatened the credibility and ultimately the continued existence of the entire company, leaving just two possibilities: either Intel could prove there was nothing wrong with the chip, or it could recall all the microprocessors it had delivered—a decision that would cost the company more than *half a billion dollars.* Ultimately Intel opted to recall the offending chips.

Looking back at the incident later in his book, Grove wrote: *"You only know that something has changed, something big, something significant, even if it's not entirely clear what that something is."*[4] Intel's management felt that it had totally lost control. Computer users, who were not even Intel's direct customers, demanded the processor's removal. What Intel thought it knew about quality and reliability suddenly no longer applied. The company had reached a *strategic inflection point,* as Grove called it: a situation necessitating a massive transformation far exceeding the scope of a normal change. Such inflection points are characterized by a drastically and extremely rapidly shifting situation and can involve *competitors, technology, customers, suppliers, complementary services, products,* or even certain *rules and regulations.*

The actual problem is not so much the fact of change as its scope and intensity. Grove himself quantified such radical shifts as ten times more intense than the changes to which an organization is "normally" accustomed.

A large proportion of Grove's highly readable book *Only the Paranoid Survive* is devoted to dealing with strategic inflection points. Incidentally, Peter F. Drucker, who only very rarely commented on books, had this to say about it: *"This terrific book is dangerous. . . . It will make people think."*[5] The point here is that the action Intel chose to take when faced with strategic inflection points *highlights the importance of constant circumspection, healthy skepticism, and a certain degree of paranoia,* regardless of whether the threats faced stem from technological progress or arise through competition.

■   ■   ■

Which specific steps can be taken to ensure that impending changes or even strategic inflection points are recognized at an early stage? The first essential step is to encourage *tough, open debate*. Only when situations, possibilities, and dangers are discussed at length will an organization have a chance to spot impending strategic inflection points, possibly even at an early stage. This step also entails deliberately aspiring to—or even demanding—differences of opinion in such discussions. Alfred Sloan was a master in this respect.

Any organization deeming this *kind of culture of debate* a necessity and wishing to embrace it will also end up without sycophants—and, for that matter, without bosses fond of surrounding themselves with people who agree with everything they say. Observation and analysis of what *competent* managers or advisory or supervisory bodies bear in mind when making staff-related decisions reveals that they like filling management posts with *strong characters* and with people who like working alongside such individuals. It has been known for some time that the quality of decisions depends primarily on a healthy culture of debate within an organization, so care needs to be taken to ensure that such a culture can arise and flourish.

Another key step entails encouraging targeted *discussions on core issues throughout your organization, across departmental boundaries*. Such exchanges could result in change or lead to strategic inflection points. Many problems and opportunities arising today are too complex for any few individual knowledge holders to have a sufficient overview of them. This is why in the future it will increasingly make sense for organizations to engage in opinion-forming and consensus-building across all departmental boundaries when issues of central importance are involved.

A further recommendation is to display healthy skepticism toward the *data* available to you and question the *assumptions* underlying your views and conclusions. At the same time, check whether the management team (including *you*) is keeping up with shifting reality. If it's not, decide what needs to be done to close the gap and "catch up." This may sound banal, but in the real world it regularly emerges that this issue has not been addressed or ends up being taken seriously only when it is almost too late to remedy the situation. Intel, too, waited a long time on both the occasions described above.

Naturally, it should be stressed that long before Intel faced any crises that jeopardized the company's very existence, it also successfully steered clear of many threats, preventing them from ever becoming really serious problems in the first place. Sensible questions to ask are: *"What can we do to circumvent crises and dangers at an early stage?" "What do we need to look out for?" "Which targets should we set for ourselves?"*

Over the past 50 years, specific *key areas* have proved their relevance for organizations to keep in mind and set targets for. Peter F. Drucker published them for the first time in 1954 in his book *The Practice of Management.*[6] Ever since, many authors have adopted, slightly altered, or based their work on them. According to Drucker, organizations should aim to meet specific performance targets and objectives in the following eight areas:

1. Market standing
2. Innovation
3. Productivity
4. Physical and financial resources (especially liquidity and cash flow)
5. Profitability
6. Manager performance and development
7. Worker performance and attitude
8. Public responsibility.

This approach has four distinct consequences: first, it sets *performance targets;* second, it defines areas that can be *appraised;* third, these eight areas create a *practical framework* from which to order and structure a wide range of real-life phenomena; and fourth, they serve to focus the systematic search for *risks* that may arise for the organization.

It is often supposed that different organizations need to cover different key areas, but in actual fact practical experience in this domain since the first publication on this issue half a century ago has shown that these areas are quite universal. In fact, they apply equally to organizations in all kinds of sectors, of every conceivable size, at every conceivable stage of development, and in any economic situation. Naturally, different organizations are likely to vary considerably in how they differentiate these areas, that is, subdividing them into variables or objectives of *secondary importance within a key area*. In addition, any such variable or objective may have to be altered to keep it in line with changing internal or external circumstances. Implementing this constant adaptation of development-driven objectives, limit values, factors to monitor, and variables is one of the main strategic tasks facing the management team.

The eight key areas listed above can be useful for neatly structuring the debate about what to look out for. Asking the following questions may be a useful way of setting the ball rolling:

- What determines our organization's *market standing*?
- How can we structure that market standing and view it in different perspectives?
- How can we define *innovation performance*? What does this performance determine for our organization's innovations, both internally and in the marketplace? How is our innovation performance developing over time? Is it getting worse or better?
- How *productive* is our organization in terms of labor, capital, time, and its exploitation of knowledge?
- What, apart from liquidity and cash flow, do we use to assess our *financial resources*? Which trends can we recognize?

- Which *physical resources* are of central importance to us?
- How high should our *minimum profit* be to ensure that we remain in business?
- How good is our *corporate culture* and how do we appraise the *performance, development, and attitude of our managers and workers*?
- In which areas do we accept *public responsibility*? In which domains do we have to decline such responsibility on the grounds that our organization would "overheat" if we *did* accept it?"

If you deal thoroughly and diligently with the eight key areas, not only will you lead your organization more reliably and with greater precision, but you will also be able to spot impending changes and strategic inflection points early on.

ACTION POINTS AND FOOD FOR THOUGHT

- Use the questions on the eight key areas to start a discussion with your colleagues. What else could you do to consolidate and improve your organization's performance in these areas?
- In which area is complacency jeopardizing lasting success?
- Where can you find the really good people you would like to have working alongside you? Can you offer them something they want as well?
- What can you do to recognize change or even strategic inflection points at an early stage? Encourage open debate? Discuss issues at the interdepartmental level? Question assumptions? Do you have any other ideas?

CHAPTER 14

Secure

Feedback

LEARNING FROM

James Watt

Most people believe that *James Watt* (1736–1819) invented the steam engine—but actually they are mistaken. The first modern steam engine was built by the English blacksmith and ironmonger Thomas Newcomen in 1712. Newcomen's engine performed a very useful task: it pumped water out of an English mine. However, Newcomen's machine was highly inefficient, earning it a reputation as a "coal guzzler." Newcomen's early design was itself based on experiments by French and English inventors who started testing ways of converting steam into kinetic energy as early as 1700 (almost 30 years before James Wattt's birth).

In 1764, when Watt set about repairing a Newcomen steam engine, he recognized how inefficient the design was and how much steam was being wasted. This fired his ambition to develop a far better machine. To fulfill that ambition, he even went so far as to study foreign languages so that he could read publications about the steam engines being built in other countries at the time. Incidentally, many people who go on to achieve greatness learn foreign languages so that they can gain access to valuable knowledge. For instance, Arthur Schopenhauer and Peter F. Drucker both learned Spanish so that they could read the original of the excellent *Oráculo manual y arte de prudencia*, published by

Baltasar Gracián in 1647, a book that Schopenhauer later single-mind-edly translated into German. The English edition of Gracián's book, titled *The Art of Worldly Wisdom*, became a bestseller.[1]

Returning to Watt, one thing is certain: in 1776 the first steam engine designed by him was put to work, and very soon it revolution-ized transport and was being used to power ships and traction engines, the precursors of trains. But to learn something about management, we will consider another of Watt's inventions, the *centrifugal* or *flyball governor*.

A governor is a device that controls and regulates the speed of an en-gine. The quicker the steam engine's pistons move, the faster the gov-ernor rotates. As a result, masses on lever arms rise against the force of gravity, activating a mechanism to reduce the flow of steam and throttle the machine's running speed. Watt used *feedback* from the centrifugal governor to keep his steam engines running at a constant speed.

Today, the principle of feedback is so widely applied that it usually goes totally unnoticed, whether in computers, for air traffic control, when performing surgery, in a production context, or when manag-ing organizations—in other words, anywhere a process has to be *con-trolled*. Yet far too few managers make sufficiently systematic use of this *essential management tool* when managing people, when manag-ing their organization, or when managing innovation.

Feedback is the key to continuous learning. As long as 2,500 years ago, the most celebrated physician of the ancient world, Hippocrates of Cos, taught that doctors should write down how they believed their patients' cures should develop, based on what they decided. Subse-quently, the *outcome* of that decision was to be compared with the doc-tor's *predictions*. You will be amazed at how much can be learned from feedback, and how quickly! Within just a few years, the decisions made by someone who previously neglected this valuable source of informa-tion will be far more competent than before.

Make sure that, as a professional manager, you *systematically* receive regular feedback within your organization on key projects and issues. This means routinely gathering information on *order confirmations, interim reports,* and *notices of execution.* If you do this consistently, you will be making a major contribution toward ensuring the functional reliability of your organization as a whole and thereby also minimizing its risks. Not for nothing is such an approach absolutely essential in domains in which people's lives are at risk, as is the case in surgery or in the context of military operations or air traffic control. There, feedback is indispensable for ensuring the safety of actions taken, and naturally the same applies to the transaction of business, too.

A perfect example of true professionalism related to feedback was provided by General Dwight D. Eisenhower at the end of World War II. After Alfred Jodl, the chief of operations for the German Armed Forces High Command, had signed the unconditional surrender at Allied headquarters in Reims, Eisenhower soberly penned this final, brief report to be sent to Washington: *"The mission of this Allied Force was fulfilled at 02.41, local time, May 7, 1945."*[2] Considering the significance of the message, what a singular display of professionalism that was.

The same approach that applies when managing an organization or managing other people can also be adopted for managing yourself. Whenever Jesuit priests or Calvinist pastors do something of significance, they are required to note down the results they expect. Then, *nine months* later they consult those records to compare what actually happened with what they anticipated, thereby guaranteeing a supply of valuable feedback. If you do the same, you will very soon find out what your strengths are, where lessons need to be learned to enhance those strengths, and where any weaknesses preventing you from ever becoming maximally efficient happen to lie. In addition, you will find out which habits you need to change in order to improve. Peter F. Drucker rigorously applied this approach for over 60 years, even at a very advanced age and always emphasized how fruitful it was for him.

ACTION POINTS AND FOOD FOR THOUGHT

- Make systematic use of feedback analysis when managing organizations, people, or innovation. When you make your next key decision, write down what outcome you expect. Then, a suitable number of months later, compare the actual situation with what you expected it to be.

- What do you need to do to make regular feedback standard practice in your organization? Who can help you establish the generation of professional feedback as a constant practice in your company?

PART 2

MANAGING
Innovation

CHAPTER **15**

Implement
Ideas

LEARNING FROM
Steve Jobs

Steve Jobs (born in 1955) has justifiably earned a reputation for innovation. But what makes him truly innovative is not that he is the *first person to come up with ideas,* but rather that he is the *first one to implement them.*

Thus, he was *not* the first person to think of:

- Developing an affordable computer for the average home.
- Developing a truly user-friendly computer with an intuitive, mouse-driven user interface.
- Making the first fully digitally animated movie and turning it into a worldwide hit.
- Developing the first computer whose design would set new standards.
- Developing a new generation of music players (whose worldwide success would dwarf that of the Walkman).
- Developing a cell phone that would epitomize a new generation of smartphones.
- Establishing a totally new global market with digital lifestyle products (in his case the *iPod, iTunes,* and the *iPhone*).

Instead, his innovation lies in spotting the true potential of great ideas and implementing them to unparalleled effect.

The advent of the *Apple 1, Apple 2, Apple Macintosh,* of the movies *Toy Story* and *A Bug's Life,* of the *iMac, iPod, iTunes, iPhone,* and *iPad* were all milestones in effective implementation, driven by a relentless will to innovate. In short, there is a clear answer to the question about what makes top people really special: *they get the right things done.* So implementation is vital. After all, it is relatively easy to come up with ideas, but *implementing* them is another matter entirely.

Innovation is the one core skill that any organization needs, be it a government organization, a nongovernment organization (NGO), a business, or a nonprofit organization. But before an organization can develop this core skill, it must first properly understand what innovation is. There is one unequivocal and uncompromising benchmark for doing this—namely the extent to which benefits are generated for customers so that the market is satisfied. Consequently innovation cannot be evaluated from within an organization, but depends solely on what customers want and whether they will be prepared to pay for it. Neither the technological nor the scientific value of innovation is decisive; nor is its originality, attractiveness, or quality, or even the top management's opinion of it. The decisive thing is the customers' verdict in the marketplace. *That* is the acid test.

Well-managed organizations systematically measure their innovation performance. Yet the starting point here should not be performance, but *observation* of the market. Consequently, the management team should ask itself:

- Which innovations have occurred in our organization's market during the period under consideration?
- Who brought these innovations to market?

- Which innovations proved particularly successful?
- Which innovations in other sectors could influence our organization's market?
- Which consequences does our organization need to draw in light of all the innovations cited above?

A profound understanding of the respective business environment is the basis on which to discuss innovations and then move on to question your organization's own achievements by asking the following:

- How many—and which—innovations have we successfully introduced?
- Are these innovations strengthening our market standing? If so, where? In existing markets where we are already established, or in major growth markets that may represent our future?
- What proportion of our sales do we earn from which products? How long have these products been available?
- Is the overall result a healthy, sustainable structure?

In addition to considering performance, however, some discussion should also focus on *non*performance, missed opportunities, failures, errors, things that were overlooked, or developments that prompted too late a response (if at all). The question to ask then is: why did this happen to us?

Strictly speaking, the answers to these questions constitute a *judgment* (rather than a *measurement*) of innovation performance. All the same, it is such assessments that form the basis of sound decision making. Indeed, managers would be making a big mistake if they relied solely on what is measurable and objectively quantifiable. Anyone who tackles the subject of innovation as sketched out above will initially have more questions than answers, but at least they are *essential* questions and the *right* kind to ask.

ACTION POINTS AND FOOD FOR THOUGHT

- Keep precise track of innovations in your market.
- Which innovations that were developed and then introduced by your organization actually generated benefits for your customers and which were merely new products or services? What needs to be done to establish closer contact with your target group?
- Does your organization ask the right questions about innovation at regular, scheduled intervals?
- What can you and your colleagues do to boost your organization's power to innovate?

CHAPTER 16

Remember, Innovations Are Rarely Welcomed with Open Arms

LEARNING FROM

Gustave Eiffel

If there is one thing you need to know as a manager, it is the fact that innovations are never welcomed with open arms. Accordingly, whenever you innovate, you will always find yourself facing an uphill struggle. The Eiffel Tower serves as a good example because if many prominent Parisians had had their way back in 1887 it would never have been built.

Gustave Eiffel (1832–1923) had already made a name for himself around the world by constructing steel bridges, various facilities, and exhibition pavilions. His most famous buildings include the first department store built of steel and glass, Le Bon Marché, in Paris (1876), designs for locks along the Panama Canal (1882–1914), and the armature for the Statue of Liberty in New York (1886). The idea of erecting a tower came to Eiffel when he was constructing metal bridge piers. The first designs date from 1884 and can be attributed to Eiffel's colleague Maurice Koechlin.

Eiffel's firm of architects won the competition launched in 1886 to develop the site for the Paris World Expo in 1889 by erecting a tower on the Champ de Mars as a kind of trademark of the exhibition. After over two years of work directed by Koechlin, the structure that has become the most famous Parisian landmark was completed. Full of joyful enthusiasm, Gustave Eiffel proclaimed: *"France will be the only country in the world with a 300-meter flagpole."*[1]

But rather than receiving a universally warm welcome, the plan for Eiffel's innovative structure unleashed a storm of protests. Indeed, leading lights like the composer Charles Gounod, the authors Émile Zola, Leconte de Lisle, Guy de Maupassant, and Alexandre Dumas, and Charles Garnier, the architect of the Paris Opera House, drew up a petition that proclaimed: *"We, the writers, painters, sculptors, architects and lovers of the beauty of Paris, do protest with all our vigor and all our indignation, in the name of French taste and endangered French art and history, against the useless and monstrous Eiffel Tower."*[2]

But once the tower had been completed, those initial misgivings soon turned to jubilation, and the structure was duly featured on paintings by Pissarro, Dufy, Utrillo, Seurat, Marquet, and Delaunay and was mentioned in poems by Apollinaire and Cocteau. And who today could imagine Paris *without* the Eiffel Tower?

As the manager of an organization, you should not necessarily expect such a dramatic switch from initial opposition to euphoric acceptance of your plans. In fact, you would be wrong to expect your innovative ideas to be met with joy, for quite the opposite is the norm. Spotting promising opportunities and seizing them for your organization is psychologically demanding: often it means abandoning old habits. Worse still, it frequently involves letting go of the very things that the organization's most capable people hold most dear. It takes unremitting efforts to overcome their opposition, strike a balance between clashing interests, and thus ensure that the innovation is successfully carried through to completion. What any innovation needs is someone who says *"I will make a success of this"* and then sets to work and does not stop until the intended breakthrough has been achieved.

Anything that has been improved or that is new needs to be

tested—on a small scale. This would have been difficult with something like the Eiffel Tower, yet the general rule still applies: market research, studies, and simulations are no replacement for real-life testing. Pilot tests are essential.

The key is to ensure that the *best and most deeply respected* people take up the challenge. Whoever is placed in charge must not be selected merely because he or she has the time. Indeed, it is likely that people with time on their hands will not be the right choice. Furthermore, the person in question does not necessarily need to come from within your organization. In many cases a good solution is to work with a customer who really wants a new product or service, is prepared to work as part of a team to establish it, and is also willing to persevere until all the inevitable problems have been overcome. If the ensuing pilot test proves successful, the risks run by going ahead with the planned innovation will usually be relatively minor.

ACTION POINTS AND FOOD FOR THOUGHT

- Make sure that your best ideas are driven forward by really good people.
- Which innovative projects should you start working on tomorrow, despite all the difficulties that are bound to crop up?

CHAPTER 17

Question Every Assumption

Nicolaus Copernicus

When *Nicolaus Copernicus* (1473–1543) was a young man, it seemed obvious to everyone that the Earth was at the center of the universe, because every night the celestial bodies could be seen revolving around our planet. Until Copernicus came along, nobody questioned such a geocentric worldview. But this persistent astronomer queried all such supposedly "proven" assumptions and constructed a worldview in which the sun, not the Earth, occupied center stage. In this heliocentric worldview, he explained the complex movements of the planets by postulating that they moved in small circles called epicycles along larger circles, called deferents, with the sun not lying at the exact center of the Copernican system, but also completing an orbit. It was only later on that the astronomer Johannes Kepler found out that planets' orbits are elliptical, not nested circles. And how did Kepler reach that conclusion? Again, by questioning the assumptions made in his day.

So what can you, as a manager, learn from Copernicus? Copernicus had the same data as everybody else and saw and heard the same things as his peers. Yet he reached totally different conclusions because he *interpreted* the data totally differently. He queried assumptions that everyone else considered to be beyond discussion. And that is precisely what you ought to do, too. Any successful company makes—and *needs* to make—assumptions about how business works.

Also when dealing with opportunities and problems, any decision you make will be based on assumptions. My advice is not to make life too easy for yourself by too swiftly accepting apparently obvious assumptions, answers, or solutions. Question them. Instead of expecting others to immediately agree with your position or opinion, try to make sure that people can follow your line of argument and understand your line of thinking. This may occasionally make life somewhat uncomfortable for your employees, colleagues, and bosses, but you will certainly end up with better solutions—and that will earn you respect.

Think back to Copernicus again. He had no problem understanding the geocentric worldview, but he did not share it, so he developed an alternative. In 1616, the Catholic Church banned Copernicanism, alleging that it contradicted the Bible. Of course, whether the ban was imposed because the Church was unable to follow the line of thinking behind the Copernican model or merely unwilling to do so is another question entirely.

ACTION POINTS AND FOOD FOR THOUGHT
- Make a point of questioning everything.
- In connection with which current problem facing you should you reconsider supposedly "established" facts?

CHAPTER **18**

Innovate
Systematically

LEARNING FROM
Thomas Edison

Successful managers do not merely sit around waiting for brilliant ideas to occur to them; they work methodically. *Thomas Alva Edison* (1847–1931) showed us how to *innovate systematically*.

When one of Edison's assistants went to see him feeling somewhat dejected after numerous experiments had not produced the desired result, the tireless inventor retorted: *"Listen, I conducted 50,000 experiments to invent a new battery. The fact that those 50,000 possibilities do not work is a great result!"*[1] Not without reason is Edison also attributed with the insight that: *"Genius is 99 percent perspiration and 1 percent inspiration."*[2]

Edison was the archetypal inventor. In his lifetime he registered over 1,200 patents, the first when just 21 years old and the last at the ripe old age of 81. Edison was self-taught, attended school for only three months, and started working when he was 12. During his lifetime he developed more than 2,000 appliances and processes. Most people think of Edison as the man who invented the light bulb, but that is not actually the case. The light bulb was invented roughly 25 years before Edison popularized it by the precision engineer Heinrich Goebel, who had used one to illuminate his New York workshop since 1854. What Edison invented was city illumination, which is something quite different, but definitely more significant, bearing in mind the benefits to its users. Edison succeeded in making the breakthrough to *mass production*. That was his achievement. And his systematic approach to innovation was legendary.

What can Edison teach us? Well, innovative managers know that innovation is sparked by an idea. But instead of suppressing "crazy" ideas, effective managers ask themselves: "*What would it take to turn this crazy idea into something sensible, something that constitutes an opportunity for us?*" So while there is no shortage of ideas, the true challenge lies in *applying* them (as described in Chapter 15 on Steve Jobs). Most ideas will turn out *not* to be worth following up. For this reason, you and your colleagues and employees should seriously ask yourselves this question: "*What do we need to find out, learn, and do before committing ourselves to putting this idea into practice?*" In so doing, focus your attention on *really essential* innovations, rather than striving for small changes and minor improvements. Edison carried out 6,000 experiments before finding the right filament for his light bulb. All the time, what kept him going was *a single big idea*. Remember, too, that big and small aspects are not at all mutually exclusive. No doubt it was recognition of this fact that prompted Edison to ask his engineers and scientists "*to invent something small every 10 days and something big every 6 months.*"[3]

To innovate systematically, you will need to be aware of the seven main sources of innovation. The first four ought to prompt action within your organization[4]:

1. *The unexpected,* such as an unexpected success, an unexpected failure, or an unexpected outside event.
2. *Incongruity* relates to a situation in which expectations regarding observable reality and reality as it "ought to be" do not tally with the actual situation.
3. *Process necessity,* such as an innovation required to meet a need intrinsic to a process.

4. *A sudden change in market or sectoral structures* that takes everyone by surprise.

The three other sources of innovation involve changes stemming from
outside the organization:

1. Changing *demographic structures.*
2. *Changes in perception, mood, and meaning* within the broader
   context.
3. *New knowledge,* both scientific and nonscientific.

If you systematically explore these seven sources of innovation, you
will go far. Nonetheless, even if you reliably spot opportunities for innovation and take excellent steps to make practical use of them, errors
of judgment are bound to occur. So bear in mind what Edison said
in 1926, shortly before one innovation achieved its worldwide breakthrough: *"I have determined that there is no market for talking pictures."*[5]—and doggedly continue your systematic approach.

ACTION POINTS AND FOOD FOR THOUGHT

■ Set a date with your key colleagues and employees to work
through the seven sources of innovation listed above in relation to your organization.

■ Which idea should you take up in depth tomorrow with a view
to assessing or facilitating its viability?

CHAPTER **19**

Exploit Success

LEARNING FROM

Dietrich Mateschitz

Not many organizations are really good at exploiting their *successes*. In fact, most of them are pretty bad at doing so. The reason for this is the belief that they have earned their success and thus attained their objective. But that is most decidedly wrong, for it is here that their work should truly begin. In this respect, you can learn a lot from *Dietrich Mateschitz* (born in 1944), the founder of Red Bull and a true master at exploiting successes.

"What do you want with this syrupy stuff?,"[1] he was asked when he launched his Red Bull brand. Worse still, his energy drink, which tasted like liquid gummy bears, was going to cost way more than a Coke or Pepsi. *"Who needs it? What's the point of it? Where is the market for it?"* were the questions he faced. To tell you the truth, there was no market. What is more, Dietrich Mateschitz was well aware of the fact: *"When we first started, we said there is no existing market for Red Bull. But Red Bull will create it."*[2] When the brand's launch proved successful, Red Bull's competitors initially claimed it was just a fad. *"But when we noticed, over time that we had 142 copycats, we stopped counting,"*[3] Mateschitz said 15 years later, in 2002.

One of Mateschitz's recipes for success is that he has always invested heavily in building the brand. In 2004 he pumped around $600 million, roughly 30 percent of his revenue, into marketing. Coca-Cola spends around 9 percent. However, instead of spending millions on enlisting the services of superstars, like PepsiCo and Coca-Cola, Mateschitz went in search of up-and-coming stars in somewhat unconventional disciplines. The result? No brand is as strongly represented in the extreme sport segment as Red Bull. Every year the company organizes dozens of events, including air shows featuring the Flying Bulls aerobatic team, kite surfing in Hawaii, downhill mountain biking, or cliff diving. And it now arranges cool cultural events, too, under the bywords *Red Bull Music and Dance.*

Red Bull's marketing is brilliant. Right from the outset, Mateschitz banked on a positively received *guerrilla marketing* approach. This meant profiling the product by adopting a creative, different strategy without deploying vast resources. No other company has made this approach such an incisive trademark. Its success has been truly spectacular, especially when you bear in mind the heavyweights the company was up against when it started out. In some countries Red Bull has achieved market shares of 80 percent in its segment; in 2004 it scored a market share of 47 percent in the United States, notching up annual growth at a rate of around 40 percent. Red Bull became Austria's first truly global brand, before Mozartkugel chocolate balls, Lipizzaner horses, or the Vienna Symphonic Orchestra. But Mateschitz more than deserves his personal and financial success; surely anyone who turns out a product that livens up parties around the world *deserves* to be a billionaire.

Dietrich Mateschitz teaches us how to *exploit success*. Any organization will tend to concentrate on problems. In fact, managers are almost

magnetically attracted to problems, causing both them and their organizations to *focus on problems instead of on opportunities.* The best
chances of thriving arise when successes are exploited and used as a
platform for further development. Sony has employed this approach on
countless occasions in the consumer electronics sector to score small
and large successes. Its Walkman is just one example among many. The
fact that the Japanese giant missed out on the iPod trend is a different
story that I touch on in Chapter 21 on Joseph Schumpeter.

Conversely, capitalizing on success does not mean simply ignoring problems. Serious problems need to be dealt with, of course. But
organizations that successfully manage change concentrate on their
successes, the rule of thumb being to *nurture successes* and *starve
problems.*

So how can you recognize successes, especially unexpected ones?
What you need is an *"additional first page"* in your monthly report, a
page listing all those results attained by the organization that exceeded
expectations: revenue forecasts, the volume of sales achieved, profit,
productivity, innovation performance, or the hiring of suitable people.
Also listed on that page every month should be any *recognized opportunities.* That page should come *before* the page on which problems are
listed. And you should spend as much time on the *opportunities page*
as you have previously done working on the *problems page.*

If you are to succeed in seizing any spotted opportunities, make
your best, most competent performers responsible for capitalizing on
them. Organizations that make this approach a monthly routine and
which demand that everyone keep his or her eyes peeled for potential
opportunities will switch from being problem-focused to *opportunity-
oriented.* And along the way they will create something that could be
described as "the pleasure and enjoyment of achieving." In other words,
the result will be a very different corporate climate.

ACTION POINTS AND FOOD FOR THOUGHT

- Draw up an "additional first page" for your monthly report, listing opportunities for your organization. Then document all those areas in which expectations regarding revenue, sales volume, profit, productivity, innovation performance, and the recruitment of suitable people were exceeded.
- Who right now are the best people to take responsibility for seizing your organization's biggest opportunities?
- What would have to be done in your organization, and what can you do, to ensure that in the future your organization is more opportunity-oriented than problem-focused?

CHAPTER **20**

Practice Purposeful Abandonment

LEARNING FROM

Herbert von Karajan

For over 30 years, the masterful conducting of *Herbert von Karajan* (1908–1989) made the Berlin Philharmonic, which he led between 1955 and 1989, one of the most highly rated orchestras performing Wagner's music. At the same time, Karajan also set new standards for the interpretation of the classical and romantic repertoire of concertos and orchestral works of Ludwig van Beethoven, Anton Bruckner, and Richard Strauss. And as if that was not enough, Karajan was rated one of the most competent interpreters of works by Giuseppe Verdi.

In addition to making almost countless recordings, Karajan also attained an unusually powerful position on the European music scene. Apart from leading the Berlin Philharmonic Orchestra, between 1956 and 1964 he was in charge of the Vienna State Opera and took on various other top jobs as well, including at the Salzburg Festival, the Salzburg Easter Festival (which he founded in 1967), and the Salzburg Whitsun Festival, which began in 1973. Through his production companies, Karajan comprehensively exploited his artistic performances across multiple media, combining live appearances, audio recordings, and videos. Karajan himself was always enthusiastic about new technical developments and was invariably among the pioneers when it came to exploiting new technology for his own ends. Another fact that should not be overlooked is that many young artists, like the violinist Anne-Sophie Mutter, largely owe their original breakthrough to Karajan's benevolent influence.

Yet as extensive as Karajan's various activities and commitments were, he was also a maestro at "purposeful abandonment," and it is in this connection that you, as a manager, can learn some valuable lessons from him.

Purposeful abandonment is a technique exploited by many people and organizations that achieve greatness. The concept is nothing new, having been discussed at length by Peter F. Drucker as long ago as 1964 in *Managing for Results* and again in 1967 in *The Effective Executive*. Nonetheless, most organizations are not systematic about practicing purposeful abandonment, despite how extremely useful it is today, faced with a glut of possibilities and the associated risk of dissipating their efforts and energy.[1]

Karajan's exceptional drive may be characterized by impressive versatility, but he was also perfectly capable of devoting his full attention to just one activity during a particular creative phase while deliberately suppressing or totally abandoning others. He was aware that no orchestra can on the same day put in world-class performances of works by composers who are stylistically worlds apart. Furthermore, even when concentrating on just a few composers, like any competent conductor, he did not overstretch his repertoire with them when he wanted to set new standards. This paved the way for excellent performances, while other orchestral pieces and composers were set to one side.

This is one reason why conductors with very broad repertoires very rarely rank among the world's best, Simon Rattle being one such exception, as you will discover in Chapter 26. Ordinarily, people are simply incapable of excelling at lots of different things. But even where genius enters the picture, sometimes there may be justification in claiming that *less would probably have been more*. This, for example, is what

Giorgio Vasari, a contemporary of Michelangelo and biographer of famous painters, sculptors, and architects of his time, wrote about Leonardo da Vinci in the sixteenth century: *"We see that to really find out what art was all about Leonardo started all manner of things, but saw barely any through to completion."*[2]

Just how important the concept of offloading ballast is can be seen from literature as well. English author Charles Dickens, whose most famous works include *Oliver Twist* and *David Copperfield*, improved his books by gradually shortening them, reviewing them over and over again. Instead of writing more text, he used different colors to successively delete words, sentences, or entire passages from his manuscript in the course of successive revisions. By the time he had finished, his manuscript could be peppered with red, green, and blue markings and be just a third of its original length!

If such eminent individuals as these saw a need to make a habit of systematically scaling back their activities, then humble managers must surely embrace the same principle. Yet the concept does not only apply to individuals, entire organizations can substantially boost their effectiveness and efficiency by practicing purposeful abandonment. In this connection, the following few *basic considerations and procedures* may prove useful.

1. Basic considerations

Neither managers nor organizations can simultaneously notch up remarkable achievements in multiple domains. This is simply a fact. Accordingly, the first and most important step must entail systematically setting aside anything that detracts from effectiveness and efficiency. If this is not done regularly and as a matter of course, *resources* will constantly be squandered on things that no longer need to be done. And not infrequently your *best people* will end up being wasted, assigned to deal with old, outdated business instead of being allowed to focus their attention on opportunities with future promise. What is more, any wasting of *time, money, or human resources* will subsequently make it-self felt in areas where urgently needed resources could otherwise have been put to very productive use.

The process of *self-renewal* through systematic, purposeful aban-donment and innovation is essential because all products, services, processes, systems, and guidelines will sooner or later become redun-dant, quite simply either because the objectives associated with them have already been achieved, or because different goals will need to be met in the future. Quite apart from this, it is worth bearing in mind that it is considerably better to actively drive forward the process of systematic abandonment yourself than only to react when forced to do so by one's competitors. Playing an *active* role puts you in a far superior position. Organizations and individuals who expedite change may take certain risks, but neglecting to make such changes at all, or only doing so too late, would definitely represent a greater risk. Organizations that are intent on making names for themselves as *change leaders* will inevitably have to undertake a rigorous process of *systematic purpose-ful abandonment* anyway.

2. Procedures

There are many different ways of setting up such a process. Two tried and tested methods are drafting a *"stop-doing"* list and scheduling reg-ular *meetings on systematic, purposeful abandonment* (called *"aban-donment meetings"* for short).

Writing a *stop-doing list* can work wonders for your own personal efficiency. Effective managers keep some kind of *to-do lists* to note tasks they wish to perform. But instead of merely listing what you intend to do, you should also write down what you plan to *stop doing* in the future. Keeping a stop-doing list will help you understand not only *what* you should no longer do, but also *how* you can go about making sure that there is no need for you to do it any longer, if it still needs to be done at all.

Be mindful in this context that many successful people swap money for time, whereas the vast majority trade time for money. And even if this still seems like only a distant notion to you, keep it in the back of your mind because you will soon find ways of buying time for money, probably on a rather limited scale to begin with, but soon, if you persevere, on a much broader scale. And you will see that the situation is very similar to that concerning interest, which generates compound interest, which in turn generates even more interest, and so on. The more time you can afford to buy, the better you will be able to concentrate on things that generate greater added value for others, which in turn will further boost your resources. Obviously, then, stop-doing lists are not only helpful for you as a manager, but more importantly can help you make your organization more effective.

The second method (holding monthly *abandonment meetings*) is based on an idea that is both simple and sensible. It entails setting aside *a fixed day every month* for a meeting at which the participants discuss any activity they feel ought to be sloughed off. Some organizations consistently hold such meetings once a month at every management level. Each such meeting focuses on a different core area, such as products, services, designated uses, markets, groups of customers, distribution channels, processes, rules, or guidelines. The aim of the exercise is to scrutinize all aspects of an organization's activities over the course of a year with a view to practicing systematic, purposeful abandonment. The general questions to be asked in so doing are these: *"Do we want to keep on doing what we are currently doing?" "What should we stop doing in the future?"*

It was in response to the following two questions that legendary General Electric CEO *Jack Welch* set his goal of ensuring that GE should be the number one or two in every single one of its companies' markets, asking: *"If you weren't already in the business, would you enter it today?"* And if the answer is no, *"What are you going to do about it?"*[3] Apply these questions correspondingly to different areas of your organization. What you should expect to happen over the year is to see significant changes regarding both *what* is done and *how* it is done. In addition, some worthwhile activities that you would like to take on are bound to crop up. And you can make the process dynamic and more effective if, in keeping with good implementation management practices, you regularly communicate what is being achieved and what has changed as a result of these abandonment meetings.

ACTION POINTS AND FOOD FOR THOUGHT

- Introduce a monthly abandonment meeting (or a meeting geared toward purposeful abandonment) and spread the word within your organization about the results of systematically following up on them.
- Keep a stop-doing list.
- Find out where you might usefully exchange money for time.

CHAPTER **21**

Practice Creative Destruction

LEARNING FROM

Joseph Schumpeter

The process of *creative destruction* is firmly associated with the economist *Joseph Schumpeter* (1883–1950). Many people are familiar with the concept, yet few organizations apply it systematically. Schumpeter's main underlying idea is set out in his book *Capitalism, Socialism, and Democracy:* "*This process of Creative Destruction is the essential fact about capitalism. It is what capitalism consists in and what every capitalist concern has got to live in.*"[1]

Schumpeter was the first influential economist to vehemently advocate the view that a *dynamic imbalance,* caused by the activities of the innovator-entrepreneur, is a far more normal situation for a healthy economy than balance and optimization. Ahead of his time, in his seminal work *The Theory of Economic Development,* published in 1911, he drew attention to the topic of *innovation,* decades before it became a key issue in all business and social organizations. Today, *creative destruction* is more relevant than ever, and *innovation and entrepreneurial activity* have become major issues for all organizations. In an age of constant change the relevant criterion is not *size,* but *strength,* and above all *adaptability* to changing circumstances.

Electronics giant Sony is an example of an organization that has at times been too slow to acknowledge the importance of creative destruction and of the need to adapt to changing circumstances. In the 1980s the company enjoyed unbelievable success worldwide with its Walkman, the world's first mobile cassette player. For around 20 years Sony dominated the market. Yet it failed to properly anticipate the threat posed by Apple, let alone respond by bringing to bear all the market power it could muster. In 2007 Apple reported that it had sold 100 million iPods, and the press spoke of the "Walkman of the 21st century." In 2009, the dominance of the iTunes store was so strong that it was estimated to command an incredible 70 percent market share of the legal American music download market.[2]

For too long Sony clung to the belief that hardware was the key to success, while Apple, displaying creative destruction, deliberately abandoned such a credo. And with everything offered in conjunction with its iPod, from easy Internet access to a significant lifestyle statement, Apple turned a good product into an excellent one that proved popular all over the world.

In an age when the *dynamic imbalance* is even greater than it was in Schumpeter's day, it is organizations that move forward by systematically innovating and achieving *stability and continuity*. At some stage, all rules and regulations, systems, procedures, products, and services have fulfilled their purpose, become outdated, and need to be renewed. Either that or they *fail* to fulfill their purpose and likewise need to be replaced.

Of course, creative destruction is not merely a useful concept in the economic domain. For instance, the composer Arnold Schoenberg (1874–1951), who developed the 12-tone technique, greatly influenced the music of the twentieth century because his music broke with tradition, prompting musicians to enter totally uncharted territory. And although Schoenberg's achievement was subsequently deemed an important milestone in the history of music, like Gustave Eiffel, he found that his innovation was not afforded a universally warm welcome. Nonetheless, demonstrating true entrepreneurial spirit, he always believed in his work, saying in 1935: *"The time will come when the ability to draw thematic material from a basic set of twelve tones will be an unconditional prerequisite for obtaining admission into the composition class of a conservatory."*[3]

Entrepreneurial activity may widely be deemed risky, which it undoubtedly is, yet it entails less risk than stubbornly continuing to optimize things that are no longer of use. If consumers want automobiles, any attempts by the last manufacturer of horse-drawn carriages to optimize his internal procedures and marketing will be in vain. Practicing creative destruction helps to ensure that resources are deployed where they prove most productive. Contrary to the cliché about daredevil entrepreneurs, managers who act in an entrepreneurial fashion are intent *not* on taking risks but on making substantial efforts to spot, avoid, and control any dangers. Entrepreneurs and managers who innovate successfully pursue opportunities rather than be audacious and take risks.

As the pace of change picks up, managers are faced with the choice of either merely reacting to changes or actively trying to shape them. *Creative destruction* is a key tool for innovation and entrepreneurial conduct because it questions things and opens up room for improvements. In addition, it underpins a corporate culture in which innovation and entrepreneurship are duly appreciated.

ACTION POINTS AND FOOD FOR THOUGHT

- In what connection would creative destruction benefit your organization? What would you change?
- Gather your best people together and discuss where you could benefit from creative destruction.
- Where do you see opportunities that are associated with relatively minor risks?

CHAPTER 22

Combine Existing Know-How with Other Knowledge to Create Something New

LEARNING FROM
Ettore Bugatti

It is very probable that technologies and solutions developed *outside* your own sector will have the greatest influence on the path taken by your organization or domain of activity. The same applies *inside* your organization, where excellent solutions await if you systematically link knowledge from different areas of activity. *Ettore Bugatti* (1881–1947) showed how effectively separate disciplines can be teamed up to produce wonderful results.

Ettore Bugatti made automobiles that combined unusual construction with highly aesthetic designs. These rolling works of art met with amazement, eliciting almost boundless enthusiasm. Bugatti succeeded in marrying different disciplines in previously unimagined ways and created something entirely new out of advanced technology, top-quality production, and truly artistic car body designs. This was how the Bugatti brand attained unrivaled, true cult status between the Golden

Twenties and the outbreak of World War II. Looking back over a long list of exceptional racing cars, like Bugatti's *Type 29* and *Type 32* or the luxurious *Type 41 Royale,* many Bugatti aficionados thought the brand's days were over when Ettore Bugatti died in 1947. Indeed, the Bugatti company was forced to stop production in 1956.

A first attempt to revive the brand was made by Romano Artioli in 1987, and just four years later the 12-cylinder *EB 110* was unveiled in Paris to coincide with the 110th anniversary of Ettore Bugatti's birth. However, the company proved unable to hold its own in the market and was forced to file for bankruptcy in 1995. When Volkswagen acquired Bugatti in 1998, the aesthetic tradition started by Ettore Bugatti was continued in the shape of a new supercar. The dream was to build a production vehicle that once again uniquely combined *aesthetic appeal* with *high technology.* The resulting automobile was intended to perform like a Formula 1 race car while at the same time being suitable for everyday use, thus marrying extreme innovation with noble tradition and great design. The outcome was unquestionably an utter masterpiece: the *Veyron 16.4,* with a top speed of 257 mph, a 1,200-horsepower engine, and acceleration from 0 to 60 mph in under 3 seconds—all wonderfully packaged in an aesthetically appealing design. *Note how this result could be achieved only by combining specialist knowledge from different disciplines.*

Technologies leap from sector to sector with breathtaking speed and end up no longer being specific to any individual field. At the same time, sectoral knowledge itself is increasingly being derived from other areas of activity. This is why you need to seek solutions in other sectors that could also prove useful in your primary business segment.

For example, fiber optic cables have revolutionized the entire telecommunications sector, yet they were invented not by a company active in that domain, but rather by the glass company Corning Inc.

The creation of NASA in 1958 also constituted an attempt to reap benefits from bringing together people from different programs and domains. NASA's inception was galvanized by the Soviet Union's launch of Sputnik, beating the United States in the race to put a satellite into orbit around the Earth. As a result, NASA organized a *research lab without walls.*

NASA is no exception. Practically *all* organizations have incredible untapped potential because they *do not adopt a systematically interdisciplinary approach* in their quest to find better, more effective solutions. If you want to make a major contribution toward your organization's development, take steps to ensure that complex problems are solved by *people from all parts of it in a truly interdisciplinary approach* and that major opportunities are properly exploited the same way. *Finding solutions without walls* can make a huge difference, whether you're striving for the swift, successful implementation of a change process, overseeing the adoption of a new strategic tack, coming to terms with a merger, targeting long-term savings, penetrating new markets, boosting the quality of products or services, or seeking to lastingly improve internal processes and procedures. To achieve any of these objectives, gather together your brightest people.

ACTION POINTS AND FOOD FOR THOUGHT

- Establish a procedure for regularly scouting other sectors for new trends, technologies, and know-how that could prove useful for your organization.
- When do you next plan to bring together the best people from throughout your organization at an off-site session to approve a bundle of measures for solving the toughest problems you face and making the most of your biggest opportunities?

CHAPTER **23**

Exploit Opportunities Arising From New Technologies

L E A R N I N G   F R O M

Larry Page

Google cofounder and current CEO *Larry Page*, born in 1973, and the company's other cofounder, Sergey Brin, strikingly demonstrated the hidden power inherent in being quick to seize on and then exploit opportunities presented by new technologies. Google not only dominates the Internet search engine market, but also the online advertising market. Today, Google has its hand in pretty much everything on the Internet, and without Page, Google would not have achieved much of it.

Once, when asked by *Fortune* magazine what the best piece of advice he had ever been given was, he answered: *"In graduate school at Stanford University, I had about ten ideas of things I wanted to do, and one of them was to look at the link structure of the web. My advisor, Terry Winograd, picked that one out and said: 'Well, that one seems like a really good idea.' So I give him credit for that."*[1] (We return to the importance of good advisors in Chapter 36 on Camille Pissarro.)

Together with his fellow student Sergey Brin, Larry Page set to work, and urged on by Winograd's suggestion, ran "Project Google," which became a company in 1998. Once the company had been founded, Page served as its CEO until 2001. Under his leadership, the company grew to 200 employees and entered the profit zone. In 2001, Page and

Brin brought Eric Schmidt, the former chairman and CEO of Novell, into the company. Ever since, Page, Brin, and Schmidt have been the company's top executives. Larry Page has personally won numerous awards, including being named a "Global Leader for Tomorrow" at the World Economic Forum in 2002. In 2009, *Forbes* estimated his personal fortune at around $12 billion, placing him and Brin, whose assets are similarly rated, in 26th place in the *Forbes* list of the world's billionaires. So recognizing and exploiting the opportunities presented by new technologies can certainly pay off financially!

When talking about *innovation,* many people almost automatically think of scientific, and especially technological, innovation. Vast amounts of money are invested in these areas, and those companies that prove successful become the darlings of the business media. *Newly acquired knowledge* in these domains often seems to be surrounded by a fascinating aura, which may bolster the impression that this is the true pinnacle of innovation. Yet many of the innovations based on new know-how are neither scientific nor technical, but have to do with social or economic factors and therefore may not be as clearly evident to the public, even though their impact is frequently far broader.

When it comes to practical applications, all organizations should find themselves asking *what opportunities might arise from their use of new technologies.* At a *general* level, of course, today there is no longer any need to highlight the importance of electronic media, but when it comes to *specifics,* many organizations are lagging way behind in their use of new technologies and in their Web presence. Tremendous opportunities go begging here. At the same time, organizations' failure to make the most of such opportunities places them at risk, totally unnecessarily, thus giving their rivals a major weakness to attack.

Moreover, this state of affairs is by no means limited to the business world. In the 2008 U.S. presidential election battle between John McCain and Barack Obama, the difference between their use of the Internet could hardly have been greater. What's more, use of new technologies is also an issue for nonprofit organizations, universities, cultural institutions, and hospitals. Managers have a free hand when it comes to deciding how they wish to recognize and exploit new technologies, and it is astonishing how greatly direct competitors differ with respect to their use of the Internet as a platform. As long ago as September 2000, *Bill Gates* expressed a view that even today gives us food for thought: "*The Internet is not just about new start-up companies. . . . The Internet is much more about existing businesses and how they take skills and customer base and move over to use these digital approaches to do things better. That's the most profound thing about this revolution.*"[2]

Larry Page and Sergey Brin succeeded in recognizing new technologies and using them to accomplish exceptional technological innovations. But even at a far more modest level, any organization can ask itself about the opportunities associated with current technological possibilities and how it could benefit from exploiting them. Bearing in mind that the Industrial Revolution turned out to be the catalyst for a long list of far-reaching innovations, we can confidently conclude that the greatest effects of the present revolution still lie ahead of us.

Despite all the praise lavished on what Google has achieved, there can be no ignoring the fact that the company's muscle and projects that enter uncharted territory are viewed in a highly critical light. And while *"Don't be evil"* may be the guideline set out in the *Google Code of Conduct,*[3] and no one could wish the company and Google's users much better than success in following that principle, there are already serious problems in answering questions like, *"What is evil?"* and, *"Who defines the answer?"*

ACTION POINTS AND FOOD FOR THOUGHT

- Where do you see opportunities in your organization to make more effective use of new technologies? Who could drive these issues forward?
- In which domains can you personally derive greater benefit from new technologies?

CHAPTER **24**

Recognize the Future That Has Already Happened

LEARNING FROM

Ray Kroc

Ray Kroc (1902–1984) can rightfully be said to have changed the eating habits of our entire planet. For many years he successfully earned a living selling paper cups before moving on to peddle milkshake machines. At over 50 years of age he then decided on a bold career change. A sales trip in 1954 took him to a hamburger joint in San Bernadino, California, run by the McDonald brothers. Ray Kroc was surprised by the number of mixers Richard and Maurice McDonald had ordered for their restaurant. But he was even more surprised when he saw his machines set up in eight banks of five, enabling 40 milkshakes to be made simultaneously. And that was not all: the entire restaurant was organized along principles similar to those governing Henry Ford's production lines. Everything was extremely efficient, so it took just 60 seconds to serve each customer. However, what probably bowled Kroc over the most was the presence of such a high number of customers.

Ray Kroc then did something remarkable. *He recognized a future that had already happened.* Kroc persuaded the McDonald brothers to sell him the license allowing him to use their name for a chain of franchised fast-food restaurants. In return the brothers would receive a certain percentage of the sales generated by each franchisee brought in by Ray Kroc. As early as 1955, he opened the first branch of McDonald's in Des Plaines, Illinois. That restaurant was soon followed by many more, but in spite of the brand's great success in penetrating the market, the company found itself in such dire financial straits during its start-up phase that it almost went bankrupt. That situation changed immediately when Kroc hit upon the idea of also buying the properties and then leasing them to franchisees, giving him control not only over the sites chosen for the chain's restaurants, but also giving him greater influence over his profits.

Like a man obsessed, Kroc perfected every detail of the concept, whereby quality, service, hygiene, and low prices always topped his list of priorities, driving both innovation and a constant striving for standardization. In 1961, he succeeded in persuading the McDonald brothers to leave the company altogether in return for a payment of just $2.7 million dollars. In business terms, that was a very farsighted decision, for here too Kroc recognized something that eluded others— the tremendous potential of the concept when combined with effective marketing.

Kroc duly launched an extensive advertising campaign, which resulted in the creation of the clown Ronald McDonald as a promotional figure and a comprehensive market breakthrough. By 1963, Kroc was already able to open his five-hundredth restaurant, and in 1967 he started expanding outside the United States. Kroc's pioneering fast-food restaurant concept changed the world. *And it all began when he interpreted what was going on differently from all his peers. He recognized a future that was already happening.*

So what can Kroc's approach teach us about how to innovate effectively? When he entered that popular and highly efficient hamburger restaurant in 1954, he recognized how perfectly the concept fit the spirit of his age. Suburbs were springing up across the United States, people were being made increasingly reliant on their automobiles, and Americans throughout the country were becoming more mobile. Comfortable, quick-service restaurants serving inexpensive food perfectly matched people's changing habits. Kroc *did* not try to *predict* the future, *he observed the present,* looking at what was going on right before his eyes. He then drew the correct conclusion, deciding that the behavior he was seeing, triggered by *developments that had already taken place,* was likely to continue.

One of a manager's most important tasks is *to recognize change that has already occurred.* And the trick here is to spot it early enough to be in a position to exploit it as an opportunity. That was precisely what Ray Kroc did—and not only once, but repeatedly, just a few examples being his recognition of the concept's potential, his establishment of the company's franchise system, his perfection of its standardization, the substantial expansion of the brand's marketing, and the group's internationalization starting in 1967. Kroc would have been proud to see what the management of McDonald's went on to achieve after him and would probably have been particularly happy about the innovation of the McDonald's-owned coffee-house-style food and drink chain *McCafé.* The first McCafé was opened in Australia in 1993 and is a perfect example of recognizing a future that had already happened.

However, recognizing change must not be left to chance. Instead, organizations need to establish a method that will enable them to spot changes and act on them to their advantage. Indeed, all the aspects of management showcased in this part of the book (including questioning assumptions, spearheading change, innovating systematically, capitalizing on success, heeding the unexpected, practicing purposeful abandonment or creative destruction, and exploiting fresh know-how) are geared toward ensuring that one of managers' most important tasks is to take *innovation* seriously and constantly seek ways of boosting an organization's power to innovate. One common thread running through the biographies of successful entrepreneurs is that they all made innovation a high priority.

McDonald's has undeniably been a momentous success, but it ought to be stressed that the company's triumph was first and foremost the result of sheer hard work. Ray Kroc reiterated that when he said: *"Luck is a dividend of sweat. The more you sweat, the luckier you get."*[1] So it will probably come as no surprise that Kroc worked for McDonald's right up until his death. In fact, even though he was wheelchair bound for the last years of his life, he traveled to his San Diego office almost every day to indulge his passion for business.

ACTION POINTS AND FOOD FOR THOUGHT

- In which current trends, events, or clear breaks with past patterns or behavior in your sector or society as a whole can you recognize a future that has already happened? What exactly do you plan to do about it?
- Seek out the future that has already happened.

PART 3

MANAGING
People

CHAPTER **25**

Focus on a Single Objective

LEARNING FROM
Michelangelo

Michelangelo Buonarroti (1475–1564) is widely recognized as one of the world's greatest sculptors and painters. His true passion was always sculpting, however, so initially he described himself as a *scultore*, only later coming to eye even this general description of his profession with suspicion, when he had developed a deeper sense of his artistic destiny. Michelangelo's feel for stone was very special. For instance, when his sculpture of Night sleeping inspired Giovanni Strozzi to pen an epigram, he duly responded in verse himself, writing: "*Sleep is dear to me, and being of stone is dearer.*"[1]

Although Michelangelo's true mastery of painting is undisputed, during his lifetime he had always been reluctant to indulge in it, deeming it, "something for women." In letters and poems he repeatedly stressed, "*I am no painter.*"[2] Had Pope Julius II not forced Michelangelo to paint, he would have stuck to sculpting. The commission to paint the ceiling of the Sistine Chapel, on which Michelangelo started working in May 1508, was something the artist felt he had been forced into, an imposition that was beneath his dignity and talents. Worse still, he felt he had been "given the cold shoulder," because the fact that Bramante had been assigned to pull down the Basilica of St. Peter and build the new cathedral for the Pope seemed to Michelangelo like a victory for his opponents. By contrast, the terse commission to paint the ceiling of the Sistine Chapel called for *"twelve apostles with a canopy of ornaments."*[3]

If there is any such thing as a "secret" to effectiveness, then it is focus on *one* thing at a time. Michelangelo was only too aware of this. He knew that all the sculptures he still wanted to create, which already existed in his mind's eye, would only see the light of day if he single-mindedly concentrated on sculpture. In other words, he was aware of his unique *strength*. For wonderful though his paintings might be, there were other wonderful painters about, whereas nobody but Michelangelo could take a raw piece of stone and so masterfully sculpt it into a *David, Bacchus, Moses,* or *Pietà.* The fact that Michelangelo also succeeded in achieving great feats outside painting and sculpting, such as taking charge of the construction of the Church of St. Peter, whose cupola he also designed, earned him the reputation as a genius—even during his own lifetime. The reverence in which Michelangelo was held among the people was reflected in their calling him *Il Divino,* "the Divine one."

Individuals or organizations out to achieve something notable have to focus. Below I expand on this key principle, first in relation to managers, and then in the context of an organization.

1. Managers

Managers always have far more things of importance to do than time in which to do them. The more competent managers are, the more things they could theoretically attend to. Yet even with the best time-management skills in the world, they will not be able to focus most of their time on single tasks, because much of it will be decided by others (like customers, superiors, colleagues, employees, or support staff) or be taken up with various company-related obligations.

Realizing this, great achievers exploit a number of valuable "secrets:" *First*, they always *focus on one thing at a time*, which enables them to deal with it in far less time than if they tried to attend to several tasks at once. *Second*, they always *do the most important thing first*, dropping lesser tasks altogether if at all possible, rather than dealing with them second. *Third*, they free up and set aside the *longest possible contiguous blocks of time in which they can work undisturbed on their most important project*. Creating such blocks of time takes effort and self-discipline, but doing so is the key to being productive, especially for knowledge workers. *Fourth*, they know that the more successfully they manage to spend the time available to them doing *what they are best at*, the more effective they will be in their endeavor.

People and organizations perform well only when they play to their strengths. Otherwise they underperform. Paradoxically, people who achieve nothing often work harder than everybody else, being unaware of the four "secrets" noted above.

If you focus your efforts, resources, and time, you will not only succeed in completing *more* tasks, you will also find yourself able to deal simultaneously with *more diverse* tasks. Both Michelangelo and Herbert von Karajan, one of the most widely admired conductors of the twentieth century, have proved that this apparent contradiction is actually nothing of the sort.

The importance of focusing is well documented. In *Adventures of a Bystander*, Peter F. Drucker wrote the following about the engineer and architect Richard Buckminster Fuller and the communications theorist Marshall McLuhan: *"[They] exemplify to me the importance of being single-minded. The single-minded ones, the monomaniacs, are the only true achievers. The rest, the ones like me, may have more fun; but they fritter themselves away. The Fullers and the McLuhans carry out a 'mission'; the rest of us have 'interests.' Whenever anything is being accomplished, it is being done, I have learned, by a monomaniac with a mission."*[4]

The authors Balzac, Flaubert, and Zola slaved away on their books like men possessed, as did Schubert, Beethoven, and Wagner when working on their music. Michelangelo was still chiseling away at his *Pietà Rondanini* until six days before he died at the age of 88. Even geniuses like Bach, Handel, Haydn, and Verdi always focused on only *one* piece at a time, which they finished before starting the next. And if they did interrupt their work, they did so deliberately to let it mature in their minds. Mozart is the big exception, for he was able to create multiple masterpieces simultaneously. But who can compare themselves with Mozart? The rule of thumb is this: *The key to success is to take on just a few, carefully selected tasks.*

Even geniuses can fritter away their time. We can be pretty sure that this was the case with that universal genius Leonardo da Vinci, who was a painter, natural scientist, engineer, inventor, and architect. Yet spreading his interests so widely meant that there was much Leonardo never finished. The following anecdote speaks volumes: Immediately after Pope Leo X commissioned Leonardo to paint a picture for him, the artist rushed off to buy the oils and herbs to distill into the liquid for the final protective varnish for the painting. This prompted the despairing Pope to exclaim: *"Alas, this man is never going to do anything, for he starts to think about finishing the work before it is even begun!"*[5]

2. Organizations

Focus is also of considerable importance to organizations. Very highly diversified companies almost invariably fail, mostly because—like individuals— their efforts are insufficiently focused. Assets that are already limited in any organization, like money, physical resources, and—most importantly—capable people, are ineffectively used up because modest advances are made everywhere instead of focusing fully on one thing in a bid to achieve a major breakthrough.

The less diversified an organization is, the easier it is to manage. One of the main advantages of a more focused organization is that people find it easier to understand the relationship between their personal performance and the contribution they make to their organization as a whole. As a result, they focus better, targeting their efforts more on attaining shared objectives and serving that "greater whole." Successfully diversified companies manage to spread themselves by focusing their various business activities, technologies, and product lines on a *shared market,* thereby creating a common basis. Alternatively, their various business activities, technologies, and product lines are based on a *shared technology.* In both scenarios, however, the result is *focus,* not diversification.

Anyone (and this applies equally to individuals and organizations) who has seen for themselves just how powerful an effect proper focus can have will never again stray from this principle. We can only hazard a guess at what a struggle it must have been for Michelangelo to paint the Sistine Chapel and how he suffered doing it. As far back as Fall 1533, Pope Clement VII had commissioned Michelangelo to paint the altar and entrance walls of the Sistine Chapel, each of which is 17 meters high and 13 meters wide. When Clement VII died the following year, his successor Pope Paul III, already an old man by the standards of his day, renewed that commission, thereby forcing Michelangelo to once again relinquish his beloved sculpting of the *tomb of Pope Julius II,* which he had only just resumed. The artist's excuses prompted the following angry outburst from Pope Paul III: *"I have had this desire for thirty years [that you serve me], and now that I am Pope, am I not to satisfy it? I will tear up this contract [for Pope Julius' tomb], and, in any case, I intend to have you serve me!"*[6]

This time Michelangelo undertook to paint the entire 738 square feet of wall by himself. He did not even attempt to seek the aid of other painters as he had previously tried when tackling the ceiling of the chapel. Only his faithful servant Urbino assisted him, grinding pigments for his master's paints. Michelangelo knew that only he could do full justice to the version of *The Last Judgment* that he saw in his mind's eye.

"Sono scultore"—*"I'm a sculptor,"* he is said to have cried out in the quarries when the Pope once again forced him to carry on with his painting. And he even painted a pitiful portrait of himself into *The Last Judgment*, portraying himself not as one of the redeemed or damned, but as an empty shell, his own pain-racked features clearly recognizable on the flayed skin of St. Bartholomew.

ACTION POINTS AND FOOD FOR THOUGHT

- First, focus on a single objective. Second, always do the most important thing first. Third, free up the longest possible contiguous blocks of time to work undisturbed on your most important project. Fourth, draw on your strengths during that time.

- To which one or two key tasks could you devote your efforts that make the biggest contribution to your organization's results?

- What can you do within your organization to prompt a discussion that specifically tightens its focus? How will you measure the success of this endeavor?

CHAPTER 26

Create a Perfect Whole

L E A R N I N G   F R O M

Simon Rattle

Sir Simon Rattle (born in 1955) is one of the most highly acclaimed and sought-after conductors in the world. He has gained numerous international plaudits—being knighted, being awarded the French order "Chevalier de la Legion D'Honneur" (Knight of the Legion of Honor), receiving several honorary doctorates, and winning three Grammy Awards, for his achievements in music —for his dedication to teaching and his social commitment. In 2007, he and the Berlin Philharmonic were appointed International UNICEF Goodwill Ambassadors in New York. Rattle's longest creative stint so far, from 1980 to 1998, was with the City of Birmingham Symphony Orchestra, where he served first as principal conductor and artistic adviser and then, from 1990 onward, as music director.

Simon Rattle not only captures attention because of his exceptional live performances and recordings, but also because of his remarkably broad repertoire, which extends from ancient to modern music. Furthermore, he has repeatedly taken on ambitious, large-scale projects, such as a TV series about orchestral music of the twentieth century, for which he won a BAFTA (British Academy of Film and Television Arts) award in 1997 for best arts program or series. On top of this, he successively staged the complete Ring cycle by Richard Wagner, starting in summer

2006 at the Aix-en-Provence Festival and concluding it at Salzburg in 2010. Hopefully, both for Rattle himself and for music lovers the whole world over, he will manage to make many more wonderful recordings, maybe even beating Sir Georg Solti's record of 32 Grammy Awards.

Conductors who master their profession as well as Rattle succeed in creating a perfect whole, something that is far greater than the sum of its parts. Their inner vision, tireless efforts, and leadership unerringly steer their orchestra toward achieving the sublime perfection that fills concert halls around the world. Like conductors, all managers must strive to create something that extends beyond the sphere of individual performance. This already holds true for small-scale enterprises, because anyone leading a team of a few employees has to make sure that the organization's overall performance is more than the sum of its individual members' contributions. Yet the same applies to anyone in charge of a sector, department, or entire organization, though they of course will bear correspondingly greater responsibility.

Conductors listen not only to the overall sound of the orchestra, but also to the performances of its individual members. This creates a kind of interdependency, for by aiming to enhance the orchestra's overall performance, they raise the ambitions of each individual musician, and by helping individuals perform better, they increase the quality of the work as a whole.

Good conductors spend a great deal of time communicating the work *as a whole* to their musicians, providing background and explaining their interpretation of the score. They do this because only when the intention behind the work and its meaning have been properly understood can individual members of the orchestra help to convey the sense of the work in its entirety through their instrument. Gustav Mahler, for instance, insisted that every musician sit in the auditorium, at least once a week, to hear the combined effect of all the orchestra's instruments. At the same time, good conductors also work intensively with individual musicians. On top of all his daily work, once a year the great conductor and peerless interpreter of Mozart, Bruno Walter, wrote a letter to each individual member of his orchestra in which he listed everything he had learned from that musician. Invariably this prompted a fruitful dialogue between Walter and his players.

Likewise, managers need to retain an overview of the performance and results of their entire organization as well as to keep track of what its individual members achieve. That way they can take appropriate measures leading to an effective overall achievement. But whereas conductors face the difficult task of interpreting a score, managers are also "composers," since their duties include *thinking through what kinds of contribution are required.* In fact, any specialist effectively faces a similar task.

It is important to bear in mind that specialist knowledge is of no use by itself: The benefit derived from it arises only when it is *integrated into a greater whole.* This is the function and purpose of organizations: to incorporate such specialist knowledge into a combined overall performance. Without the organization, the specialist know-how of the knowledge worker—and therefore the individual in question—would remain ineffective. The organization itself can only be effective if it succeeds in channeling specialist knowledge toward the fulfillment of a shared purpose.

However, people in an organization will not automatically strive toward a common goal. On the contrary, any specialization conceals the inherent danger of knowledge workers who are experts in specific fields exclusively focusing on their particular domain and thereby losing sight of the bigger picture. In addition, organizations' *hierarchical structure* means that every level has, or even *must* have, its own view of things, because only in that way can it fulfill its designated role. Accordingly, *management by objectives and self-control* is essential if everyone is to pull in the same direction. In this connection, you, as a manager, must make sure that the *organization's objectives*—geared toward achieving a perfect whole—have been understood at all its various levels. The individuals involved must see the big picture and understand what they have to do to help their organization attain its overriding goal.

One rule for managers advocated by legendary General Electric CEO *Jack Welch* was this: *"Leaders make sure people not only see the vision, they live and breathe it."*[1] Until this message has permeated every level of an organization and lodged itself in the minds of all employees, you may well need to display a great deal of patience. Indeed, as Jack Welch said about himself: *"There were times I talked about the company's direction so many times in one day that I was completely sick of hearing it myself."*[2] Nonetheless he persevered.

If you, as a knowledge worker, ask yourself what you should be contributing, you can make certain that you are aiming to achieve the right results. People who fail to ask themselves this question often work harder, but end up performing less effectively for their organization. In addition, asking the question effectively broadens individuals' focus and places their personal contribution in a wider, more comprehensive context. The aim here is not to create generalists, but to *enable specialists* to make a fruitful contribution to the greater whole, the *joint performance*, just like in an orchestra. In other words, effective "generalists" are specialists who successfully forge links between their specialty and other areas of knowledge.

ACTION POINTS AND FOOD FOR THOUGHT

- How are you contributing toward the attainment of your organization's overall objectives?
- Considering the *big picture*, where does performance need to improve and what exactly needs to be done to bring this about?
- Where can each *individual* area of the organization improve and what impact would that have on the organization as a whole?

CHAPTER 27

Be Results Driven

LEARNING FROM

Michael Schumacher

On July 29, 2009, *Michael Schumacher* (born in 1969) announced his Formula 1 comeback, but just a few weeks later, with a heavy heart, he had to put the brakes on that plan. In 2010, both the motor racing fraternity and Formula 1 fans were tremendously excited to see how successful his comeback with Mercedes would turn out. One typical feature of Formula 1 is the tendency to sum up pretty much any conceivable result in some kind of statistic, and a defining character trait of Michael Schumacher is having almost every significant figure at his fingertips. The long list of records he holds in the sport is truly impressive, and a comparison with his closest rivals in this respect reveals an astonishing gap[1]:

Most world championship titles
- 1st place: Michael Schumacher, 7 titles
- 2nd place: Juan Manuel Fangio, 5 titles (the last won in 1957)

Most Grand Prix victories
- 1st place: Michael Schumacher, 91 victories
- 2nd place: Alain Prost, 51 victories

Most victories within one season
- 1st place: Michael Schumacher, 13 wins
- 2nd place: Michael Schumacher, 11 wins
- 3rd place: Michael Schumacher, 9 wins (2001)
- 3rd place: Michael Schumacher, 9 wins (2000)

121

- 3rd place: Michael Schumacher, 9 wins (1995)
- 3rd place: Nigel Mansell, 9 wins (1992)

Most appearances on the victory rostrum

- 1st place: Michael Schumacher, 154 times
- 2nd place: Alain Prost, 106 times

Most points in a career

- 1st place: Michael Schumacher, 1,369 points
- 2nd place: Alain Prost, 798.5 points

Fastest lap times

- 1st place: Michael Schumacher, 74 laps
- 2nd place: Alain Prost, 41 laps.

Gradually it has become clear to the public that a good racing driver needs to be ambitious and very, *very* sure of himself. Applying himself with skill, diligence, stamina, meticulousness, and a strong desire to achieve perfection, Schumacher strove to improve every detail of his performance—and the results bore out his approach.

In addition to setting all these records, he leads a commendably scandal-free life. Furthermore, in 2006 he achieved something that many sports stars fail to do: choosing the right time to pull out of the profession, retiring when he was runner-up in the Drivers' Championship.

So managers can learn valuable lessons from Schumacher's consistently results-driven approach.

Management is all about results. This may sound rather banal, yet it is amazing that the focus of many people working for an organization is more on *input* than *output*. The common characteristic of people who consistently perform remarkably well is their single-minded orientation toward results—as opposed to concentrating on effort, stress, or input.

One of the clearest indications of this is that when the going gets tough, instead of "making do" with what has already been achieved, top performers put in the extra effort required to attain their objective. In other words, they "go the extra mile." At the same time, they do not look for alibis or excuses if something has not worked out because they know that setbacks or failures have to be faced and that giving up in the face of adversity is not an option. This will not guarantee them the attainment of all their goals, but embracing the principle of adopting a systematically results-oriented approach does get them very far—much farther than those who are laxer about focusing on achieving results.

Michael Schumacher's obsession with detail is a prime example of someone who genuinely strives for the best possible results in every domain of his work. He is remarkable for being so demanding of himself in areas where other racing drivers content themselves with far less. For example, he doggedly acquired extensive technical knowledge so that he could serve his team by ensuring that its technicians could do their level best based on the feedback he gave them.

The significant fact here is that *focusing on the end result* and asking yourself how you can help to achieve the outcome alters the answers to questions about what you can—and *need*—to do. This is a mark of good managers; they are results-oriented and see how what they accomplish contributes to the overall result.

Management must give its organization direction. To that end, it has to think through and define the organization's business mission and its specific purpose. It must also set appropriate objectives and organize the available resources in such a way that those objectives can be reached. The ensuing results then indicate just how effective the management's actions really are. *Every organization will grow stronger by clearly defining its objectives.*

Taking detailed measurements in Formula 1 has the advantage of enabling very accurate comparisons with initial objectives. It enables the team to ascertain where it is working effectively and where there is still even the slightest room for improvement. This approach not only provides a sound basis for correct decisions, but also makes the organization as a whole more effective because it highlights where potential improvements can be made. It is therefore wise to ensure that clear objectives are set in your area of responsibility and that it is made just as clear which variables will be used to measure and judge the results.

When doing all this, the objectives in question should meet the following conditions: First, they *should not* be *easily attainable*. If no real effort is required, the target has been poorly set. Second, the desired results should of course nonetheless *be attainable*. Setting unrealistic objectives at the outset is not just demotivating, but even damaging, because it undermines the credibility of managing by objectives. Third, the *relevance* of the set objectives should be clear. They should make a meaningful contribution to the whole. It ought to make a difference whether the result is achieved or not. Fourth, if possible, the result should be *measurable*—at the very least, it must be possible to judge the *degree* of attainment.

The areas where objectives need to be set and results achieved in the context of managing organizations is discussed in Chapter 13 on Andy Grove: market standing, innovation, productivity, physical and financial resources, profitability, the performance as well as the development and attitude of the people in the organization, and public responsibility.

Especially if things do not go according to plan, the result needs to be taken seriously. Throughout his long career, Schumacher has impressed everyone by showing what a master he is at recovering from setbacks—the sign of a true professional. That said, it is important to remember that being results-oriented is a principle of management, not of life. Michael Schumacher pursues numerous interests not with results in mind, but simply because they give him pleasure and enjoyment.

ACTION POINTS AND FOOD FOR THOUGHT

■ Focus on results, not effort.

■ Are the benchmarks for evaluating performance in your organization appropriate and sufficiently clearly defined? If not, how can you change this?

CHAPTER **28**

Draw on Your Strengths

LEARNING FROM

Albert Einstein

Albert Einstein (1879–1955) loved nothing more than playing the violin: *"I often think in music. I live my daydreams in music. I see my life in terms of music. . . .I know I get most joy in life out of music."*[1] Opinions differed, however, about how good a violinist Einstein actually was. Most people thought he was not especially talented, although somewhat more charitable contemporaries said he played "with feeling." In truth, Einstein probably had good reason for deciding to become a physicist rather than a musician. Nevertheless he managed to find a way of enjoying both pursuits: In his career he concentrated on his strength—physics—while in private, where no damage could be done, he continued to indulge his passion for violin playing. *"Music,"* Einstein wrote, *"does not influence research work, but both are nourished by the same sort of longing, and they complement each other in the release they offer."*[2]

Similarly, one of the central tasks of all managers is to *enhance the performance* of their organization by drawing on their strengths. Three areas in particular are deserving of attention: drawing on your *own strengths*, harnessing the strengths of your *colleagues*, and drawing on the strengths of your *organization*.

1. Drawing on your own strengths

Your first step toward greater effectiveness is to *ascertain your own strengths.* To do this, look back at your past achievements and results and try to spot a pattern. What did you find relatively easy to do, while others would have had considerably more difficulty completing the same task? In which areas did you perform exceptionally well, compared with others? Using *feedback analysis,* as described in Chapter 14 about James Watt, is a pretty reliable way of identifying your strengths.

Once you are aware of what those strengths are, focus on them as much as you can, and put yourself in a situation in which you can draw on them. Seek out corresponding tasks within your organization. At the same time find out which tasks are *not* suited to your strengths, and then avoid them! Decide unequivocally what you would be well advised *not* doing. Focus on playing to your strengths.

In addition, you need to constantly *develop your strengths.* After all, the difference between middling and excellent managers is that the latter always endeavor to improve at whatever they are *already* very good at. This is just as true of managers as it is of musicians, athletes, politicians, or physicians. Feedback analysis will very quickly show you where you lack ability and what you need to improve. If you lack the knowledge required to develop your strengths, acquire it. By boosting the necessary *skills* and building up the *knowledge* you need, you will successfully deploy your strengths to the fullest effect.

Finally, you should also make sure that your strengths are deployed *in keeping with your values.* Albert Einstein suffered for the rest of his life after contributing to the development of the atom bomb, in violation of his pacifist ideals: *"But the probability that the Germans might work on that very problem with good chance of success prompted me to take that step,"*[3] he said. After World War II he campaigned intensively for disarmament and peace, and shortly before his death he signed a manifesto against nuclear weapons.

2. Harnessing the strengths of your colleagues

You will never perform well if you start out from *areas of weakness,* regardless of whether the weaknesses in question are your own or those of your subordinates, colleagues, or superiors. Results are achieved by making strengths productive. This is a fundamental aim of any organization, since doing so opens up major opportunities and potential. If you have people working for you, you must enable them to combine their performances effectively. The best way of achieving this is to deploy people in such a way that they can *draw on each other's strengths*. At the same time, make their *weaknesses* become *irrelevant*. One slogan perfectly encapsulating this approach was used in the United States to support disabled people looking for a job: *"It's the abilities, not the disabilities, that count."*[4] And no slogan better sums this up than that of one American organization for the disabled: *"Don't hire a person for what they can't do, hire them for what they* can *do."*[5] Is there any better, more characteristically human way of describing how human beings should be deployed?

On the other hand, you need to be able to *recognize your own weaknesses and those of your subordinates* in order to make sure that neither you nor they are used in areas where weaknesses could prove a hindrance. Because if this happened, it would not only result in mediocre performances by the individuals involved, it would also damage the organization as a whole. One interesting fact worth noting is that people with major strengths almost invariably exhibit major weaknesses as well (*"The higher the peak, the deeper the valley,"* as one famous Alpine skier saying so aptly puts it). Of course, your job as a manager is not to *change* people, even if that is at all possible and morally justifiable, but to deploy them in the organization in as carefully considered a manner as possible, in a way that maximally draws on their *existing strengths*. This means that decisions about who should fill a *vacancy* or assume responsibility for *key tasks* must always be based on what the person in question *is already capable of*, where his or her *strengths lie*, and which *specific requirements* the incumbent of the job or assignment in question needs to meet at that particular time. The appointment will prove successful only if the strengths of the individual are *appropriate for accomplishing* the key task at hand.

3. Developing the strengths of your organization

Just as most people do not have the good fortune to be blessed with numerous talents, organizations do not tend to be truly competent in many different areas. On the contrary, a majority of the most powerful and healthiest companies on the planet are highly specialized world-beaters. A very readable book by Hermann Simon, *Hidden Champions of the 21st Century*, provides numerous examples.

So identify and develop the strengths of your organization, because in those few core skills lies the key to success. Naturally, the organization must perform well in many different areas, but it must excel in at least *one* domain if it is to attain any significant degree of success. Focus your organization's efforts and establish a niche or activity in which you can outperform your competitors and where you are better at meeting market demand.

Incidentally, it was not least due to Albert Einstein's extraordinary abilities in physics that he had to endure the occasional derisive remark about his somewhat less-than-perfect violin playing. One afternoon, so the story goes, when Einstein was playing through some sonatas with the world-famous pianist *Arthur Rubinstein*, he missed his cue and came in too late, earning the following rebuke from Rubinstein: *"Albert, can't you count?"*[6]

ACTION POINTS AND FOOD FOR THOUGHT

- What are your strengths? Use feedback analysis to identify them. Work on consolidating your strengths and making them work most effectively in your favor.
- When hiring staff members, focus on their capabilities. Make sure their particular strengths match the key task they are being recruited to perform.
- Discuss the following question with your colleagues: "What do we need to do together to make more of, and build on, the strengths of our organization?"

CHAPTER **29**

Manage by Objectives

LEARNING FROM

Gustav Mahler

The world premiere of the Symphony No. 8 in E-flat major by *Gustav Mahler* (1860–1911) in Munich on September 12, 1910, was a grandiose event involving no fewer than *1,030* people, including Mahler himself, who had no intention of letting anyone else conduct the first performance of the work. Yet Mahler's symphonies only really became widely popular in concert halls and as records in the 1960s, during a veritable *Mahler renaissance*. One factor that prompted this resurgence in Mahler's popularity was a speech given in Vienna, the *"Wiener Rede,"* in 1960 by Theodor W. Adorno, commemorating the centenary of the composer's birth. Another factor was the ardent backing of Mahler's works by the great conductor Leonard Bernstein. The fervor for Mahler's music stirred up back then has lingered to today among conductors and audiences alike.

On August 18, 1906, after completing his Eighth Symphony, Gustav Mahler penned a gushing letter to the conductor Willem Mengelberg, writing: *"I've just finished my Eighth—my greatest work to date. And so unusual in content and form that it defies description in words. Imagine the universe starting to ring and reverberate. These are no mere human voices resounding, but those of planets and suns. . . ."*[1]

Just as it is almost impossible to describe the delight of delicious food, the beauty of a picture, or the sense of exhilaration upon hearing a wonderful opera, even the composer was at a loss for words to adequately describe his latest piece. Things like that simply need to be experienced. It comes as no surprise, then, that those who attended the world premiere of Mahler's Eighth Symphony, author Thomas Mann among them, reported the overwhelming impact of the performance. But how was that impact created? What makes an undertaking like that succeed? How does a performance have to be conducted to elicit a perfect result from 1,030 people?

In management, the "secret" behind such a masterly feat is management by objectives and self-control. *Management by objectives and self-control* enables hundreds of musicians and their conductor, who is akin to their CEO, to synchronize their performance of even the most complex works with absolute precision. It is the fact that they *share the same score* that enables so many specialists in the orchestra to make such an effective contribution to the overall performance. And this, of course, is nothing other than a figurative description of how to go about using objectives in an organization.

Objectives provide the human beings in an organization with the information they need to make effective contributions as specialists. *Management by objectives* makes clear to the people in an organization what management expects the organization as a whole to achieve, as well as what it expects of each division and of each specialist who constitutes a part of the larger unit.

In addition, clearly spelled-out objectives enable every staff member to *autonomously* compare those expectations with their own performance because they enable them to exercise *self-control*. In organizations in which knowledge work plays a central role, this situation is particularly important. Often, a superior is unable to tell a specialist *how* to execute the task at hand, just as only a few conductors can play the violin, let alone show their first violinist how a piece should be played. Conductors can guide players in a way that harnesses the knowledge and skills of a violinist for the benefit of the overall result and produces wonderful music, but the violinist needs objectives and must be allowed to use self-control to implement those instructions.

The importance of *management by objectives and self-control* really cannot be overestimated, since it *gives human beings control over their own performances*. Within set limits, managers have the freedom to decide which course of action is right. This results in better performances and boosts motivation.

Management by objectives and self-control forces managers to *make high demands* on themselves. Aiming high is much more likely to make them ask too much of themselves and of their subordinates, rather than demanding too little. The concept assumes that people *want* to assume responsibility, contribute, and achieve. Managers may experience a few disappointments, but in most cases the response will be exactly what they are hoping for: *responsible behavior, valuable contributions, and great performances*. By acting in this way, they lay some of the essential foundations for a healthy corporate culture—a culture based on trust, responsibility, a results-oriented approach, and performance.

If objectives are to be effective, they must meet a string of criteria. They should always *derive from the goals of the enterprise* and *be worded clearly and unequivocally*. *Specific deadlines* need to be set for the attainment of objectives, which must also be assigned to *one particular individual* who is responsible for their attainment. "*Who needs to do what by when?*" is the key question to ask when deciding on which measures to implement to achieve the desired outcome.

Another thing to spell out is which *results* are to serve as a basis for *measuring* the attainment of objectives. It is helpful if results can be quantified. Often, it will neither be possible nor make sense to *exactly* quantify the attainment of objectives. In such instances, you will have to decide which criteria to use to *judge* the degree of attainment.

Accordingly, if management by objectives and self-control is to prove effective, managers must be given more than just targets, namely regular *feedback*—that is, *information*—on the current situation regarding the attainment of objectives. And they need it quickly enough to enable them to make any changes required to ensure that the objectives in question are attained. Only if this information is provided can they judge *their own* performance, and only *then* can self-control function properly.

Management by objectives and self-control is one of the most important components of effective management. Everyone in an organization makes his or her own specific contribution, but each individual contributes something different. Management by objectives and self-control effectively channels these various contributions toward a common goal. It turns individual achievements into an overall performance. It encourages people in an organization to see the bigger picture, to bear in mind what can only be jointly achieved—an excellent overall performance.

Mahler, too, conducted his Eighth Symphony using a *single* score, and all the musicians knew what they had to do.

ACTION POINTS AND FOOD FOR THOUGHT

- Manage the area for which you are responsible with objectives and self-control.
- What can you do tomorrow to ensure that greater use is made of self-control and that it functions efficiently?

CHAPTER 30

Plan Meticulously

LEARNING FROM
Napoleon Bonaparte

Although his campaigns did not always go as he had wanted, nothing could stop *Napoleon Bonaparte* (1769–1821) from planning them all meticulously. It was this comprehensive planning and the associated thorough thinking through of every conceivable scenario that made his numerous victories possible.

Napoleon was held in high regard as a general and commander. His troops deeply revered him, and his adversaries tried to emulate him. He made full use of the possibilities offered by techniques of war and brilliantly incorporated them into his plans: quick marches, surprising concentrations of troops at strategically decisive places, and the systematic use of artillery were just some factors behind his success.

Great commanders have always lavished attention on the *thorough preparation and planning* of their campaigns. This applied just as much to Caesar as to Frederick the Great or Sunzi (Sun Tzu), who in *The Art of War* advises making meticulous plans before taking action. Frederick the Great's *Military Instructions, Written by the King of Prussia, for the Generals of His Army* was the first coherent treatise on strategic theory and practice of the modern era, a document that Frederick wrote shortly after the Seven Years' War and repeatedly revised up until his death in 1786. Most of his strategic principles were concerned with planning and organization.

The most important strategist of the modern era was the Prussian officer Carl von Clausewitz, whose book *On War* remains standard reading for cadets even in today's military academies. Strongly influenced by Kant and other German philosophers of the Enlightenment, Clausewitz applied methods like critical argumentation to war. In so doing, he linked the theory and practice of war and set about explaining the psychological and moral aspects of war. He wrote: *"Once it has been determined, from the political conditions, what a war is meant to achieve and what it can achieve, it is easy to chart the course. But great strength of character, as well as great lucidity and firmness of mind, is required in order to follow through steadily, to carry out the plan, and not to be thrown off course by thousands of diversions."*[1] And according to Clausewitz, very few human beings have all these qualities.

One of the main reasons why it is difficult to stick faithfully to a plan is a phenomenon that Clausewitz calls *friction: "Everything in war is very simple, but the simplest thing is difficult. These difficulties accumulate and end by producing a kind of friction that is inconceivable unless one has experienced war. . . . Countless minor incidents—the kind you can never really foresee—combine to lower the general level of performance, so that one always falls far short of the intended goal."*[2]

In other words, the innumerable, unforeseen minor troubles that constitute friction jeopardize implementation of the plan. Yet Clausewitz does *not* conclude from this that no plans should be made—on the contrary. One of his best pupils, Helmuth von Moltke, famous for being a skillful planner himself, wrote that no plan survives the first contact with the enemy.

The lesson that you, as a manager, can learn from this is to *assume that any plan will change*. Only if you always make meticulous plans and preparations for the situation facing you, always *thinking through everything to its conclusion*, including every conceivable scenario, will you be in a position to react flexibly in your thinking and adaptably in your implementation to all the imponderables that are bound to crop up.

Embrace the principle of viewing *objectives, means, and measures* together. This will open up the way for several things at once: First, you will *gain a deeper understanding* not only of a given problem as such, but also of your organization as a whole. Second, you will *set more realistic objectives* because the most important resources you need in order to attain your objective will have been taken into account from the outset. And third, you will increasingly *think on a larger and more holistic scale*—like a true entrepreneur.

The following should also be borne in mind: long-term planning is often treated merely as an uncritical continuation of current situations and trends—naturally with a positive outlook. Try a different approach by considering whether your present markets, products, services, and technologies might not end up looking very different in the future. If you believe they will, start allowing for this new future *now*. The future is taking shape today. After all, most aspects of any long-term plan are realized through a number of short-term decisions and plans. Turned around the other way, a correct short-term decision can be made only if it contributes toward a long-term plan. If, in the context of such thinking, you can succeed in regarding objectives, means, and measures together, you will have made a decisive step forward toward setting *realistic* future objectives that are genuinely attainable.

There is an extensively tried-and-tested method for steadily improving your decision-making and planning abilities: use *feedback*. Compare your *original expectations* when you made a decision and drew up a corresponding plan with the *actual results* achieved. To this end, at the outset you need to write down your decision, listing any intended measures, what you expect them to achieve, and the reasons that prompted you to take them. You can then compare these written records with the results. If you do this consistently, in time you will become a truly competent decision maker and also improve your ability to develop realistic plans.

ACTION POINTS AND FOOD FOR THOUGHT

- What do you need to do to plan an imminent decision more meticulously?
- Review your standards and aspire to more meticulous planning and preparation.

CHAPTER **31**

Be True to
Your Own Values

LEARNING FROM

Winston Churchill

"I have nothing to offer but blood, toil, tears and sweat. We have before us an ordeal of the most grievous kind. . . . You ask, what is our policy? I will say: it is to wage war, by sea, land and air, with all our might and with all the strength that God can give us: to wage war against a monstrous tyranny, never surpassed in the dark, lamentable catalogue of human crime. That is our policy. You ask, what is our aim? I can answer in one word: It is victory, victory at all costs, victory in spite of all terror, victory, however long and hard the road may be; for without victory, there is no survival."[1]

WINSTON CHURCHILL (1874–1965) ON MAY 13, 1940,

IN HIS FIRST SPEECH AS BRITISH PRIME MINISTER

Churchill's forceful "no" to Hitler in World War II effectively altered the course of history. It was his powerful oratory skills that triggered such firm resolve among the British people to offer such uncompromising resistance. Without Churchill, that "no" would not have been as resounding. Churchill gave Europe faith in the rightness of sensible conduct; he embodied moral authority and strengthened people's beliefs in *values*.

Looking back today, when we consider the decisive role Churchill played in world history, it seems barely conceivable that anyone else could have served in his place. But back in early 1939 the situation was anything but clear-cut. After a military and political career with major highs and lows, between 1929 and 1939 he held no political office whatsoever. Only after the outbreak of World War II was he reappointed First Lord of the Admiralty. And on May 9, 1940, when the pressing question was, who should succeed Neville Chamberlain to become prime minister, nobody wanted Churchill: not the King, not Chamberlain himself, and none of the three main political parties. Everyone preferred Edward Halifax, and Churchill refused to press his case. Again that same day, when Chamberlain asked Churchill whether he would be willing to serve as a minister in a government led by Halifax, Churchill said nothing—and kept silent for a very long time. There was no way that silence could be interpreted as a yes. And since the British people at the time would never have accepted a government from which Churchill was altogether absent, Chamberlain had no option but to drop Halifax and accept Churchill. So Churchill prevailed "*and within a few hours all those who had opposed Churchill were very grateful that they had been defeated,*" Peter de Mendelssohn wrote about that important turning point. "*The most powerful orator of his time, never short of an apt word or rousing turn of phrase, had won through by remaining silent.*"[2]

Why did the British people give Churchill an almost unlimited vote of confidence at such a pivotal moment in history? There is a fascinating answer to this question: The British people were ready, without hesitation, "*To forget the long list of Churchill's acts of folly, blunders, and errors of judgment, even though his worst acts of folly stemmed from his inability to understand the people. The people were willing to do this, because they instinctively felt that Churchill more uncompromisingly than any other political leader personified a deep-seated personal,*" *unspoken rejection of submitting to Hitler's Nazi Germany*."[3] To them, Churchill's deep-seated conviction embodied something he himself termed "*world responsibility*." Is there any more convincing example in history of the power of living out one's values?

Just like people, organizations have values too. Every organization needs the individuals working for it to *commit to shared values* and the *attainment of common goals*. No organization can unleash its full force or function in the long run without this voluntary commitment. One of any management's key tasks, then, is to *think through* these values, *prescribe* them as binding, and *lead by example*. Leading by example is particularly important, because whenever human beings notice a difference between what is *said* and what is *done*, they gear their own standards to the example set by those at the top.

This is one reason why it is so important that managers' conduct be exemplary. Their behavior shapes individuals' *faith* in the management of their organization. And the more senior a manager is, the more important this role-model function is. In large organizations, *exemplary conduct* is even more important, and every top executive needs to be aware of this fact. Top managers do not only affect the people within their organization. They also affect how the public sees the economy and business and determine individuals' views on what being a manager is all about. Any inappropriate behavior at higher levels not only has damaging consequences within the organization, but also fuels hostility to business and foments mistrust of managers.

Even individual cases that attract intensive media interest can convey the impression that dishonorable behavior among managers is the norm. The resulting negative feeling toward senior managers cannot be in the interest of modern society. After all, the development of that society hinges on having as many competent people as possible who are positively disposed toward management in general.

■   ■   ■

There is another important point to bear in mind here. There is every reason to assume the existence of a largely unchanging gap between the performance at the top of an organization and the performance of most of its employees. Consequently, if the level of performance at the top of the organization goes up, the overall level of performance will rise with it. If values are not taken seriously by top management, how can it expect the human beings in the organization to act any differently? Likewise, if an organization's top managers set a poor example in terms of their standard of performance, how can its staff reasonably be expected to perform, let alone put in an excellent performance?

People decisions regarding senior management posts have far-reaching consequences because they set the standard for the entire organization. Therefore, the managers and bodies responsible for such decisions should pay particularly close attention to making sure that high standards are set at the top of the organization. There is no more direct way of enhancing the performance level of the organization as a whole.

One reason why Bill Gates, Steve Jobs, Jack Welch, Michael Dell, Larry Ellison, Jeff Bezos, and similar top managers are so valuable to their organizations is that to some extent they set its pace of development and performance level—and even influence the entire sector their business is in. They substantially determine their organization's business mission, set objectives and values, and color the organization through the example they set. If an organization is to be effective, its *shared values, business mission,* and *objectives* must be clear to the people who work for it. Accordingly, these values must not only be straightforward and readily understandable, they must also be *constantly reinforced.*

Values are also extremely important for the effectiveness of individuals, whose own values should be *compatible* with those of their organization. They need not be identical, but individuals' values should fit within their organization's overall system of values. Conflicting sets of values will almost inevitably leave individuals feeling frustrated, prevent them from realizing their full performance potential, and cause the results they achieve to invariably fall short of the level they could otherwise attain.

Ask yourself this question: *"What are my values?"* A clear answer will benefit you in two ways: just as a conflict of values can hinder performance, acting in harmony with your values can be both truly empowering and highly motivating. Fundamentally, there is a rather simple, though not always obvious, link between strengths, performance, and values. In areas in which human beings have *strengths*, they will *find it easy to perform well*. This may be readily understandable, but it does not say anything about whether the application of those strengths matches the individuals' *values*, and this fact is frequently overlooked. As described in Chapter 28, Einstein's contribution to the development of the atom bomb rankled him his whole life long. Why? Because his strengths were deployed in a domain that was seriously at odds with his pacifist values.

If you end up in situations where your strengths and values clash, always follow the principle that you will be able to mobilize the necessary reserves of energy and performance only if you act in keeping with your values. The same applies when, at a given moment, you find yourself unable to see the *sense* in applying your strengths, with the result that every minute spent seems like wasted time. Here again, heed your values (the issue of sense or "meaning" is taken up separately in Chapter 47 on Viktor Frankl). If you ensure a match between what you do and what is important to you, this will have a marked positive impact on what you achieve.

On numerous photographs we see Winston Churchill, certain of triumph, flashing his now legendary "V for victory" sign. He started using this comparatively small hand gesture in around August 1941, and it epitomizes what he believed in and what he was fighting for. He felt certain that what he was striving to achieve was something worth fighting for. His "V for victory" sign visibly communicated that conviction around the world, clear for all to see. Stand up for your values!

ACTION POINTS AND FOOD FOR THOUGHT

- What are your values?
- What values are upheld in your organization? If there is a discrepancy between theory and practice, what exactly do you and your colleagues within the organization need to do together to change this?
- Insist on exemplary behavior and high performance standards within your sphere of influence.
- Bring in strong, competent people at the top level to boost your organization's overall performance.

CHAPTER 32

Surround Yourself with Good People

LEARNING FROM

Jack Welch

John Francis "Jack" Welch (born in 1935) became General Electric's youngest ever CEO at the age of 45 in 1981. During his 20 years at the helm, he really took the company forward by introducing many management innovations. His management skills earned him legendary status. Indeed, in 1999 *Fortune* magazine named him "Manager of the Century," and the *Financial Times* recently listed him as one of the three most widely admired company CEOs today.

Welch had little time for bureaucracy and outmoded forms of company leadership and management. His radical questioning and drastic realignment of existing structures and practices often won him no friends, but the results (almost) always proved he had been right.

Continuing a tradition established by his seven predecessors, Welch made *solid management training* a trademark of the company. As CEO, he personally invested a massive amount of time and energy on training up-and-coming managers, among other things by being a frequent speaker at the training center in Crotonville, New York, and attending numerous other events worldwide. To this day, the quality of GE's managers and their training are largely characterized by Welch's influence, which constitutes a benchmark of professionalism and effectiveness in the best tradition of good management.

One of Welch's great strengths was to surround himself with really good people. Personnel decisions are crucial for guiding a company's development because it is the human beings working for an organization who determine its overall performance. The quality of its employees determines the quality of the *performance for customers*, as well as determining how *efficiently* and *effectively* things are done within the organization. In addition, it is the people in the organization who live out its *values*, visibly reflecting the *integrity* and *trust* that characterize its *corporate culture*.

In a knowledge society, the most important resource—knowledge—is brought into an organization by its staff and is then deployed for the benefit of customers. Organizations that *fail* to implement the values set out in any mission statement will lose those employees who can freely choose where they work. The problem with this is that the people who have such a choice are always the good ones. And organizations cannot afford to lose them.

The extent of staff turnover is less important than the question of *who* leaves the organization. If large numbers of good people leave, this is an alarm signal that the organization's top management needs to take very seriously. I expect good people in particular to start valuing a *healthy corporate culture even more in the future*, as the perceived importance of experiencing a culture of trust, of integrity, and openness, performance orientation, professionalism, effectiveness, and responsibility increases, along with a sense of community of purpose. After all, why should good people who can choose where they want to earn their money make do with an unsatisfactory corporate culture if they are unable to change it?

Jack Welch always set great store by a healthy corporate culture, and during his 20 years as CEO of General Electric, he made a tremendous effort to ensure that such a culture actually thrived. He knew that he could fulfill his ambitious plans for the company only if he had really good people to help him. The prerequisite for realizing such a corporate culture, which also boosts the organization's capacity to perform, is a *consistent policy of recruiting, developing, and promoting the best people.*

Every people decision must follow a set procedure. Rather than focusing on "insights into human nature," the emphasis should be on a sober, conscientious procedure that is allowed the necessary time and carried out with due care. Below we examine the basic premises underlying this approach.

First basic premise: Good at what?

Start out from the basic premise that people are not good *in a general sense.* The question must not be: *"Is this a good staff member?"* but rather, *"What is this staff member good at?"* Effective managers are characterized by an ability to productively harness people's strengths. Accordingly, when hiring or promoting staff, they always aim to make use of individuals' strengths while rendering their weaknesses irrelevant. Since people always have very few strengths, they must first be identified so that the individual in question can subsequently be deployed precisely where these strengths are needed. Find out the *one* area where each person performs remarkably well; do not look for people whose performance in many areas is only passable. Once you know for certain where their greatest strength lies, set them to work in that domain and insist that they do best what they are most capable of.

Second basic premise: People and assignments must match

When filling a *post*, the question to ask is not what work it generally entails, but rather which *specific key task* or *assignment* is to be fulfilled there. Very different strengths may be required, depending on how that specific assignment is defined for the next 15 to 24 months or so. *People and assignments must match*—this is one of the key "secrets" to effective people decisions. (This is explored in greater detail in Chapter 37 on General George Patton.)

Third basic premise: Always choose between several candidates

When you're hiring staff, always—I repeat, always—give serious consideration to several candidates. If you cannot find *at least between three and five candidates* for a post that needs to be filled, make *no decision*. You would simply be confirming the appointment of someone you had not actually *selected*. Jack Welch personally experienced the toughness and pressure associated with such a selection process for senior positions. His predecessor, Reg Jones, who was chairman and CEO of GE for nine years, left the decision about who should succeed him open for a long time. Welch ultimately won the tough, but fair, battle against two other candidates who had also stayed the course. And when the time came for him to decide who should step into his shoes, he made sure there were also several top candidates in the running (that particular race was won by Jeff Immelt, who became the company's chairman and CEO).

It should be obvious that making such decisions is often difficult; for Welch the choice of his successor was one of the most difficult decisions he ever had to make, not because of the person he had favored, for good reason, but among other things because he had to reject two esteemed top-quality candidates, people who had worked alongside him for a long time.

Fourth basic premise: There are no unimportant people decisions—give yourself time to make people decisions

People decisions should either be thoroughly and painstakingly thought through or not made at all. Alfred Sloan, Jr., for many years the CEO of General Motors, was once asked by Peter F. Drucker how he could afford to spend four hours deciding how to fill a somewhat low-level management post. Sloan replied: *"This corporation pays me a pretty good salary for making the important decisions and making them right . . . . If we didn't spend four hours on placing a man and placing him right, we'd spend four hundred hours on cleaning up after our mistake—and that time I wouldn't have."* Sloan then concluded by saying: *"The decision about people is the only truly crucial one. You think and everybody thinks that a company can have 'better' people; that's horse apples. All it can do is place people right—and then it'll have performance."*[1]

Fifth basic premise: Surround yourself with people who are better and brighter than you

For Jack Welch it was a sign of exceptional competence if managers surrounded themselves with people who were better and brighter than they were. Whenever GE found itself in a tight spot, he resorted to a special method: *"Every time we had a crisis at GE, I would quickly assemble a group of the smartest, gutsiest people I could find at any level from within the company and sometimes from without, and lean on them heavily for their knowledge and advice. I would make sure everyone in the room came at the problem from a different angle, and then I would have us all wallow in the information as we worked to solve the crisis."*[2]

As a rule, those discussions proved extremely lively. The questions raised and differences of opinion expressed not only identified the really important issues, they also prompted reconsideration of the assumptions underlying them. As Jack Welch blithely put it, *"A good leader has the courage to put together a team of people who sometimes make him look like the dumbest person in the room!"*[3] The key point here is that the aim was to determine *what*—not *who*—was right.

Effective managers surround themselves with *strong people* because opposition is essential for good decisions. There are countless examples of this in books and biographies by top managers. Bill Gates had Microsoft staff totally question his Internet strategy; Alfred Sloan, Jr. discontinued meetings at GM if there was no disagreement about key decisions; and at Nestlés Helmut Maucher always stressed the importance of involving his staff in decisions. This list could be extended almost indefinitely. Seeking differences of opinion with a view to making better decisions is an essential part of competent management. Managers who surround themselves with yes men are not competent. And remember, good people will leave organizations that favor toadying.

Sixth basic premise: Good people need breathing space

Whenever Jack Welch found good people, he gave them a lot of space to run the divisions for which they were responsible in the way they wanted. The condition always attached to this leeway was that the managers in question fulfill the "*GE Culture,*" a familiar concept within the company, and above all that they comply with the GE principle of constantly seeking change and improvement.

Seventh basic premise: Integrity is absolutely indispensable

Integrity alone is not enough to achieve anything. Yet if it is lacking, nothing can compensate. For Jack Welch the question about someone's integrity was always the first he asked himself when making people decisions.

Once you have found really good people, you may occasionally end up in a similar position to the one in which Sergey Rachmaninov found himself when he heard the young pianist Vladimir Horowitz play the Piano Concerto No. 3 that Rachmaninov had composed. At the time, a totally content and relieved Rachmaninov said: "*Now I don't have to play any more.*"[4]

These days, Jack Welch and his wife Suzy are devoting their time to sharing profound insights into effective management. His books and talks on this subject are a success worldwide.

ACTION POINTS AND FOOD FOR THOUGHT

■ Are the seven basic premises listed above practiced in your organization? If not, what exactly can you do to change this?

■ What do you need to do to attract really good people to your
organization and keep them there? What is the first measure
you will implement to achieve this?

■ Campaign to ensure that your organization draws up management principles and behavioral standards that have to be followed by its staff. If such principles and standards exist, but
are not being heeded, launch a discussion to find out what you
and your colleagues can do together to ensure that a healthy
corporate culture ensues.

CHAPTER **33**

Create a Culture of Effectiveness

LEARNING FROM

Herb Kelleher

A great deal is said about the relaxed, entertaining, laid-back style of the corporate culture of *Southwest Airlines,* but these comments overlook the key point. For underlying that apparently effortless approach is an unrivaled *culture of professionalism and effectiveness.* The airline's former CEO *Herb Kelleher* (born in 1931) created a *corporate culture* in which *customer value, performance,* and *responsibility* are top priorities. This is the company's real "secret."

Many reports about the company and its eccentric CEO focus on Southwest's unconventional corporate culture. Indeed, it is frequently suggested that this was the *mainstay* of the company's success. But that is not the case at all. *In the marketplace and where customers are concerned,* the company is not successful because of the *unconventional aspects of its corporate culture* but thanks to its *first-class performance.*

The reason for this is a commonly encountered and widely accepted fallacy about effective management: the tendency to focus on *how* things are done instead of *what* is done. Yet the *style* of management is relatively unimportant for determining the company's success, as is evident from the fact that there are many excellent and successful airlines which, though also professional and successful, are managed in a *different* style. Many such companies are larger than Southwest

Airlines and operate on more complex routes all over the world, not only in the United States. This does not diminish the performance of Southwest, but it does direct our attention to factors that merit it.

Dressing casually to go to work at Southwest's corporate headquarters, celebrating at every conceivable opportunity, employing flight attendants with a sense of humor, and presenting safety briefings in the form of stand-up comedy definitely create a special corporate culture. I am not ruling out the possibility that in the case of Southwest Airlines all this may go *some* way toward explaining the airline's success, but it is definitely not the key to its success in general and can most certainly not simply be carried over to other companies.

Airline customers want to arrive safely and punctually, and where Southwest is concerned, for relatively little money. The keys here are professionalism and reliably excellent performance, not the fuss surrounding it. Or would you board an airplane that was flown by a very witty, but incompetent pilot? And how often can your baggage go missing before you switch airlines?

What is impressive about Southwest is not the peculiarities of its corporate culture, but its performance record. Ever since the U.S. Department of Transportation started recording customer satisfaction in the aviation sector back in 1987, Southwest has led the way in the industry, eliciting the fewest complaints per passenger conveyed while at the same time achieving excellent financial results. In this connection, Herb Kelleher said, *"We tell our people, "Don't worry about profit. Think about customer service. Profit is a by-product of customer service. It's not an end, in and of itself. It's something that's produced by your efforts and by the way that you treat each other and the way you treat the outside world."*[1]

The fruits of this form of management geared toward customer value, performance, and responsibility are clear to see. In 2010, for the fourteenth year in succession, the annual study on companies' reputations published in *Fortune* magazine paid tribute to Southwest. Again in 2010, Southwest was the only airline to make the Top 20 in *Fortune* magazine's prestigious annual list of the "World's Most Admired Companies" and was also deemed one of the most admired airlines. In 2008, *Forbes* magazine listed the company as America's most reliable airline. One study published at *TIME.com* listed Southwest as the friendliest airline, and in 2007 and 2010 Southwest made *Business Week*'s list of "Customer Service Champs." This is just a small selection of the company's successes, which were outshone by its achievement of reporting a *thirty-eighth successive* profitable business year in 2010.

Herb Kelleher and Southwest Airlines can teach us a vast amount about corporate culture, namely about how to create a *culture of professionalism, focused on effectiveness, performance, responsibility,* and *trust.* A corporate culture of this kind is nothing more than the *result* of *effective management.* Or put the other way around: *effective management creates a desirable corporate culture.*

Anyone setting out to offer professionalism, effectiveness, and excellent performance will end up cultivating effective management. Viewed in this light, the issue of corporate culture becomes very *easy to operationalize.* In other words, there are many specific measures that can be taken to build up a corporate culture that will benefit the organization.

This book advocates a division into three domains that need to be taken into account when developing a *culture of effectiveness:* the *management of organizations,* the *management of innovation,* and *the management of people.* A beneficial corporate culture is not just a combination of several separate things, but rather derives from the professional mastery of the three domains, each comprising numerous modules, and from the interplay between them. Ultimately, a *culture of effectiveness* is the sum of the quality of its building blocks and how well they work together.

As Helmut Maucher, the long-serving CEO of Nestlé, once said in connection with the tasks of company management and corporate development, *"'Be close to your products, be close to your people' and be close to your customers.' If you take this to heart you cannot go wrong all along."*[2] However, this advice can be adopted as the core of a corporate culture geared toward effectiveness, performance, professionalism, and responsibility.

ACTION POINTS AND FOOD FOR THOUGHT

■ In which of the three domains—*the management of organizations, the management of innovation,* or *the management of people*—can you make a big step toward a culture of effectiveness if you wish to progress in this area? What specific action will you now take?

■ Genuine interdepartmental cooperation *throughout your organization* can help you make a major contribution toward a culture of effectiveness. At one of your next off-site meetings, ask your managers to focus on this single question: *"What do we need to do together to establish a corporate culture of effectiveness?"* Substantial progress will be made if you focus the ensuing discussion on the three domains listed above.

CHAPTER 34

Nurture and Develop People

LEARNING FROM
David Packard

Together with *Bill Hewlett*, in 1939 *David Packard* (1912–1996) founded the *Hewlett-Packard Company*, with seed capital of just $538. In the manner befitting a high-tech legend, Hewlett-Packard began in a garage in *Palo Alto*, Silicon Valley. The garage is still standing today, at Addison Avenue 367, near Stanford University and is a historic landmark, whose memorial plaque bears the venerable words "*Birthplace of Silicon Valley.*"

Right from the start, the two founders of the company gave their employees tremendous room to maneuver, which was anything but typical for the form of management practiced at the time. "*We recognized that employees achieve more if they are given the opportunity to make use of their talents and abilities,*"[1] David Packard said, looking back at those early days. The extensive powers he gave the company's employees made him a pioneer in what would today be described by the buzzword "empowerment." However, it is more appropriate, and in many respects simply better, to say that Packard fostered a *corporate culture of performance and responsibility*, long before such a culture was adopted by the majority of effectively and efficiently managed companies. In the corporate culture he and Bill Hewlett established, he always attached great importance to nurturing people. The fact that these individuals were given important assignments and great responsibility was a key element of this approach.

For this chapter I could have picked any one of a huge number of leaders to epitomize the *nurturing of people*, because it is such a fundamental part of good management. For instance, one of Winston Churchill's strong points was that he vigorously nurtured young politicians right up until the end of his life. Likewise, the celebrated conductor Bruno Walter, who was admired for his interpretations of Mozart, Bruckner, and Mahler, was well known for his commitment to strongly encouraging the musicians in his orchestras, a characteristic common to all exceptional conductors. Many musicians, too, are deeply devoted to encouraging their peers and emerging stars. For example, the world-famous "wonder violinist" Yehudi Menuhin was an extremely active teacher who sought to pass on his own perfect technique to his students, while at the same time giving them invaluable guidance on maximizing their personal interpretation. General George Marshall was another possible candidate, having forcefully advocated the nurturing and development of people on countless occasions. For instance, one of Marshall's decisions with extremely far-reaching consequences was taken in the mid-1930s, when he quite deliberately arranged for the still young Major Dwight Eisenhower to be posted to the War Department. Although Eisenhower's work there did not turn him into an excellent strategist, it did help him develop a systematic, strategic understanding and make him respect strategy and appreciate its importance. Subsequently, when Eisenhower was a general and later on president of the United States, this previous experience helped him to appoint the country's best available people to teams working on strategic issues. Generally speaking, one of Eisenhower's great strengths was his ability to put together excellent teams.

There are countless examples of people deliberately and successfully being nurtured. In fact, one characteristic of good, effective managers is that they personally deal with the issue of nurturing people. *People constitute the most important resource an organization has.* What makes David Packard a particularly pertinent example above all is that almost every organization in the world has a product that could not have come about without what he did or without following his principles.

But let us now turn to their actual implementation. The following elements should always be kept in mind when you are nurturing and developing people:

1. Organizations foster people's development with positive or negative results

If people are nurtured within their organization, they have a chance to develop in a positive way. However, if the organization neglects to nurture their development, then their skills, talents, and ultimately their attitude will atrophy, and they will develop in a negative way.

Organizations cannot escape exerting an influence one way or another. In fact, it is in the interests of organizations and individuals alike that people *be* properly nurtured. For organizations always depend on hiring independent, competent managers for their own effectiveness, strength, and growth. At the same time, people's performance, self-improvement, and success all hinge on their organization's willingness to attribute high importance to nurturing its employees. When all is said and done, *people can only develop themselves;* they have to motivate themselves and produce their own performance and results. Nonetheless, *organizations can create an environment* conducive to these individuals' development.

2. Set demanding tasks to elicit high aspirations

People grow with the tasks assigned to them. Consequently, which tasks are assigned is the key element when seeking to nurture people and encourage their development. This is far more important than any course they could be sent to complete. Courses are complementary instruments for ensuring that an assigned task can be fulfilled.

The assigned task should be *bigger and more demanding* than previous tasks completed by the person in question. The task should prove *demanding* and urge the person to question previous performance limits. Whenever there seems to be a chance of exceeding these limits, this is precisely when it is worth making additional efforts, for example, by providing an accompanying training program.

Remember, *aspirations about performance can easily be lowered at any time, while raising them is nearly impossible.* If high standards have already been firmly set and people are accustomed to try to meet them, usually an organization's employees will urge each other to do so.

To cite but one example, Gustav Mahler used to make extremely high demands on his musicians, and still did so when he was placed in charge of the Vienna State Opera. Once, when Emperor Franz Joseph I of Austria, who was also King of Hungary, attended an orchestra rehearsal directed by Mahler, the composer placed such inhumanly high demands on his players that the Kaiser called out to him, asking, *"Don't you think you're overdoing it?"* to which Mahler replied, *"Your Majesty, my demands are nothing compared to the demand the musicians now make on me because they play so much better."*[2]

Facing up to an extremely demanding task is another common feature on the résumés of successful people.

3. Draw on people's strengths

To nurture people, you need to constantly draw on their *existing strengths.* Since there is no way of knowing what children at school will be doing in 10 or 20 years, it is important to make sure that they adequately master all the basic skills. As a result, schools make intensive efforts to iron out any weaknesses in their students. By contrast, organizations hire people to *deploy their strengths* with a view to *attaining goals.* There *is* no other path to achievement. So, when nurturing people, care must be taken to ensure that they develop their strengths and therefore enhance their skills, know-how, and conduct—not in a general sense, but with a view to enhancing those existing strengths. On the other hand, efforts to diminish weaknesses should be made only if these weaknesses prevent individuals from fully developing or deploying their respective strengths.

4. A suitable post and the right superior are crucial to personal development

Closely linked to the task and strengths is the question of which *type of post* will be most conducive to a person's development. Posts should be chosen to fit their occupants' *personality*. And for the purposes of nurturing and development, consideration ought to be given to whether an employee will perform most effectively in a *line position* or a *staff position*. Does the person in question need plenty of *routine* or a highly *innovative and frequently changing environment*? Is the individual good at handling *details* or better at working with *concepts* and *fundamentals*? Does he or she work well *alone* or does this person function better in a *team*? Last, but not least, a person's designated *superior* exercises considerable influence over the subordinate's subsequent development. Younger employees in particular will tend to model themselves on a successful superior, so integrity is absolutely essential, as is always the case when managing people.

Many successful people had idols whom they set out to emulate. As this role model exerts such a strong pull, it is essential for people's individual development to make sure that their superior sets an example worth following. Not in a general, overall sense, but rather with respect to the tasks to be fulfilled in the organization and with an eye to professional management, specifically the superior's *expertise, commitment, professionalism, attitude toward the company, readiness to assume responsibility, trust of others*, and—last, but not least—the *integrity* mentioned above.

5. Assess individuals' performance and development

As stated above, people develop themselves. So the responsibility for that development lies primarily with the individual in question. However, the organization can create favorable conditions that facilitate personal development. For this reason it is well worth sitting down together at regular intervals with the people who are being nurtured to *assess their progress*. Key questions to ask in this connection are:

"What did you take upon yourself a year ago, and how much of it have you achieved? What was a success for you and us, and what should we therefore build up further in the future? What do you need to learn in order to draw on your strengths even more effectively?"

Although the points listed above have been proven valid a long time ago, not all organizations give nurturing and development the status they deserve, even though it is crucial that all managers accept measures in this domain as part of their basic duties and should systematically endeavor to promote them.

Today, Hewlett-Packard is one of the world's largest companies and has for years figured near the top of the Fortune 500 list. In the 1990s the company went through a difficult phase, and even though the corporation's two founders, Bill Hewlett and David Packard, were already nearing 80, they both heavily involved themselves in initiating HP's recovery. By implementing a *back-to-basics strategy*, the company sought to regain the power to innovate that had made it so strong in the first place. This involved the company's founders personally falling back on the tried-and-tested method of their early years in business: *management by walking around*. Is there any better example of the fact that not everything has to be *new* to be *good*?

ACTION POINTS AND FOOD FOR THOUGHT

- Nurture and develop your employees. Make sure that they are assigned demanding tasks, and deploy their strengths, check that they are well matched to their post and superior, and regularly assess their performance and development.
- If you set yourself personal development targets, regularly assess your progress. What will you do based on what you learn from this?

CHAPTER **35**

Invest in Training

LEARNING FROM

Alexander von Humboldt

Alexander Freiherr von Humboldt (1769–1859) was one of the most respected scientists of his time, and today he is often described as the last great polymath because of his tremendously wide-ranging interests. From a management perspective this fact alone is not particularly noteworthy; the remarkable fact is that he *actively put his extensive knowledge to work to accomplish his various projects.*

After completing his studies, which focused on science and technology, he worked as an assessor of mines and later as senior mine manager in the Franconian principalities of the Hohenzollern family. In the summer of 1799, together with the French botanist Aimé Bonpland, Humboldt set about realizing his vision of exploring the entire region of Latin America, which was still virtually uncharted territory to scientists at the time, by completing a broadly conceived, self-financed expedition devoted entirely to science. The trip took a full five years, and before embarking on it, he and his team secured the unusual privilege of free passage through Spanish South America and permission to pursue their research unhindered, even though the Spanish colonies had previously not been accessible to foreigners. Humboldt was a humanist, and his aim was, *"To turn the unfamiliar into the known, using reason and suitable methods."*[1] In a farewell letter to a friend, the euphoric explorer wrote, *"I will collect plants and fossils and be able to make astronomical observations using excellent instruments;. . . I will perform chemical analyses of the air. . . . However, all that is not the main aim of my expedition. I will constantly observe the interaction of forces, the influence of the inanimate world on animal and plant life. My eyes will constantly focus on this harmony! . . . Mankind must strive for the great and the good."*[2]

To conduct their research, Humboldt and Bonpland transported numerous instruments thousands of kilometers through Central and South America. They identified countless geographical features, described some 3,500 new plant species, studied the exotic fauna, and documented the customs and history of native peoples. On the way back to Europe in 1804, Humboldt visited U.S. President Thomas Jefferson, and the two men discussed the idea of constructing the Panama Canal, though Jefferson ended up rejecting the idea because he considered the terrain impassable.

After his return, Humboldt spent decades analyzing the many botanical, geological, and mineralogical materials he had collected and published his findings in a 35-volume work titled *Voyage to the Equinoctial Regions of the New Continent*[3] (*equinoctial* being the favored term for *equatorial* in Humboldt's day). During the last major creative phase of his life, Humboldt also produced his five-volume *Cosmos*, in which he attempted to sum up what was known about the Earth in his time, adopting a holistic, cosmological viewpoint.

Humboldt devoted his life exclusively to tackling a mammoth task of his own choosing. Such total dedication to a specific endeavor is characteristic of all top achievers. In his work, Humboldt always combined his *broad general knowledge* with a *clear specialist focus*. His almost encyclopedic knowledge set an example to many of his contemporaries. In fact, the grandiose poet Goethe found Humboldt such a knowledgeable dialogue partner that he described him admiringly as a *"seemingly neverending fount of knowledge."*[4] *"Such a versatile mind!"*[5] an exhilarated Goethe is said to have exclaimed.

For the purposes of this book, the interesting fact for you as a manager is that, in addition to specialist qualifications, knowledge traditionally regarded as *general* will (once again) come to be seen as very important. The reason for this becomes apparent below.

The title of this chapter highlights the need to invest *in training*. Whether you wish to invest in *education* is a *personal* decision. As a manager, the latter is *not* imperative for attaining your objectives. All the same, some arguments in favor of a solid education are presented below, after the following comments on training. It makes sense to distinguish two domains in which people are trained with a view to working effectively for their organization: first, *management training*, and second, *training to acquire specialist knowledge and expertise.*

People don't query the systematic accumulation of *specialist knowledge and expertise* any more than they ask questions about continuing training in this connection. Those working in the health-care sector; in education, culture, or administration; in information technology, commerce, or the financial sector; or in any other profession for that matter, will acquire the specialist knowledge and expertise required to exercise that profession. And that specialist knowledge and expertise are constantly updated and consolidated as a matter of course. All this indicates professional competence and, as such, is perfectly understandable.

But it is far less self-evident for people to adopt the same rigorously methodical approach to *management training*. As a result, very few executives have received systematic instruction in how best to manage. So they may have built up their background scientific, technical, legal, or economic knowledge, but generally speaking they will not have acquired any notable management know-how. Extensive management courses are taught to economics students at universities and colleges, but nowhere else. Consequently, what makes most competent managers so able is the fact that they have *taught themselves* the necessary management skills *on top of* their specialist and expert knowledge. People intent on ensuring an effective organization and guaranteeing their own personal effectiveness should attribute special importance to the acquisition of management know-how. This is because organizations are never about specialist knowledge and expertise *as ends in themselves,* but rather about *applying* such knowledge in a bid to *bring about* results that benefit customers. Yet this know-how about how to apply knowledge and attain results in an organization is *management know-how.* In other words, *both* kinds of knowledge are needed. So organizations and people who focus on this will have a very clear competitive edge as they will be able to apply their specialist knowledge and expertise *more effectively* and *more efficiently* in practice.

While the first two domains, *training to acquire specialist knowledge and expertise* and *management training,* are key in determining the effectiveness of the organization, *the acquisition of general knowledge* is a third domain that is a personal matter, not imperative for performing effectively. You can manage a business area competently without having an appreciable store of general knowledge. Nonetheless, it is a conspicuous fact that some of the best companies obviously attach importance to this issue. For instance, the section in *The Nestlé Management and Leadership Principles,* headed "The Nestlé Leadership: Adding Value," explicitly states that in addition to their professional skills, practical experience, and focus on results, high-level managers are also selected for their *"broad interests"* and *"good general knowledge,"* among other things.[6]

For the grandparents of people starting their careers today, it was perfectly natural to strive for a good general education. Among the generation of people who graduated from high school before World

War II, the best students attributed great importance to general education, which they cultivated and nurtured as part of their own personal identity.

Today, that attitude is less widespread and self-evident, even though our present knowledge society undoubtedly needs educated people. Not as an end in itself, and not to realize some kind of humanistic educational ideal, but rather with a view to gaining a deeper understanding of reality and coming to terms with it more effectively. In this context, a general education should make it easier for people to think their way into different disciplines, cultures, and religions and recognize the links between them. Organizations do not need polymaths who easily master multiple disciplines; they need people who at least have a basic grasp of several domains and can find their footing in any of them. All this should help to ensure that effective managers make good decisions, that risks are spotted before it is too late, and that opportunities are seized. The higher a manager's position within an organization, the more important these skills become, because problems and opportunities can be seen and understood only for what they are in their respective context.

To reiterate, the distinction to make is this: whereas managers can run their business area perfectly well and be very well grounded in their specialization without having an exceptional command of general knowledge, the more senior they become, the greater their need for background knowledge, including an understanding of other disciplines, will be if they are to make *effective* decisions.

Changes in one sector or domain often stem from innovations arising in another area or discipline. In the future it will become more and more important for managers to draw on such know-how from other domains. Accordingly, it can only become increasingly advantageous to undergo continuing training constantly and expand your own personal horizons. Put the other way around, you will also have to be able to make your own special discipline accessible and understandable to others so that they too can benefit from what you know.

Few people have set such a powerful example of how learning and teaching can complement each other so well as Alexander von Humboldt.

ACTION POINTS AND FOOD FOR THOUGHT

■ What are you doing to foster your training and continue your training, and which specific objectives do you intend such measures to attain?

■ What are you doing to expand your horizons? Where might this knowledge prove useful?

CHAPTER **36**

Seek Wise
Dialogue Partners

LEARNING FROM

*Camille Pissarro
and Paul Cézanne*

Camille Pissarro (1830–1903) was one
of the leading pioneers of French *Impressionism and Neo-Impressionism.*
As a mentor and teacher he exerted
great influence over younger painters,
like *Paul Cézanne* (1839–1906), Paul
Gauguin, and Vincent van Gogh.

Pissarro constantly sought to
exchange views and ideas with the
leading artists of his day. During his formative years as an artist in
Paris when he was a private pupil of the teaching staff from the École
des Beaux-Arts and Swiss Academy in around 1860 he already got to
know not only Paul Cézanne but also Claude Monet and Jean-Bap-
tiste Armand Guillaumin. Guillaumin and Vincent van Gogh subsequently formed a close friendship. Pissarro himself had been a student
of Camille Corot, whose figurative works served as models for works
by Edgar Degas, Georges Braque, and Pablo Picasso. In 1865, together
with Alfred Sisley and Auguste Renoir, Pissarro left the confines of his

studio to paint from nature in the forest of Fontainebleau. Like Monet and Renoir, he developed and steadily refined the art of open-air painting, constantly experimenting with increasingly brighter, less broken colors and sketchily applied paint. The paintings he created during this period, like *Landscape at Louveciennes*, were largely instrumental in the emergence of Impressionism.

Pissarro also cultivated fruitful exchanges with artists outside his own discipline. For example, the author Émile Zola was a prominent admirer of his work. Pissarro regularly attended meetings of Édouard Manet's "Batignolles Group," in which painters and critics discussed avant-garde art. After returning from exile in London during the Franco-Prussian War of 1870 to 1871, Pissaro engaged in an intensive exchange with Paul Cézanne. Together the two artists developed an increasingly unconventional style of open-air and landscape painting.

Cézanne himself was not only a pugnacious artist, constantly at odds with the Paris art establishment, but he was also frequently misunderstood and derided in his lifetime. Early on in Cézanne's career Pissarro became a key mentor to him, setting an example for him to follow. Under Pissarro's guidance and tutelage, Cézanne reflected on the skills he needed and thus refined his use of Impressionist techniques. In the medieval tradition of great artists, Cézanne started off by copying pictures painted by Pissarro, but their relationship soon blossomed into a stimulating give and take, with each artist learning from the other, and they spent hours discussing their views and theories in *"Père Pissarro's"* house. *"As for Pissarro, he was a father to me, a man to consult and something like the good Lord,"*[1] Cézanne said. But like all good mentors, Pissarro advised Cézanne not just to produce sterile copies of his (Pissarro's) works.

Today, Cézanne is regarded as one of the greatest painters in the history of art, even as a precursor for new styles, like *Fauvism* and *Cubism*. For example, references to Cézanne are apparent in Henri Matisse's Fauvist works, and in the summer of 1908 Georges Braque and Pablo Picasso painted geometricized landscapes in L'Estaque, following in Cézanne's footsteps. The paintings they produced there are heralded as the birth of Cubism. For Henri Matisse, Camille Pissarro was not just inspirational, he was also a valuable advisor, recommending for instance that he study the works of William Turner in London.

At the same time, Pissarro was not just a teacher and mentor, but also forcefully advocated his view of art. As a protest against both the prevailing conservative policy on art and salon juries with antiquated views, Pissarro joined Edgar Degas, Claude Monet, Auguste Renoir, and others to form an artists' initiative that organized eight group exhibitions of works by avant-garde painters between 1874 and 1886. The art critic Louis Leroy mockingly derided the members of the group as "Impressionists," a play on the title of a canvas exhibited by Monet entitled *Impression, Sunrise*. The term Impressionists duly stuck, sealing a firm place in the history of art for Leroy, though probably not the kind of legacy he would have hoped for. Pissarro, along with Degas, remained a driving force in this community of artists to which he introduced many younger artists including Cézanne, Gauguin, Seurat, and Signac.

However, Pissarro did not just bring together a large number of artists and serve as a precious mentor and teacher to younger artists; he also let *them* inspire *him*, the most striking example of this being Georges Seurat, a man almost 30 years his junior. It was Seurat who, after intensive study, painstakingly developed a new technique that would come to be called Neo-Impressionist. In 1885, Paul Signac, one of the most prominent Neo-Impressionists alongside Seurat, brought Camille Pissarro and Georges Seurat together. At the time, Seurat had nearly completed one of his most famous works, *A Sunday Afternoon on the Island of La Grande Jatte*. The painting so impressed Pissarro that he immediately adopted the technique that would later be described as Neo-Impressionist—though not without taking the opportunity to offer his younger fellow artist a few welcome practical tips.

Some people today regard Pissarro as one of the best teachers of painting and regard him as a *prototypical mentor,* devoting a large proportion of his energy to promoting talented young artists, without ever being too aloof to learn from his protégés and students.

So what can Camille Pissarro teach us about management? What Pissarro and the outstanding group of artists with whom he associated teach us above all is something that is apparent in all disciplines, in all areas of society, and naturally also in the management of organizations: *the importance of icons, mentors, teachers, and trusted dialogue partners.*

However, we must differentiate here, because by no means everyone who went on to achieve greatness could—or wanted to—fall back on mentors or teachers. Many of them made strides all by themselves. And not everyone has always valued dialogue partners highly: Cézanne himself was very much a loner for lengthy spells of his life. Indeed, his friendship with Pissarro was exceptional. But virtually everybody has had people they looked up to, as countless biographies make clear.

The first and possibly most important lesson of this chapter is that *icons were—and still are—a driving force for many great people.* Usually mentoring is considered a one-sided relationship, with younger individuals taking their example from people older than themselves, and this is no doubt regularly the case, as with the relationship between Cézanne and Pissarro, for example. But at the same time, Pissarro shows us that a teacher-student relationship can also work the other way around, for he was sufficiently open-minded to draw sustained inspiration from the Neo-Impressionist style of Seurat, who was a full generation younger than Pissarro himself.

Second, although not all the greats made use of the possibilities opened up by having a mentor, *very few of those who achieve greatness manage to do so without any teachers or patrons whatsoever.* Even Michelangelo had the Medici family and six pontiffs sponsoring him, especially Pope Julius II, who gave Michelangelo some major opportunities in the form of his most challenging assignments. The safe assumption that the Pope and Michelangelo must—at times—have loathed each other is another issue. The fact remains that the Pope *did* give Michelangelo his support.

Jack Welch frequently reiterated the importance of mentors in shaping his own career and his own life. In so doing, he underscored one very important point: *"People, it seems, are always looking for that one right mentor to help them get ahead. But in my experience, there is no one right mentor. There are many right mentors."*[2] This is something that many sports stars, artists, scientists, business leaders, and politicians can confirm.

The third lesson is that the importance of *inspiring dialogue partners* must on no account be underestimated. For many of the artists connected to Pissarro, he was neither a teacher nor a mentor but more of a *trusted* and—when necessary—*critical dialogue partner*. At first sight this may seem banal, but its true value emerges at the very latest when we bear in mind the high level of the peers from whom he sought both contact and above all constructive, critical debate.

The discussion group led by Édouard Manet and the corresponding Impressionist circle co-founded by Pissarro pursued this kind of critical dialogue, which is precisely the type of exchange sought by effective managers and takes place on well-run advisory boards. In a nutshell, *the best people seek critics*. They *want* their positions, opinions, and theories to be challenged because they know that only the ensuing critical dialogue produces *tangibly better solutions*. Whether an advisory board or supervisory body is used for this purpose, as is often the case in business, or whether an informal discussion group or valued friends fulfill it, is not important. What really counts is that such discussions take place *at all*, for they are extremely valuable. In short, competent managers will always deliberately open themselves up to such critical dialogue.

The important thing is that the people involved are independent, and it was just such circles that Pissarro sought out. And *independent advice* of this kind can not only prove extremely valuable for *organizations*. The biographies of practically all great historical figures show that they constantly cultivated solid trust with certain individuals and sought an additional opinion or good advice from them.

Good management just happens to be far more commonplace than some people would have us believe. Yet it is—and will continue to remain—important that such meetings of advisory boards or supervisory bodies do not become mere "showcase events" or pleasant, but ultimately ineffective gatherings. Instead, serious critical exchanges need to take place there, though this outcome is by no means self-evident. One thing is clear: the best people definitely make very vigorous efforts to ensure the effectiveness of such bodies and discussion groups.

The examples set out below indicate just how much the brightest business minds have been influenced by advice. In this connection, *Fortune* magazine asked prominent business leaders: "*What was the best advice you ever got?*"[3] Maybe one or more of the following tips can prove useful to you as well.

- *Howard Schultz,* chairman and CEO of Starbucks: "*Recognize the skills and traits you don't possess, and hire people who have them.*"
- *Warren Buffett,* chairman of Berkshire Hathaway: "*You're right not because others agree with you, but because your facts are right.*"
- *Alan G. Lafley,* chairman of Procter & Gamble: "*Have the courage to stick with a tough job.*"
- *Richard Branson,* founder of the Virgin Group: "*Make a fool of yourself. Otherwise you won't survive.*" (This piece of advice came from an entrepreneur Branson had befriended and was intended to highlight a possible strategy for competing against the massive advertising budget of British Airways.)

- *Andy Grove,* former chairman and CEO of Intel: *"When 'everyone knows' something to be true, nobody knows nothin.'"*
- *Jack Welch,* former chairman and CEO of General Electric: *"Be yourself."*
- *Jim Collins,* management author: *"The real discipline comes in saying no to the wrong opportunities."*
- *Peter F. Drucker,* pioneering management thinker: *"Get good—or get out."* (This is what one boss told a roughly 20-year-old Drucker.)
- *Ted Turner,* founder of CNN: *"Start young."*
- *Hector Ruiz,* former chairman and CEO of AMD: *"Surround yourself with people of integrity, and get out of their way."*
- *Herb Kelleher,* founder and former chairman and CEO of Southwest Airlines: *"Respect people for who they are, not for what their titles are."*

ACTION POINTS AND FOOD FOR THOUGHT

- Which dialogue partners do you surround yourself with?
- Spend your time being an interested person, not an interesting one.

CHAPTER **37**

Clearly Define Jobs and Assignments

LEARNING FROM

General George Patton

George S. Patton (1885–1945) is among the most successful generals of World War II. After the attack on Pearl Harbor triggered the United States' entry into the war, the then Major-General Patton, under the supreme command of General Dwight Eisenhower, successfully led the Western Task Force in Operation Torch during the American landings in North Africa in November 1942. Promoted to the rank of lieutenant-general, he then commanded the U.S. Seventh Army during the invasion of Sicily in July 1943, remaining in charge until January 1944, when he was reassigned to command the U.S. Third Army in France, where he most decisively contributed to the Allies' success. In recognition of Patton's achievements during World War II, he was honored with the rank of a four-star general.

Notwithstanding all these successes and his proven competence as a commander, Patton cut anything but an uncontroversial figure. He repeatedly incurred public disapproval and criticism from General Eisenhower, no less, because of his somewhat heavy-handed political diplomacy. At decisive moments, Chief of Staff General George

Marshall stepped in to protect Patton, even though he, too, frowned on some aspects of Patton's conduct. In addition, Marshall lobbied hard for Patton's promotion to the rank of a four-star general. Marshall knew that although Patton was a "difficult" general, for the situations faced in 1942—and to be faced thereafter—Patton was the best man for the job.

Patton is a prime example of the perfect match between a *person* and the *assignment*. Achieving such matches is one of the key "secrets" of effective people decisions, as already explained in Chapter 32 on Jack Welch.

General George Marshall was a true master at making effective people decisions. In the course of World War II hardly anyone had to make as many—and such important—people decisions as he. And Marshall's unerring ability to pick the right man for the job made an important contribution to the Allies' victory and ultimately led to Marshall becoming the only partner of Roosevelt, Churchill, and Stalin to succeed in being viewed by them as a respected equal. Following the basic premises already set out in Chapter 32 on Jack Welch, when making his people decisions General Marshall usually proceeded in the following steps.

Step 1: Think through the assignment

Marshall always thought through assignments very thoroughly. —An *assignment* can be defined as the highest-priority task to be fulfilled in the foreseeable future. The period in question will usually comprise 15 to 24 months, though this should only be taken as a rough figure as its exact duration will depend on the actual assignment. Judging from experience, it is usually possible to maintain a pretty reliable overview of the next 18 months. *Assignments* change more frequently than *jobs* and *job descriptions*, which can remain unaltered for a long time.

Job descriptions define *tasks* which, in organizational terms, constitute part of the job in question and are thus expected to be fulfilled by its incumbent for an unlimited duration. However, no priorities are set within the job description, for that happens only when the job incumbent is given an *assignment*. The assignment should crucially lead to concentration, with the person involved being attributed as few key tasks as possible, ideally just *a single* assignment: for the more assignments there are, the greater the risk that they will not be fulfilled effectively.

Step 2: Always consider several candidates

Marshall made sure that he always considered several candidates for a job, his main concern being that the *person* should be a good match for the *assignment*. This did *not* entail looking for some kind of *general compatibility* between the *person* and the *job*; it meant ensuring that the selected candidate was suitable for the *specific task* at hand.

This often poses a problem in corporate management today, because the concept of hiring people for *jobs* with specific *assignments* in mind is still not universally adopted. Where the concept *is* consistently applied, it relatively swiftly results in efficient units and organizations.

Step 3: Study people's track record

Since *strengths* are prerequisites for accomplishment, Marshall always endeavored to ascertain his candidates' strong points. George Patton is an excellent example of this. In 1942 it was clear to both Marshall and Eisenhower that Patton's strengths as a commander would be needed for the imminent Operation Torch assignment, namely the landings in Morocco and Algeria. It was equally apparent to them that the same skills would be particularly important later on as well, as indeed turned out to be the case, for instance in Operation Overlord—the Normandy landings.

Marshall was only interested in initial question marks hanging over candidates or their weaknesses if they were relevant to the domain to which the people in question were to be assigned. In practice this meant that he was unable to prevent occasional gaffes by Patton—a fact naturally pounced on by the British or American press—but he *could* limit the damage they caused. Above all, in this way Marshall was able to ensure that the respective *assignment* would be fulfilled as competently as possible by the best-suited candidate in the U.S. Army.

Step 4: Speak with former colleagues and superiors of potential candidates

Marshall was of the view that the best, most reliable information about people emerged from informal talks with their former superiors and colleagues, so he always spoke with such individuals before making a people decision.

Step 5: Make sure the selected candidate understands the assignment

Marshall's top priority was to ensure that the selected candidate had *fully* understood the assignment, so this was something to which he paid special attention. In practice it proved useful to let the selected candidate think through the assignment in depth and then summarize it in writing; 100 days later that summary was re-examined to make certain that the assignment had indeed been properly understood and described in light of the deeper insight gained by the candidate in the meantime.

Step 6: Guide and monitor the fulfillment of the assignment

Managers who are strong on implementation consider it extremely important to follow up systematically. Every two months, at the least, you should assess the progress made in the domain in question and discuss the current state of affairs with the worker. In so doing, it is vital to ascertain whether that person is indeed working on the priority assignment, or whether day-to-day duties have reeled him or her in again. Do not rely on standard reports, but *go to where the work is actually being done and take a look yourself.*

Step 7: Assume full responsibility for incorrect decisions

Marshall was one of those generals who vehemently believed that *a soldier has a right to competent command.* As a result, he put a great deal of thought into all his people decisions. If those decisions turned out to be wrong, he always assumed full responsibility for them. Furthermore, he then personally ensured that the soldier in question was removed from his post, rather than leaving this work to others. This did not mean the soldier in question had to leave the organization for having performed badly: rather, Marshall, as his superior, blamed *himself* for having made the mistake of putting the soldier in a position that was ill-matched to that individual's strengths. The fact that Marshall swiftly and consistently rectified such errors of judgment earned him great credibility and trust.

ACTION POINTS AND FOOD FOR THOUGHT

- Make sure that the assignment is clear before you discuss which candidates may be suitable for a job.
- Make sure that the selected candidate's proven strengths match the assignment.
- How are the seven steps outlined above implemented in your organization? Where is there room for improvement? What exactly do you need to do to move forward?

CHAPTER **38**

Establish Effective Cooperation

LEARNING FROM

Joe Biden

Even the second most powerful man in the world still has a boss. In fact, apart from a small minority, everyone in society has somebody above them. People who do not have a boss constitute a relatively small proportion of the working population; that includes such professions as self-employed lawyers, doctors, consultants, and owner-managers of companies. This chapter will show what U.S. Vice President *Joe Biden* (born in 1942) can teach us about working effectively with a hierarchical superior.

Biden is a veteran politician. He joined the U.S. Congress as one of its youngest ever senators back in 1973, and is today one of America's most experienced politicians. Biden's extensive experience was definitely one of the main reasons why Barack Obama chose him as his running mate. Under the U.S. Constitution, the vice president is president of the Senate, the upper house of America's bicameral legislature.

The U.S. vice president automatically steps in for any president unable to discharge his duties. This happened in April 1945, for example, when President Franklin D. Roosevelt died while in office and was replaced by Harry Truman. Truman had virtually no foreign policy experience because Roosevelt had barely involved him in that domain. This makes Truman's achievements all the more impressive, because he took office during the difficult final phase of World War II, and his subsequent performance proved him to be a competent president in all respects. Another occasion when a vice president took over the top job was after John F. Kennedy was assassinated on November 22, 1963, and Lyndon B. Johnson had to step up to the plate.

There is no doubt that Joe Biden could competently assume the mantle of president. Usually it is the incumbent president who decides how much political largesse to give to his deputy.

What can Joe Biden now do if he is interested in cooperating effectively with his colleagues and staff? And what can he do to manage his boss, Barack Obama? Contrary to the popular assumption that only bosses are responsible for managing their workers, *people in charge also need to be managed.* There is absolutely nothing new about this idea: Peter F. Drucker described it in detail as long ago as 1967 in his book *The Effective Executive,* and even that description was based on the thoughts about organization and collaboration set out in 1954 in a previous Drucker book, *The Practice of Management.* Nonetheless, it remains a strangely neglected notion, one that bosses themselves are loath to pass on, even though it is surely very much in their interest to do so, as will become apparent below.

At the same time, not only bosses need managing. Many people fail to see that *colleagues need to be managed,* too, which is of course a far more challenging task than managing *workers* who are your subordinates. Since workers are aware that their superiors are authorized to issue them instructions, they tend to make sure their boss has no need to do so.

Anyway, if a boss frequently manages by decree, there is a more fundamental problem on one of the two sides involved. The four recommendations set out below should help to guarantee effective cooperation in practice.

1. Draw up dependency lists

One characteristic of today's knowledge society is that most people actually have several bosses. For instance, they will have a direct superior, but if they are working on a project, they will also have a project manager above them in that connection. In the context of their own work, these people are dependent on the results that *you* achieve, and at the same time you will be dependent on others. You would be very well advised to begin by drawing up two such dependency lists, the first titled *"People on whom I depend (with regard to my results),"* and the second headed *"People who depend on me (with regard to their results)."*

Lists of this kind should not remain limited to dependencies *within* the compiler's organization. Many partnerships in business fail because dependencies *outside* the organization in question are not sufficiently kept in mind or taken seriously. So make sure that you include customers, joint ventures, strategic partnerships, and any other scenarios in which you and others might be mutually dependent. Dependent relationships most definitely do *not* stop at the outer limits of an organization. Many people know this but fail to act on it, even though doing so would yield them a ready benefit. The questions you should discuss with the people on your lists are:

- "What can I do, and what do you need to work effectively?"
- "What am I doing or what is our department doing that makes it difficult for you to attain your objectives?"

Also let your *dialogue partners* know what results you need from them to achieve your targets, though in most cases they should ask themselves this question anyway. Update your *dependency lists* at least once a year and every time you switch jobs or whenever your job changes or fresh assignments are assigned to you.

2. Make your boss effective

The most important principle for effective cooperation with your superior is to *make your boss effective.* Pay attention to the working methods used by your boss and gear your approach accordingly. Attempts to make your boss change will not succeed. If ever you feel uncertain about something, simply *ask* your boss how she or he wants things to be. You may end up facing a not entirely pleasant acclimatization phase, but only in this way will your efforts be effective.

Both Obama and Biden were clever to enter into their partnership as president and vice president. Before Biden was appointed, he criticized Obama's lack of foreign policy experience. In one interview Biden said that Obama was superior to John McCain in every domain *"with one exception: political experience. That is something people think a president should have more of."*[1] Then again, such an impressive track record in the foreign policy domain, among others, happens to be Joe Biden's major strength. If Obama is to be an *effective* president, he needs partners just like Biden, people who can help Obama draw on his strengths and deploy their own wherever the president's are not yet strongly established. The "secret" of good managers is that they make their boss effective. Of course, the same applies to colleagues, workers, and any other people featured on your dependency list.

3. Exchange information

If a boss is to prove effective, he or she must know where things stand at any time. In other words, your boss needs to be informed, know what your objectives are, and be aware of where your priorities lie. You must never forget that your boss is in turn accountable to a superior and needs such information to form and convey a realistic picture of the situation. A self-assured Joe Biden said he would, *"Be Obama's 'top advisor."* adding: *"I'll be in the room whenever he makes an important decision."*[2] From the viewpoint of ensuring the reliable flow of information, itself an essential prerequisite for good, effective decision-making, this can only be good news. But of course good, dependable exchanges of information are just as significant for the other people on your dependency list.

4. Never underestimate bosses

There is a reason why your boss is your superior and not vice versa. Younger employees in particular often tend to have problems with this notion. It is very easy to see what bosses are *unable* to do, but it takes a great deal more experience to spot—and learn to appreciate—their strengths. In this connection, younger people would be well advised to seek out intensive contacts with the older generation. In human history, knowledge and experienced have always been passed down from one generation to another, so why should that practice have lost its validity today?

Never underestimate your boss. Should you repeatedly experience difficulties with your boss, take heed of what Jack Welch had to say about the issue: *"Generally speaking, bosses are not awful to people whom they like, respect, and need. If your boss is being negative to you— and mainly you—you can feel pretty confident that he has his version of events, and his version concerns* your *attitude or performance."*[3] So think about *your* results and attitude.

ACTION POINTS AND FOOD FOR THOUGHT
- Draw up the two dependency lists as explained above, the first titled *"People on whom I depend (with regard to my results),"* and the second headed *"People who depend on me (with regard to their results)."*
- Speak with the people featured on the lists and discuss the questions set out above.
- Make the people featured on your dependency lists effective and keep them informed.
- Seek dialogue with people from other generations.

CHAPTER **39**

Recognize the Most Important Promotion

LEARNING FROM

Barack Obama

Most people believe that promotion to the top of an organization is the most important promotion. Let us critically examine this assumption and learn from U.S. President *Barack Obama* (born in 1961).

Undoubtedly, promotion into the circle of top managers is fabulous for anyone intent on a great career. However, instead of viewing this as the *most important* kind of promotion, I suggest classifying it as the *highest* promotion. When deciding how to fill top jobs, management selects people from among a small, preselected group. For the executives involved, their highest promotion is often also their *last*. Meanwhile, at the other end of the spectrum, the *first* promotion is equally overvalued, even though it may seriously affect the person's career. So the *truly decisive* promotion entails an individual's *acceptance into the ranks of those from whom the top executives of the future will have to be selected*, because at some point in the hierarchy of any organization the pyramid suddenly narrows very sharply. Below that point, large organizations often have 30 to 40 suitable candidates for a single job, whereas for posts above that level mostly just 3 or 4 candidates come into question. So *this* is where the really decisive promotion lies.

When planning your advancement, be aware that careers, especially those of *knowledge workers*, will in future be defined less and less in terms of *how often you have been promoted or how high you have ris-en*, and judged more and more in terms of *how important the tasks are* that you will take on. This constitutes a shift to building a *career by big tasks*, as opposed to a shaping a *career by promotion*. Not everyone can become the leader of an organization, but many people can take on very important duties and thus make tremendous contributions. If you are intent on having a career and perhaps also a meaningful professional life, it is worthwhile thinking about such big tasks and seeking them out.

If you belong to the group that decides which individuals to include in the circle of people from whom future top executives will be recruited, you have a tremendous responsibility to select the *right* people, which is a more important and challenging task than is often assumed for this group. Decisions about which assignment to entrust to whom, and—more importantly—about who will be promoted, sends out very strong signals indeed, both within and outside the organization. There is no clearer indi-cation of *what the organization stands for*, what it *demands*, and what it *values*. So if the effectiveness of your organization and a healthy corpo-rate culture are very important to you too, focus on people's *performance* and *character* rather than on whether or not you like them.

So what does all this have to do with Barack Obama? Well, take a look at his career from the viewpoint sketched out above, and you will soon see that his path to becoming a *possible* president of the United States of America began much earlier than most people believe. Not just when he announced that he would be *standing* for the presidency or when he won the nomination of the Democratic Party to be its can-didate for the top job. And certainly not just during the *election* itself. No, the tipping point occurred, at the very latest, back in January 2005, when Obama took up his duties as senator of Illinois. *That* was when he joined the circle of people potentially eligible for the highest office. In actual fact, the decisive moment could be said to have occurred even earlier, when Obama was a serving as a member of the Illinois State Senate, because he was catapulted into the *national* political arena in 2004 after delivering an inspirational speech at the Democratic National Convention in Boston, where John Kerry won the party's presidential nomination.

Think about the decisions that could shape your trajectory; in most cases your career path will begin earlier than you might initially imagine. If professional development is what you are after, seek out big tasks, and do so *without* expecting a promotion to result. If you do a good job, others will almost certainly want to further your advancement anyway.

Also think very carefully about which direction you want your career to move in. Many people allow themselves to be lured into a career by the attraction of associated power, status symbols, or social recognition. If the kind of activities, the anticipated level of pressure, and the private sacrifices this would involve are incompatible with your value system or your idea of a meaningful life, then you should change your tack. So think very carefully about whether you really want to become a manager. Many top specialists in their field have deliberately decided against management, preferring instead to continue working in their specialist domain.

Many people take too one-sided a view, considering only the positive aspects of new, bigger tasks. It is important to bear in mind that recognition also brings responsibility that you will have to fulfill. This responsibility constitutes a major opportunity, but you must decide for yourself whether you are willing and able to take it on.

Accordingly, Obama does not regard the Nobel Peace Prize one-sidedly, as just an honor, but above all he sees it as a responsibility.

ACTION POINTS AND FOOD FOR THOUGHT

- Focus on the performance and character of your employees, not on whether you like them. Use your influence to make sure that the *right* people fill senior management posts—for those are the people who represent what the organization stands for.
- Which major tasks should you take on?

CHAPTER **40**

Embody Integrity

LEARNING FROM

General George Marshall

In 1953, General *George Marshall* (1880–1959) became the first *professional soldier* to receive the Nobel Peace Prize for the United States' economic aid and reconstruction program for Western Europe that was named after him—the Marshall Plan. Marshall was held in high esteem for his integrity the whole world over.

His military career began in 1897 when he was 17 years old, and just a year later he was already an active participant in the Spanish-American War in the Philippines. During World War I he led military operations by the U.S. Army in France. In 1936 he was promoted to the rank of brigadier-general, and in 1939 he was appointed chief of staff of the U.S. Army. In that capacity, among other things, he was in charge of preparing for the United States' possible involvement in World War II. When the United States entered the war toward the end of 1941, Marshall became responsible for training, organizing, and stationing U.S. troops. His performance record in making people choices during that period is a splendid example of great management. He was personally responsible for hundreds of decisions on filling leading posts, and the high quality of those decisions was instrumental in the success of the Allied forces.

As a close advisor to President Franklin D. Roosevelt, Marshall also took part in the Allies' conferences in Casablanca, Quebec, Teheran, Yalta, and Potsdam. In 1944, Marshall was appointed *General of the*

Army, supreme commander of the U.S. Army, a very rare distinction.

After World War II, newly elected President Harry Truman appointed Marshall special ambassador to China, entrusting him to mediate between the two adversaries Mao Zedong and Chiang Kai-shek. Marshall duly rose to the task, which demanded not only the highest credibility on both sides, but also presupposed deep trust in him as a person. It was between 1947 and 1949, when Marshall was U.S. Secretary of State, that he initiated the European Recovery Program alluded to above, which is better known as the Marshall Plan. This was an exceptional management achievement and a major contribution toward resolving conflicting interests. When this source of aid was curtailed in 1952, industrial production in Western Europe was already higher than it had been before the war. In 1950 and 1951 Marshall continued to work for President Truman as U.S. Secretary of Defense. In 1959, on top of his 1953 Nobel Peace Prize, Marshall was awarded the prestigious International Charlemagne Prize of Aachen for his outstanding contribution to European unification.

Let us now take a look at one of the most important characteristics of any manager, here exemplified by George Marshall: *integrity*.

Marshall exercised his duties as chief of staff, special ambassador, and minister under the toughest domestic and foreign policy conditions. Sometimes he faced not just opposition, but open enmity, as on the part of the Republican politician Joseph McCarthy, who indirectly accused him of treason.

The clearest indication of the special esteem in which Marshall was held and of his true status are perhaps the fact that Roosevelt, Churchill, and Stalin accepted him as a fourth member of their inner circle, affording him equal standing. Churchill himself once even wondered if, *"Perhaps he [Marshall] was the greatest Roman of them all."*[1] High praise indeed from such a distinguished historian, who subsequently went on to earn a Nobel Prize for Literature essentially for his accounts of historical events.

Marshall always adopted the same *straight, open approach* when dealing with people from all kinds of interest groups. He treated his workers, colleagues, bosses, and even the most deeply hostile parties in the same *upright* manner, displaying the same *integrity.* It was this that prompted people to place almost unlimited trust in him and repeatedly enabled him to establish dialogue and instill consensus even when the clash of interests could not have been greater. One distinguished biographer, Ed Cray, summed up George Marshall's trustworthiness by saying that, *"Marshall had become an icon of integrity."*[2]

Management *skills* and *know-how* can be acquired, but *integrity* cannot be learned: it is something a manager must have and bring to the job. Integrity is a fundamental prerequisite for managers. The management of an organization may have only a few ways of influencing the degree of integrity displayed in it, namely *leading by example, selecting appropriate staff,* and *setting clear rules of conduct,* but they are extremely important.

1. Leading by example

People in organizations follow the lead set—and above all exemplified—by those at the top. So the *spirit of the organization* is shaped at its very *summit,* and it is from there that a corporate culture of integrity, high performance, and responsibility must emanate. Since there is no way of compensating for a lack of integrity, the standards demanded at the top of an organization must be high. Where no such positive example is set, the organization will be unable to develop an effective corporate culture that creates trust.

2. Selecting appropriate staff

Nowhere is an uncompromising commitment to integrity clearer than in staff selection, which both tests and provides evidence of whether required standards are actually being met. One simple, but also very profound question is this: *"Would I want my son or daughter to work for this person? Would I want my children to follow his example?"* Since strong managers, particularly if successful, shape others through the example they set, it is important to decide if the organization—and especially the younger people in it—can justify following such an example. People who set an indefensible example do not belong in management, regardless of how intelligent or successful they may be. Organizations that compromise on integrity are already on the wrong track.

3. Setting clear rules of conduct

Organizations must have clear, reliable rules of conduct that are consistently applied in practice. Where these rules, or somebody's word, or a pledge cannot be relied on, the trust in the organization and its leadership will be destroyed. Conversely, certainty that an organization will behave *reliably* and *predictably* creates the kind of *solid trust* that is essential for enabling a calm, constructive response to inevitable occasional errors.

Human beings forgive many weaknesses and errors, but not a lack of integrity. They will absolve neither the individual who acted without integrity, nor the manager who appointed someone lacking integrity as their boss. Nor will they pardon the fact that the person in question is being allowed to continue managing. The credibility of management will hinge primarily on how seriously it demands unconditional integrity.

ACTION POINTS AND FOOD FOR THOUGHT

- ■ Make sure that integrity plays a pivotal role in people decisions. Ask yourself whether you would like your child to work for the person in question.
- ■ When you take up a new post, decide whether you are willing to follow the example set by your boss.
- ■ Act with integrity yourself, and make sure your organization embodies integrity, too.

CHAPTER **41**

Harness the Potential of Women

LEARNING FROM

Hillary Clinton

Hillary Rodham Clinton (born in 1947) always considered herself an independent political player. That attitude earned her limitless admiration and intense disapproval in equal measure. For millions of women around the world, she is an example of how one woman's achievements, strength of will, thirst for knowledge, and discipline can take her to the very pinnacle of world politics and enable her to assert herself there, overcoming all obstacles strewn in her path.

The present U.S. Secretary of State studied at Wellesley College and Yale. As a successful attorney she drew attention to herself in the late 1980s, her name figuring twice in the list of the 100 most influential lawyers in the United States. In 1983 she made her first appearance on the political stage, drafting a school reform plan for her husband, who was governor of Arkansas at the time, though her concept drew plaudits way beyond the boundary of that state. While Bill Clinton was U.S. President, from 1993 to 2001, she was the most active First Lady the United States had ever seen, supporting her husband on social policy issues in particular. She was very popular with many voters and in 2000 launched her own political career, successfully securing election as a senator from New York State and then engineering her reelection in 2006. In 2007, when the Democrats decided to nominate not her, but Barack Obama, as their presidential candidate, Hillary Clinton vigorously backed him and his running mate, Joe Biden, in the final stages of the presidential campaign.

You are bound to have noticed by now that far too many of the icons figuring in this book are men. This is not because there is any shortage of women who set excellent examples. On the contrary, many of the issues featured could have been covered perfectly well with reference to the biographies and achievements of women: *Clara Schumann*, the pianist and composer who was also one of the leading musicians of the nineteenth century, could have provided numerous examples. Then there is *Steffi Graf*, winner of 22 grand slam titles, seven of them at Wimbledon, who topped the world rankings for 377 weeks, longer than any tennis professional before her. Or *Marie Curie*, the Polish-French chemist and physicist, the first woman to be awarded a Nobel Prize, or rather two: in 1903 the Prize for Physics together with her husband, Pierre Curie and teacher Antoine Henri Becquerel, and in 1911 the Prize for Chemistry by herself. Another great woman was *Maria Theresa*, archduchess of Austria, queen of Hungary and Bohemia, who in 1746, in the face of stiff opposition, embarked on a series of domestic reforms to restructure her empire, updating the school system, among other things, giving her subjects access to a general school education, and founding the University of Vienna. *Anita Roddick*, too, the exceptional entrepreneur and founder of the cosmetics company The Body Shop, was way ahead of her time, not just because of her shrewd strategy, but because of her marketing concepts, which were based primarily on word-of-mouth advertising. And how about *Simone Young*, one of the most celebrated conductors of our age, winner of numerous awards and honors, who in 1993 became the first woman in history to conduct the Vienna Philharmonic, which at the time was an all-male orchestra? Last, but not least, much of what was achieved by the French author *Simone de Beauvoir*, reputed to be one of the leading theoreticians on women's issues and a figurehead of women's emancipation, could be said to reflect a sound grasp of what are now recognized as key management principles. If anyone can be said to be the *driving force behind innovations* in the domain of gender equality, then surely it is she and no other. Her groundbreaking book *The Second Sex* was published in 1949, no less. Her views on sexuality, motherhood, and abortion unleashed a storm of indignation, and the Vatican placed *The Second Sex* on the Index of Forbidden Books. But the book was rediscovered by the women's movement in the 1970s, sold millions of copies around the world, and is today considered one of the most important feminist works. *All these examples could have perfectly served to illustrate key aspects of effective management.* Yet our society still has a great deal of catching up to do when it comes to appointing women to top jobs.

In view of the large number of possible examples, it could be said, while on the subject, that the choice of Hillary Clinton was somewhat arbitrary. If that is how you choose to see it, then yes, other exceptional women could easily have been selected; but I opted to showcase her because at the time of writing this book she was probably the most famous woman fulfilling a leadership role.

Anyway, this book quite intentionally reflects the disproportional representation of women in leading positions, compared with men. One look at the list of contents of this book is enough to see how sobering an effect such inequality can have. The proportion of women covered in the book is under 10 percent, just about as dramatically low as in top jobs in business. This is totally unacceptable! In terms of *performance and results*, the key criteria for management, this state of affairs is neither explicable nor justifiable. Moreover, leaving such valuable potential unexploited entails adopting a non-results-oriented and less efficient approach that clashes with the notion of effective management.

The fact that the actual proportion of female managers varies from study to study, depending on how large the company is and on different descriptions of what constitutes a "senior" management post, does nothing to alter the overall picture and the fact that there are simply too few of them.

To avoid any misunderstandings in this connection, let me state quite unequivocally that the political imposition of a mandatory quota would probably be the wrong path to follow. People decisions should be made *in the interests of the company*, not to fill quotas stipulated by politicians. Instead, it is in the best interest of the *company itself* that the responsible executives in its management constitute a structure that matches the *realities of its market and customers*. So let me reiterate: the responsibility for the shaping of the company's management structure lies with its top managers and its supervisory bodies. No company can be managed in a sensible, truly sustainable manner if it is run in the interests of particular groups of people: it must be managed in the company's own interests.

Perhaps you, too, will be amazed by the fact that some of the best companies, including many less well-known world market leaders, have a *disproportionally high ratio of women* in their top management posts.[1] Do you believe that this is mere coincidence? Perhaps it is. Good performance is not dependent on race, gender, religion, nationality, or marital status. But even if these achievements by unknown world market leaders (or *"hidden champions"* as Hermann Simon calls them) are deemed unconvincing or coincidental, the difference in gender distribution certainly remains striking.

Around half of the working population in the United States and Europe is female, including many highly qualified knowledge workers, whose know-how makes them mobile. They will go to work for organizations where women are given equal opportunities, where the best people in a country will gather as a result. No deep understanding of management is required to realize that in a knowledge society having the best people constitutes a major competitive edge.

If this prognosis regarding organizations' attractiveness to intelligent women seems too speculative for you, just take a look at the Internet. Over the last few years, use of the World Wide Web has changed significantly. Every conceivable kind of interest group has become organized on the Web, including *women interested in achievement*; indeed, this trend started a considerable while ago. Good people will go where they have opportunities, and this kind of information can be swiftly obtained and passed on via the Internet. Those organizations that ensure that intelligent, achievement-oriented women want to work for them will have a clear competitive advantage. This will come about of its own accord—precisely *because* the best people get themselves organized. The know-how and skills of the best women will guarantee such organizations a decisive edge over their rivals. Indeed, the *opportunity* beckoning for a society that succeeds in drawing on the largely unused potential of women cannot be overemphasized. Every step is valuable, and fundamental changes are never easy; they take time and require a steadfast approach by the relevant decision makers.

It speaks very much in favor of Hillary Clinton that she agreed to serve in Barack Obama's administration. The example she is setting is just as inspirational to millions of women all over the world as the examples set by other competent female heads of government and business leaders. Today, in these top corporate jobs and at the summit of government they are still pioneers, but *they are changing people's views about what is possible.*

When the Italian Reinhold Messner scaled Mount Everest in 1978 without supplemental oxygen, it caused a sensation around the world, while for today's leading mountaineers it is a perfectly normal scenario. The pioneering achievements of women like Hillary Clinton and other leading politicians and business people in the highest offices and posts today are—and will remain—of inestimable value for reshaping society as we know it.

ACTION POINTS AND FOOD FOR THOUGHT

- What specific joint action can you take in your organization to ensure that more women occupy management posts?
- If you are a women intent on achieving professional success, what exactly can you do to make headway together with like-minded individuals?

CHAPTER **42**

Make Intelligent Use of Your Time

LEARNING FROM

Stephen Hawking

Time is the main factor that limits achievement and is utterly irreplaceable in your life. Since everything you do takes time, what you achieve and how effective you are will depend directly on *how* you use your time. If you do not manage your use of time, you will not be able to manage anything else effectively. Making effective use of time is a prerequisite for great achievement. If there is one characteristic common to people who have achieved excellence, it is the fact that they always made fastidious use of their time.

Stephen Hawking (born in 1942) is regarded as one of the greatest mathematical geniuses alive today. The work done by this British mathematician and astrophysicist concerns the origin and development of the cosmos. In 1988 he published a popular science book called *A Brief History of Time,* which described the origin of the universe and became a bestseller.

Hawking's aim is to connect general relativity theory and quantum mechanics into a *unified theory.* Hawking has not allowed his severe disability to prevent him from achieving excellence in science, and his professional, but especially also his human achievements, make him an inspirational example to many people. Shortly after his twenty-first birthday Hawking was told he had an incurable disease that would probably lead to his death within a few years. This is what he wrote about himself: *"Before my condition had been diagnosed, I had been very bored with life. There had not seemed to be anything worth doing. But shortly after I came out of hospital, I dreamt that I was going to be executed. I suddenly realised that there were a lot of worthwhile things I could do if I were reprieved. . . . In fact, although there was a cloud hanging over my future, I found, to my surprise, that I was enjoying life in the present more than before."*[1]

Seriously sick or disabled people impress us by showing how extraordinarily effective they can be by making wise use of their time. Harry Hopkins, a confidante and close advisor of U.S. President Franklin D. Roosevelt in World War II, is another example. Since Hopkins was gravely ill, any movement cost him tremendous effort, so he could work for only a few hours every few days. This forced him to desist from any activities that were not strictly necessary. In this way, Hopkins remained formidably effective in spite of his terrible illness, and few people achieved as much as he did during those years in Washington. Winston Churchill later admiringly called Hopkins *"Lord Root-of-the-Matter."*[2]

If you want to work more effectively, you must start by making better use of your time. You need to realize that all other key resources can be multiplied: money can be procured, and people can be hired, but time *cannot* be stored or regained. Once past, it is gone. Since time is *always* in short supply when you wish to achieve something, many successful managers follow these steps when apportioning their time. Maybe you will find them useful, too[3]:

1. Find out where your time goes.
2. Eliminate things that waste your time.
3. Delegate whatever you do not need to do yourself.

4. Make sure that available time is used effectively and efficiently.

5. Bundle the time at your disposal and use it to work on key tasks.

1. Find out where your time goes

There is only one way to find out what your time is being used for: over an unbroken four-week period meticulously write down *everything* you do.

Make sure you note down *every* activity throughout the day as you do it, rather than reconstructing your day that evening. If need be, have an assistant help you keep track of your activities. By keeping such very precise, down-to-the-minute records of all your activities, you can find out where your time really goes. Once the four weeks are up, evaluate your notes and then rethink and reapportion your time. You will often be amazed at the results.

2. Eliminate things that waste your time

Comb through the log book kept as part of step one above, looking for things that *did not need to be done at all* and were thus a waste of your time. Then ask yourself this question about all your activities: *"What would happen if this was not done at all?"* If the conclusion you reach is "nothing," drop the respective activity in the future.

3. Delegate whatever you do not need to do yourself

Like any manager, when analyzing your log book, you will find that there simply is not enough time to do everything you feel is important—to say nothing of the things you would *like* to do. It is only by delegating everything that can be done by somebody else that you can work on truly important things.

Most people exchange *time for money*. Do the opposite and exchange *money for time*. If you go about this cleverly, you will end up with more of both, which is precisely what very wealthy people do. If you believe you cannot afford to adopt such an approach, start off very modestly.

You will find that the shrewd investment of any time you gain really does pay. Above all, it will also change the way you think, prompting you to seek opportunities for using your skills more productively.

4. Make sure that available time is used effectively and efficiently

Making better use of your time is a really crucial key to effectiveness. Make a habit of constantly improving your working methods. This is by no means an issue just for younger managers. Observe top performers in this connection, and you will see that they are very tough on themselves, constantly striving for even greater effectiveness. You will also find that many top performers behave this way, exhibiting what might almost be called a passion for self-improvement right up to the end of their lives.

Avail yourself of the literature on the subject or copy proven methods used by other managers. There is no need to reinvent the wheel; instead develop your very own *personal working method*. Do not let anyone tell you that there is one ideal working method that works for everyone. People who claim that this is the case simply have no idea what they are talking about. No two people work the same way!

Another aspect of this fourth step entails finding out what you can do to help your organization improve its procedures and also demanding that the people reporting to you be professional about their use of time. Professional meeting management, the use of routines, standard procedures, and checklists, well planned flows of information, and the clear assignment of responsibilities are just some examples of what can be done. Furthermore, check how you use the time of your colleagues, workers, and bosses. Ask your colleagues occasionally, *"What do I do that squanders your time without helping you attain your objectives?"*

When working with your boss, start out from the basic premise that *one minute* of his or her time requires *ten minutes'* preparation on your part. If you are the boss, demand the same from your workers. If this concept is unfamiliar to you, it may sound slightly bizarre. But the true professionals among top managers work this way because they know how valuable their time is. You will not believe how quickly you will start working better and more productively if you, as an employee, prepare in this way or, as a boss, are able to devote your time to things that really matter.

5. Bundle the time at your disposal and use it to work on key tasks

To become effective at what you do, you must *create the largest possible blocks of contiguous time.* With such blocks of time you can then concentrate on your key tasks and work on them uninterrupted. So take the time that your records suggest is both at your disposal and under your control and bundle it into large, unbroken units. *How* you bundle your time in this way is not important—the main thing is that you actually do so. It is of secondary importance whether you spend one or more days working at home, concentrate all your meetings into two weekdays, or regularly set aside time during your mornings.

In addition to this, regularly *adopt a long-term view,* laying down key objectives two or three years in advance. That way you will be able to make fundamental changes even if your job demands a great deal of your time. Most busy managers have no real influence over their own short-term schedule.

You can learn how to make the best use of your time by constantly practicing and regularly checking that your time is wisely spent. Regard it as a playful challenge: *"Practice makes perfect!"* as the saying goes.

ACTION POINTS AND FOOD FOR THOUGHT
- ■ Work on your use of time. Regularly run through the five steps presented above and use them to gauge your effectiveness.
- ■ Use your time wisely.

CHAPTER **43**

Perfect Your Own Working Methods

LEARNING FROM

Benjamin Franklin

Benjamin Franklin (1706–1790) is one of those rare people who can definitely be said to have achieved greatness in many, very different domains. He was a politician, a scientist, an author, a qualified printer of books, a newspaper publisher, and an inventor. In addition, he was a leading figure in the American independence movement. In 1729, he started championing his enlightened-puritanical ideals in his publications. He also started becoming more involved in politics, first as a minute-taker in 1736 and later, from 1751 to 1764, as a member of the Pennsylvania Assembly. He was involved in planning a North American Union and between 1757 and 1762 and again from 1764 to 1775 represented the interests of Pennsylvania, Georgia, New Jersey, and Massachusetts as agent to the British crown in London. Of course, his name is etched into our collective memory as a coauthor and cosignatory of the Declaration of Independence in 1776. Franklin was highly successful as an ambassador to France, among other things bringing about France's entry into the American Revolution in 1778, but also negotiating the peace treaty with Britain, known as the Treaty of Paris, in 1783. The United States Constitution of 1787 also bears his signature.

Alongside these impressive achievements in the political sphere, Franklin also devoted his time to extensive scientific experiments on electricity, hydrodynamics, magnetism, thermal conductivity, and heat radiation. He drew the first map of the Gulf Stream and recommended its exploitation by shipping. He also made a name for himself in Europe as the inventor of the lightning rod. Other inventions of his include bifocals and also the glass harmonica, for which Mozart and Beethoven even wrote pieces of music. As an author, too, Franklin gained widespread recognition, preferring to pen shorter works like maxims, essays, and satirical pieces, which he worded in humorous, elegant, and invariably clear prose. His widely read autobiography is still being reprinted today.

Goethe admired Franklin, seeing in him a quintessential ideal combining creative energy with versatility. Should you happen to embody similar genius and achieve as much as Franklin did, then maybe one day your image will grace the American 100 dollar bill as his does now. Genius, unfortunately, cannot be learned, but what Benjamin Franklin *can* teach us is the value of *working methodically*. This was something he perfected. Otherwise he would not have been able to achieve so much in so many different areas.[1]

1. Fundamentals on working method

Contrary to widespread belief that there is one optimal way of working that suits everybody, a working method is actually highly *individual* and *personal*. Just as no two signatures are the same, no two people work in exactly the same way, even if both employ very sound working methods. A person's adopted working method will depend on the general conditions under which the work is done and the specific circumstances associated with it, including the respective:

- Duties
- Powers associated with the job
- Responsibilities
- Travel requirements

- The number of employees
- Boss's way of working
- Availability of assistance
- Infrastructure
- Size of the organization
- Modus operandi of the organization
- Sector
- Individual's personal life situation and phase of life

There is a rich literature on working methods and no shortage of seminars on the subject, too. The key is to adopt a critical attitude and remember that *no single* method works for *everyone*. Consequently, the ideas about practical implementation you should select are those that suit you best *personally*. *What* needs to be done can be defined, yet *how* a situation is to be handled *cannot* be generalized. So experiment and optimize until you find a solution that suits you.

True top performers fine-tune their chosen working method right up until late in life, constantly adapting it to changing circumstances. In so doing, they leave as little as possible to chance, just as they do when deciding how things are to be done in their organization, where they make sure that the working methods used meet the highest standards of professionalism.

2. How do I perform?

An astonishing number of people do not know how to perform. As a result, they employ working methods that do not suit them and thus fall way short of their potential. Often they are not even aware that different people work in different ways, which has catastrophic results, especially for knowledge workers, because taking the wrong approach almost always guarantees a weak performance. Look at yourself and find out how you perform and how capable you are of working well. If you have some professional experience, you will not find this hard to do. So all that remains is rigorous self-organization, which many people find more challenging.

3. How do I absorb information—by listening or reading?

The first thing you need to do is ascertain whether you are a *reader* or a *listener*, when absorbing information. Dwight (Ike) Eisenhower was a reader. When he was commander in chief of U.S. troops in World War II, his aides made sure that all the questions to be asked of him at press conferences were submitted to him in writing half an hour in advance. That way Eisenhower had everything under control; in fact he excelled at press conferences, performing with exceptional eloquence.

Later, when he became president, he succeeded two listeners, Franklin D. Roosevelt and Harry Truman, and made the big mistake of adopting *their* way of holding press conferences, rather than insisting that questions needed to be submitted in advance. This led to journalists complaining increasingly vociferously that Eisenhower never answered their questions and instead talked about other matters altogether. Eisenhower was evidently unaware that he was a reader.

By contrast, John F. Kennedy was keenly aware that he was a reader, so he surrounded himself with excellent writers, who prepared topics for him in writing before discussing their memos in person. Franklin D. Roosevelt and Harry Truman were equally aware that they were listeners, so they made certain that things were read out loud to them before dealing with anything in writing. Truman trained himself so well in the finer points of foreign policy and military matters through his daily briefings and discussions with General George Marshall and Dean Acheson that he became a true master in both domains.

4. How do I learn?

People learn in many different ways. Some learn by *writing*, like Winston Churchill or Ludwig van Beethoven, who wrote thousands of pages in sketchbooks. Others learn by *hearing themselves talk*.

Many excellent professors, legal and medical experts, and authors learn this way, Peter F. Drucker was among them. Yet others learn by *reading*, like John F. Kennedy as mentioned above, or by *listening*, as is the case with many politicians, like Lyndon B. Johnson, who became president after JFK's assassination. Finally, there are people who learn by *doing*.

Most people are aware of how they learn, *but very few consistently act upon this knowledge.* If you know that you learn best by hearing yourself talk, you should act on that knowledge and set up your learning process accordingly. Doing anything else would be like using your left hand to write even though you are right-handed. Learning the way that suits you is the key to performing effectively, especially if you are a knowledge worker.

5. How do I work?

Do you work well *with others* or do you work best *on your own*? If you are able to work well with others, you need to find out *how* you can do this to optimal effect. Some people make excellent leaders at the very top level; Winston Churchill was undoubtedly one such person. Others are brilliant managers, but not quite at the top level. For example, General George Marshall once said of General George Patton, the most outstanding U.S. troop commander during World War II, that Patton was *"the best subordinate the American Army has ever produced, but he would be the worst commander."*[2]

Are you a good *decision maker* or a good *advisor*? Some people make great advisors, but cannot handle the pressure or responsibility of decision making. Others can self-confidently justify what they decide, but need advisors or people to bounce their ideas off, to help them properly think through their decisions. Some people make great mentors; others are clearly not cut out to be mentors. Likewise, some people make tremendous contributions when in a team, but barely deliver an average performance if left to their own devices.

Do you work well under *time pressure* or perform best if you are left to work in peace and quiet? Do you need a well *structured environment* or draw energy from *constantly changing situations?* Which *kind of organization* would suit you best? Do you belong in a large *organization* or are you at your most successful when working for a *small organization?* It is extremely rare that people achieve the same level of excellence in both types of organizations. Some individuals who lead major organizations with as much virtuosity as a world-class pianist brings to playing the piano would be hopelessly wasted in a small organization. And the reverse may also apply. So where do *you* belong?

6. Which methodological tools do I use? How efficiently do I use them?

Your best bet for finding the tools that best suit your personal needs is to refer to specialist literature on the subject. For good reason there are plenty of books on the subject, suggesting every conceivable kind of tips and tricks. Treat such advice as a source of inspiration and then devise your own *personal working method.* There is no one "right" way, so experiment and find *yours.* The issues you should definitely consider in this connection include the following:

- Time management
- Scheduling and preparing for appointments
- Processing input
- Systematic follow-up
- Storing and filing knowledge
- Using the telephone, conference calls, and other methods of communication
- Computer use
- Checklists for routine procedures
- Systems for cultivating relationships

- Working together with assistants, including via the use ofdictation equipment
- Drawing up reports and other documents

Be resourceful, optimize your approach, and derive genuine pleasure from attaining a new level of productivity, like many others before you.

A good working method forms the basis for achievement and success. People who do not take this issue seriously will squander their potential and may even miss out on a successful career. *Yet people who really get on top of this issue will find themselves holding an important key to success.*

ACTION POINTS AND FOOD FOR THOUGHT
- Perfect your own personal working method.
- Which issue do you intend to work on this week? How about next week? And the week after?

CHAPTER 44

Create
Trust

Levi Strauss

In 1847, *Levi Strauss* (1829–1902) emigrated from Germany to the United States, where he first settled in New York. When the gold rush started, he followed the hordes to California, but instead of prospecting for gold, he made a smart decision to set up a textile wholesaling business. Between 1850 and 1870 he very successfully expanded that business, repeatedly enlarging his company, which was based in San Francisco. At the time, gold prospectors were faced with the problem that the pockets of their work pants kept ripping open under the weight of the nuggets they found, so the tailor *Jacob Davis* came up with a clever solution: he used copper thread to rivet together the pants' lining. Davis, who bought his materials from Levi Strauss in San Francisco, suggested that the two of them take out a joint patent on the copper-riveted denim pants, which were proving extremely popular, because he could not afford to pay the $68 fee himself. On May 20, 1873, Strauss and Davis were finally awarded the patent for copper-riveted jeans. That date is generally considered the day on which Levi Strauss & Company was born, and thus began the success story of a product that has become an integral part of everyday life today.

Levi Strauss and Jacob Davis built up a company in which trust played a very prominent role. On April 18, 1906, a few years after Levi

Strauss died, when a major earthquake hit San Francisco causing fires that destroyed the city, the corporate headquarters of Levi Strauss & Company and two of its factories burned to the ground. How did the company respond? It extended lines of credit to its major customers to help them recover from the disaster and continued paying wages to its workers while a new central office and factory were built. Again, during the Great Depression in around 1930, instead of dismissing workers, Levi Straus & Company deployed them at another site, to lay new flooring. How deeply did the company's workers and suppliers trust the company in the wake of such decisions?

Such dramatic events are by no means prerequisites for creating trust. On the contrary, *trust has to be an integral part of everyday working life.* Without trust there can be no effective, efficient management. Flying in the face of the widespread assumption that trust grows very slowly and comes about of its own accord or not at all, trust is something you can *consciously embrace and develop.* Doing this by no means requires falling back on moral justifications, because purely economic considerations make it worthwhile. Just one condition applies: *to earn trust you must always show it yourself first.* So follow the two specific steps described below to substantially boost the trust in your organization.

1. Embrace trust

Most people maintain that trust takes time to grow. This is sometimes true, for instance, if you make your degree of trust dependent on how well you know somebody. However, if an organization is to function efficiently, it cannot afford to wait for trust to build up slowly so that it can reap the benefits of such goodwill. Instead, you and the other employees must consciously embrace trust. Make a principle of expecting a cooperative attitude to be reciprocated. Expect others to be well-meaning, competent, and to act with integrity. This is not blind or naive trust, nor does it entail treating everyone the same way. Also, trust is not divorced from an assigned task. It is perfectly possible to show more or less trust in individuals, and you are bound to think hard about which tasks to entrust to which person. Perhaps the following maxims can be of use to you: *Trust everyone as much as you can. Go to the limit of what you can justify.*

2. Show trust

So what can you do in practice? You are familiar with the full range of "trust-building measures," which all have more to do with common sense and decency than directly with management: *honesty, dependability, credibility, fairness, loyalty, discretion, the ability to listen, predictability, and honoring promises.*

If you want trust in your organization to build up quickly, you must show it first, taking things as far as you can justify. The risk you run in doing this is the potential damage that could result, and the greater that potential damage, the more trust you will be showing in advance—in other words, the greater your "up-front investment" in the relationship of trust will be.

The first step toward creating trust consists of removing or curbing checks, though this does not mean abolishing *all* means of control. Rather, it means creating room for people to maneuver, perhaps even giving really extensive leeway. There is no universally applicable procedure to follow, but your approach should include working with target agreements, while leaving open how the targets in question are to be attained; curbing the checks in place; loosening the reins a little; and limiting internal reporting to the minimum required instead of striving for what may seem like a tempting maximum. In short: cut people some slack.

However, this does not mean blindly giving employees boundless freedom. Since you must always fulfill your *responsibility* as a manager, you have to ensure that you hear of any *abuses of trust*. At the same time, everyone must be aware of what the inevitable, serious consequences of such misconduct will be. People are perfectly capable of judging whether you are imposing checks that are essential for ensuring reliable operation or whether your actions are motivated by fear and mistrust. Assume that people will understand your obligation to do your duty and that, in any cooperative effort based on trust, people will help you fulfill your responsibility. Giving leeway requires a sense of proportion, and nobody has ever said that management is easy. It is always you who has to take the first step: *Show some trust up front.* If you are mistrusting at the outset, mistrust is precisely what you will get in return. *If you show trust, people will trust you.* Without trust you will be unable to manage any organization effectively and efficiently.

ACTION POINTS AND FOOD FOR THOUGHT

- Invest your trust, taking it to the limit you can justify.
- What exactly can you do to build up trust in your organization? Discuss this with colleagues.

CHAPTER **45**

Make a Life Plan: What Will Your Most Important Contribution Be?

LEARNING FROM

Peter F. Drucker

What will your most important contribution be? What do you want to be remembered for? This chapter is about these two very central questions—questions that only you can answer. What makes them valuable is that they direct you to see yourself as the person you *can become*. For *Peter Drucker* (1909–2005) the question, "*What do you want to be remembered for?*" was the question that brings *self-renewal* into people's lives.

Drucker constantly asked himself both questions throughout his life. But this chapter, instead of expounding on them at length, provides a few background details about the man who was the greatest management thinker of our time and concludes by presenting an example of what he said that speaks volumes about him.

Many people consider Peter Drucker to be the *inventor of management*. Indeed, words to that effect have been printed in the most distinguished media, including *The Economist, Forbes, BusinessWeek,* and *The Wall Street Journal*. Yet Drucker himself never accepted that description, even if he less vehemently contested it toward the end of his life. Correspondingly, he once remarked on this subject that if someone had to be named the inventor of management, the individual selected should be the CEO of Pyramids Inc., the manager who in 2600 BC oversaw the construction of the Pyramid of Cheops. To be precise, *no one individual* invented management; it is a joint achievement of humankind. Drucker was the first person to *put management into words.* And in that endeavor he succeeded like nobody else.

With characteristic modesty, Drucker only described himself as a "writer," a remarkable self-image coming from a man who may rightfully be called the greatest management thinker of all time. He authored over 30 major works, and wrote countless articles for the most prestigious publications, including *The Wall Street Journal, Harvard Business Review,* and *The Economist.* In 2002, he was awarded the Presidential Medal of Freedom by President George W. Bush.

Drucker's achievements cannot be valued too highly. Before he wrote his books, hardly any works on management were available. His first two books, *The End of Economic Man,* (1939) and *The Future of Industrial Man* (1942), which combined political and social analysis with the question of what constituted a healthy, functioning society, were followed in 1946 by *Concept of the Corporation,* which gained widespread recognition primarily because it established management for the very first time as an independent discipline and research domain.

Drucker's life work spanned around 65 years and covered every facet of the complex field of *management*: the *individual,* the *organization,* and *society.* An overall understanding of *management* can be achieved only if all three factors are brought together and taken into account. At the same time, a *healthy, functioning society* can be understood only if management's *function, importance,* and *mode of action* are likewise appreciated.

Over the decades, Drucker himself was repeatedly asked which of his books was the best (a question to which he always gave a startling answer, as you will see in Chapter 46 on Giuseppe Verdi). However, toward the end of his life he did finally reveal which six books, out of all those he had written, he deemed most important. Most of his choices are incontestable, but those familiar with his work may well be surprised by one or two of them, not to mention astonished by the absence of some works that they would have expected to see included on the list. The books Drucker selected were as follows[1]:

- *Concept of the Corporation* (1946)
- *The Practice of Management* (1954)
- *Managing for Results* (1964)
- *The Effective Executive* (1966)
- *The Age of Discontinuity* (1969)
- *Innovation and Entrepreneurship* (1985)

If you wish to acquire a profound and serious understanding of management, you cannot bypass Drucker. And you should not only read his works, you should also study them in detail, understand them, and—most important of all—*apply* them. There simply is no more worthwhile reading.

If you are looking for an introduction to Drucker's ideas, try reading his *Management, Revised Edition,* a book that came about when his long-standing colleague, Joseph A. Maciariello, performed the invaluable task of revising and updating Drucker's standard 1973 work titled *Management: Tasks, Responsibilities, Practices.*

If you want to find out more about Peter Drucker as a human being and gain an insight into some of his personal thoughts, read the wonderful book by Jeffrey Krames, *Inside Drucker's Brain.*[2] This work not only clearly brings out Drucker's genius and wisdom, but above all highlights his humanity. Another splendid book about him is *The World According to Peter Drucker* by Jack Beatty.[3]

Finally, here is an outstanding example from Peter Drucker himself, summing up *his own* most important contribution. Drucker viewed the question, "*What do you want to be remembered for?*" as crucial for bringing *self-renewal* into people's lives, and the potentially enormous impact of the answer to that question is self-evident. This much is clear from the fact that Drucker's works, published between 1939 and 2006, are still immensely influential today[4]:

What do I consider to be my most important contribution?

- "That I early on—almost 60 years ago—realized that *management* has become the constitutive organ and function of the *Society of Organizations*;
- "That *management* is not 'Business Management'—though it first attained attention in business—but the governing organ of *all* institutions of Modern Society;
- "That I established the study of *management* as a discipline in its own right; and
- "That I focused this discipline on People and Power, on Values, Structure, and Constitution; *and above all*, on responsibilities—that is, focused the Discipline of Management on *management* as a truly liberal art."

—*PETER F. DRUCKER*
JANUARY 18, 1999

ACTION POINTS AND FOOD FOR THOUGHT
- What will your most important contribution be?
- What do you want to be remembered for?

CHAPTER 46

Be Demanding of Yourself and Strive for Perfection

LEARNING FROM
Giuseppe Verdi

How can you stand a good chance of achieving something truly remarkable in your life? Devote yourself body and soul to just one thing. Be as demanding of yourself as you can be, and never stop striving for perfection. One frequent characteristic of exceptionally successful people is that they are very tough on themselves. They never tire of raising the bar ever higher; they focus on reacting to constant social, economic, and technological changes; and they continue developing throughout their life.

Giuseppe Verdi (1813–1901) provides a wonderful example of this kind of attitude. He rose from modest origins and thanks to his precocious talents, he had the good fortune to find a patron, Antonio Barezzi. This enabled Verdi to take music lessons, first in his hometown of Le Roncole and then, from 1832, in Milan, where he began his career as a composer of operas in 1839.

Just three years later his opera *Nabucco* enjoyed tremendous success. Bursting with energy, Verdi went on to write another 12 operas for various theaters before 1850. His masterpiece *Rigoletto* marked the peak of his glorious creativity in 1851, and the triumphant success of its premiere in Italy was repeated in other countries as well. Ever since, *Rigoletto* has been one of Verdi's most frequently staged operas. Yet in spite of this great success, Verdi was desperate to achieve more, having set himself the goal of writing the *perfect* opera.

After *Rigoletto* he went on to write other famous works, including *Il Trovatore* (1853), *La Traviata* (1853), *Don Carlos* (1867), and *Aida* (1871). At 74 years of age—living at a time when even healthy men could not expect to survive beyond 60—Verdi gave the world his master-piece *Otello*, seemingly crowning what his contemporaries deemed a more than accomplished career. Then, in 1893, at the age of 80, no less, Verdi wrote his last opera: *Falstaff*—a work full of vitality and zest for life. When asked why he, a famous man considered one of the most highly regarded opera composers of the nineteenth century, had once again taken on the exacting task of writing another opera at such an advanced age—and *Falstaff*, an extremely demanding work at that—he replied: *"All my life as a musician I have striven for perfection. It has always eluded me. I surely had an obligation to make one more try."*[1]

Peter F. Drucker, the greatest and most influential management thinker of our time, was familiar with Verdi's words and described how deeply they affected him as a young man: *"I have never forgotten these words—they made an indelible impression on me. . . . [Aged 18 at the time,] I had no idea what I would become. . . . It was not until 15 years later, when I was in my early thirties, that I really knew what I am good at and where I belong. But I then resolved that, whatever my life's work would be, Verdi's words would be my lodestar. I then resolved that if I ever reached an advanced age, I would not give up, but would keep on. In the meantime, I would strive for perfection even though, as I well knew, it would surely, always elude me."*[2]

The interesting thing about Verdi is that he was perfectly aware of his achievements. His successes earning him substantial public acclaim, but all the same he strove to make his next work even better. In the same vein, when Drucker was asked which of his books he considered to be the best, he sometimes gave the coquettish response: "*The next one.*"

Do you see how both these men differed from the norm by setting the bar higher than the vast majority of other people? Verdi not only wanted to write *popular* operas, but he wanted to write a *perfect work*, the value of which might well be beyond the ability of his contemporaries to appreciate. People like Verdi and Drucker believed that even the greatest of accomplishments could be topped.

Perhaps Verdi was modeling himself on Phidias, the greatest sculptor in Ancient Greece, who in around 440 BC created the statues for the pediments of the Parthenon in Athens. When Phidias presented his bill to the city's accountant, the comptroller refused to pay it, saying: "*These statues are standing on the roof of the temple on the highest hill in Athens. We can only see their front. Yet you are submitting a bill for fully completed statues, including their backs, which nobody can see.*"

"*You are mistaken,*" Phidias retorted; "*the gods can see them.*" Whether the gods were duly enchanted by Phidias' statues or Verdi's operas is a question we cannot answer, but we can say this: 2,500 years later the statues are still standing and have elicited wonderment from many subsequent generations, as have Verdi's operas.

As is pointed out above, the thing that makes Verdi, Phidias, and Peter F. Drucker stand out is the *high demands they placed on themselves*. They both had a guiding star they doggedly followed for many years. During that time, their characters matured, but they did not grow old inside. They all produced work that shone well above the average, and they all yearned for *perfection*.

ACTION POINTS AND FOOD FOR THOUGHT

- Strive for perfection in your work—even if you know that you can never attain it.
- In what domain do you aim to achieve perfection in the long run?

CHAPTER **47**

Find Meaning; Then Use It!

LEARNING FROM

Viktor Frankl

Viktor Frankl (1905–1997) was a psychologist and psychiatrist who gained worldwide fame as the founder of *logotherapy*. This form of existential analysis is regarded as the "third Viennese school of psychotherapy," alongside Sigmund Freud's psychoanalysis and Alfred Adler's individual psychology.

Frankl was born into a Jewish family in Vienna. After finishing school, he studied medicine, developing a strong interest in cases of depression and suicide. At the age of 15 he was already personally in touch with Sigmund Freud, and it was at this time that the two started corresponding. In 1924, at Freud's express recommendation, one of Frankl's first publications appeared in the German language journal of psychoanalysis *Internationale Zeitschrift für Psychoanalyse*. As a student, Frankl was also in close contact with Alfred Adler. Frankl's work centered increasingly on the *search for meaning*, especially in connection with his commitment to suicide prevention. In 1926, he also started using the term *logotherapy* in lectures as a concept based on the premise that *individuals' prime motivation in life is to find meaning*. From 1933 to 1937, Frankl worked as a doctor at the psychiatric hospital in Vienna, where he looked after some 3,000 suicidal women a year.

After the Nazi occupation of Austria, Frankl was given only limited permission to work. Risking his life, he used false diagnoses to sabotage the Nazi-ordered euthanasia of the "mentally ill." In 1939, he allowed a valid exit visa for the United States to expire so as not to abandon his elderly parents. In 1941 he married Tilly Grosser, and a year later the Nazis forced the couple to abort their child. In 1942 the pair was arrested and sent with Frankl's parents to the Theresienstadt ghetto, where his father died of exhaustion six months later. Frankl, his wife, and shortly after his mother, too, were all deported to the extermination camp at Auschwitz, where his mother died in the gas chambers. Frankl was separated from Tilly when she was moved to the concentration camp at Bergen-Belsen. In 1944, Frankl himself was moved from Auschwitz to another concentration camp, Türkheim, a subcamp of Dachau, where he remained until the camp was liberated by U.S. troops on April 27, 1945.

Frankl's observations of his fellow inmates under the extreme conditions in the concentration camps confirmed his hypotheses about the search for meaning in human life.

When he returned to Vienna after being liberated, within a few days he learned about the death of his mother, wife, brother, and sister-in-law. Overcoming his despair, in 1946 he started working at the Vienna Policlinic of Neurology. That same year, in just nine days he dictated the book about his concentration camp experience as seen through the eyes of a psychologist, titled *Ein Psychologe erlebt das Konzentrationslager* (the English title is *Man's Search for Meaning*). More than 9 million copies of that book had been sold by the time Frankl died in 1997, and the Library of Congress in Washington lists it as "one of the ten most influential books in America."

How can Frankl's findings be extrapolated to management? In surveys, nearly 90 percent of all managers list *motivation* as one of their key tasks in people management. Yet the essential teachings of Viktor Frankl are almost completely unexploited in business. Frankl's core message is that *people are motivated by meaning.* In other words, the search for meaning is a person's main motivational force. If people can see meaning in something, they will also be willing to perform to the best of their ability and even make sacrifices and forgo certain things. Conversely, people who no longer sees any meaning in their life will be neither willing nor able to perform and may even be prepared to relinquish their life. The decisive issue here is that nobody except the individual can give *meaning* to his or her own life by seeking and finding what, for them, constitutes such meaning. The remarkable fact here is that everybody *is capable of* finding meaning in their life, and Frankl cited three main ways of doing so[1]:

1. *Serving a cause,* whereby the individual contributes to a perceived whole: In management this is the most important way. Peter F. Drucker repeatedly stressed the importance of individuals' contribution to their respective organization to achieve performance and results. The aim of serving a cause is also what spurs individuals to create a life's work, to single-mindedly pursue an objective, as so many great people did through history. However, in this connection Frankl also cites the importance of experiencing something.

2. *Loving somebody or feeling devoted to a person*: Here, people find meaning by being there for their family, partner, friends, or people who are dependent on assistance. This primarily applies in people's private and personal sphere.

3. *Turning suffering into an achievement:* Whenever human beings are faced with a destiny that cannot be altered—an incurable disease or a hopeless situation—they can do that most human of all things, namely endure a difficult fate with dignity, transforming suffering into an achievement. Frankl saw in this *"the secret of the unconditional meaningfulness of life: that man, especially in existential borderline situations, is called upon to bear witness, as it were, to what he and he alone is capable of."*[2]

As mentioned already, in spite of extensive scientific evidence demonstrating the applicability of Frankl's views in different social domains and especially also in borderline situations concerning human achievement potential, the core ideas behind his work have barely been heeded in business circles. Yet it has been demonstrated in connection with many organizations and many managers that Frankl's basic ideas can make a considerable contribution to corporate culture, to the understanding of management, and to managers' personal development.

Time and time again, almost "superhuman" achievements in all domains confirm what Frankl said, quoting Nietzsche: *"He who has a 'why' to live can bear almost any 'how.'"*[3]

ACTION POINTS AND FOOD FOR THOUGHT

- Motivate yourself by drawing on the meaning of your work.
- Examining Viktor Frankl's ideas is a highly worthwhile exercise. Why not take a longer, closer look at his gripping book *Man's Search for Meaning* or at his work *The Will to Meaning: Foundations and Applications of Logotherapy* in which he provides a deeper insight into the subject?

CHAPTER **48**

Harness the Power of Discipline

LEARNING FROM

Thomas Mann

The lesson to be learned from one of the most important writers and best-known Nobel Prize laureates is about a virtue that attracts far too little attention in connection with achievement: *discipline.*

Thomas Mann (1875–1955) was extremely disciplined, and surely no manager could help but wonder at the results the author achieved through his systematic approach to work. Mann worked on his current novel *every day* from nine in the morning to noon. If things were going well, during that time he managed to produce between one and one-and-a-half pages. He did this *always*, wherever he happened to be. When England and France declared war on Germany on September 3, 1939, Mann was traveling through Sweden, and his diary entry for that day states: *"I'm writing my page, as usual."*[1] In 1941, when he moved from Princeton to California, the furniture removal company packed up the contents of his apartment while he wrote his customary page. This way he produced 400 pages in the course of a year, enabling him to complete a monumental novel every three years.

Remarkably, Mann's very first novel, *Buddenbrooks*, subtitled *Decline of a Family*, published in 1901, made him world famous. The psychological novellas *Tonio Kröger* (1903) and *Death in Venice* (1912) were also tremendously successful. Mann spent no less than *11* years working on his masterpiece *The Magic Mountain*, which was published in 1924. In 1929, Mann was finally, somewhat belatedly, awarded the Nobel Prize for Literature for *Buddenbrooks*.

Of course you cannot learn how to write like a Nobel Prize laureate, any more than you can learn to paint like Michelangelo or Adolph von Menzel or compose music like Ludwig van Beethoven. However, there are great lessons to learn from their *systematic approach:* Michelange-lo spent seven years working on *The Last Judgment*, the 19-meter-high fresco on the altar wall of the Sistine Chapel; Menzel, to produce his masterpiece *The Iron Rolling Mill*, spent weeks of long days in such an environment, busily sketching away; and Beethoven left us more than 5,000 pages of his musical sketchbooks, an impressive testament to the meticulous way he honed his works right down to the finest detail.

However, Thomas Mann was not just a perfectionist in his scrupu-lous use of time; his discipline also extended to an extremely *painstak-ing approach to content and ideas*: nothing was lost! The idea for his novel *Doctor Faustus* had already come to him in 1901, along with the basic notion of transferring the contents of the Faust legend to a mod-ern setting. More than 40 years later, he took up the idea again, and the novel was duly published in 1947.

The story behind the completion of the picaresque novel *Confes-sions of Felix Krull, Confidence Man* is equally remarkable. Thomas Mann started work on it in 1910, but he interrupted it to write his novella *Death in Venice*. The first part of *Felix Krull* was published in 1922, the second in 1937, yet he only completed the book between 1951 and 1954. Mann hinted at a sequel to the abruptly ending book in its subtitle *Memoirs, Part* 1, and a note found among his papers contained a synopsis of four more parts that were left unwritten, because Thomas Mann died a year later, at age 80.

Mann was very much aware of his discipline, describing his most comprehensive work, *Joseph and His Brothers*, the day he finished it as *"a monument to tenacity."*[2] He wrote the tetralogy between 1926 and 1942.

Even for a genius it only *seems* easy to achieve greatness. As *Schiller* once wrote to *Goethe*, *"If only the critics, ever ready to judge, and frivolous dilettantes knew what it takes to produce a decent work."*[3]

I would like to wrap up this chapter by sharing a personal anecdote with you. After one of my presentations on management, an elderly gentleman approached me and said, *"You spoke about discipline. I liked that. It may be the most underestimated of success factors."* I later found out that the man in question started out as an entrepreneur employing around a dozen people some 50 years ago, whereas today his company is active worldwide, employing many, many thousands of people—a success he largely attributes to discipline.

ACTION POINTS AND FOOD FOR THOUGHT
- How important to you is discipline?
- What exactly can you do over the next six months to gain experience in this domain?

CHAPTER 49

Motivate Yourself

LEARNING FROM
Roger Federer

We are gradually running out of superlatives to describe *Roger Federer* (born in 1981), who has already won everything of significance in his sport. In fact, leading figures in the tennis world already agree that he is the best player of all time. Could anyone else teach us as much about motivation?

Let us start off by summing up his achievements, which tell us more than many words could: on *Sunday, July 5, 2009*, Federer won his sixth Wimbledon and fifteenth Grand Slam title. A month before that, his victory at the French Open in Paris had given him his first actual career Grand Slam, meaning that he had won all four Grand Slam tournaments at least once. In 2009 he reclaimed his position at the top of the world rankings, winning Wimbledon and the Roland Garros tournament; and in 2010 he cruised to victory in the Australian Open, setting again a new record by racking up his sixteenth Grand Slam title. Just stop for a moment and think how powerfully motivated he must have been to have achieved the accomplishments listed in Table 49-1.

Few management issues are as prone to misunderstandings as motivation. The expectations placed on bosses are usually just as exaggerated as the "motivational programs" in organizations are misguided and ineffective. So here is the most important fact to note, at

COMPETITION	2003	2004	2005	2006	2007	2008	2009	2010
Australian Open	Last 16	Winner	Semifinal	Winner	Winner	Semifinal	Final	Winner
French Open	First round	Third round	Semifinal	Final	Final	Final	Winner	Last 16
Wimbledon	Winner	Winner	Winner	Winner	Winner	Final	Winner	Last 16
U.S. Open	Last 16	Winner	Winner	Winner	Winner	Winner	Final	Semifinal

TABLE 49-1

the outset: *If you wish to achieve something, you must always moti-vate yourself.* In other words, remarkable achievements do not come about by depending on others to motivate you. So first of all you must make a conscious choice to *want* to motivate yourself. Only then can you fall back on a few very useful approaches on *how* to do so or how you, as a boss, can create conditions conducive to motivating others.

1. Derive motivation from results and through an awareness of contributing to a whole

It is a question of attitude whether you opt to concentrate mainly on your *input* and *efforts* or on your *results*. Even the greatest effort be-comes easier if you know what the end result ought to look like. *The thrill of achievement* is one of the strongest motivators. If, on top of this, you see the results you achieve as a contribution toward a greater objective or *bigger picture*, you will have very good chances of remain-ing motivated *in the long run*.

In a management context, contributing to a whole stands out as one of the chief lesser-known sources of motivation. For many managers, competently fulfilling a task that makes a contribution to a perceived whole is a source of *meaning*, and therein lies by far the greatest moti-vating factor. Since meaning is so valuable for effective self-manage-ment and people management, the topic is covered in greater detail in Chapter 47 on Viktor Frankl.

2. Concentrate on strengths and focus your efforts

If you want achievements to come easy or if you are to achieve anything notable in the first place, you must *concentrate on your strengths*. Little can motivate you as much as performing in a domain in which you can make full use of your strengths.

In addition, focus your efforts on very few endeavors. This way you will notch up remarkable achievements. No mere mortal can be successful in numerous domains. Or as tennis legend *Jimmy Connors* once put it: "*In modern tennis you are either a clay court specialist or a grass specialist or a hard court specialist—or you are Roger Federer.*"[1] And *John McEnroe*, who does not exactly have a reputation for extreme modesty, had this to say about Federer: "*Thanks, Roger, for downgrading us all to the status of average players. Never in my life have I seen such a gifted player.*"[2]

Unless your bosses and colleagues talk about your managerial skills in similarly admiring terms, you should concentrate on very few things, because this will yield results and thus motivate you.

3. Have high expectations about actual performance

Having major tasks to attend to and high expectations to meet can be top motivators. *The more intent you are* on successfully completing a task, the *more attention you will have to lavish* on that endeavor. In turn, dealing more intensively with something makes it more *interesting* overall and easier to achieve as time goes by. It also enhances the results attained and sets in motion an ever more powerful cycle. Deriving pleasure from your own performance capabilities, experiencing personal effectiveness, and taking pride in these things are pleasant consequences that will influence your development as a human being and give your motivation a tremendous boost.

4. Think constructively

Encourage yourself to *adopt a positive, constructive view of things*. Do not be naively blind to real problems, but be constructive in how you actively go about fulfilling your task. Consciously *seek out opportunities*, even when all there seems to be are problems, and then *take action,* instead of idly waiting for solutions to materialize. Thinking constructively is also an ability to derive enough strength from scant successes to carry you through any difficulties. No sports star could afford *not* to take such an approach. At the same time, do not underestimate the possibility of *talking yourself into* being motivated to a certain extent. Sport, in particular, is a domain in which the impact of *positive thinking* is clear to see. The fact that Roger Federer has perfected his mental strength like no other is apparent in almost all the finals he plays.

5. Make correct people decisions and ensure meaningful job design

Motivation in this domain stems initially from *careful people choices* and the painstakingly *prepared deployment of personnel.* Both these things are discussed in greater detail in Chapters 32 and 37 on (respectively) Jack Welch and George Patton. As a manager you have an opportunity to make good people decisions to create conditions that boost motivation. If you deploy people in such a way that *their strengths match the task to be fulfilled,* not only will you stand a good chance of seeing that task competently executed, but the people in question should find it easier to motivate themselves to fulfill it. Naturally, there is no guarantee, but this is a tool that you, as manager, can and should be able to use.

Job design also has a considerable impact on people's motivation. Jobs can be too broad, too insignificant, or altogether lacking in responsibilities. In some jobs, workers will be more likely to fritter away their time, whereas other jobs will be linked to challenges to which nobody can rise because they are either too exacting or too disparate. The key impact of job design on motivation is often overlooked.

6. Foster good communication and pass on relevant information

The main thing to establish here is *which information you need to pass on* to your team, colleagues, and boss to enable them to discharge their duties effectively and efficiently. You also need to ask yourself *which information you need from them,* so that you can fulfill your tasks professionally. Good communication alone does not motivate people, but lack of communication will almost inevitably demotivate them.

7. Apply a carefully designed remuneration and promotion system

The situation here is similar to the one regarding good communication. Better remuneration and promotions cannot in themselves motivate people, but systems that have been poorly thought through or are perceived as unfair will almost inevitably demotivate people. Decisions about remuneration systems and promotions must always be made scrupulously and with the utmost care.

In a nutshell, motivation is a product of your own behavior and of competent management. To a very considerable extent, the responsibility for motivation lies with you. Many people are astonished to discover *just how greatly* they can influence their own degree of motivation if they *make a conscious decision* to do so and apply themselves to remaining motivated. Thus, the matter is in your own hands. However, it has also become clear that you, as a manager, can considerably influence the level of motivation in your organization by creating *conditions* that facilitate the build-up of motivation. Thus, motivation is a consequence of competent management.

ACTION POINTS AND FOOD FOR THOUGHT
- What can you do to boost your own personal motivation?
- Where will you take steps to help boost motivation within your organization?

CHAPTER 50

Derive Enjoyment from Your Profession

LEARNING FROM

Leonard Bernstein

True achievers love what they do. This does not mean that they like *everything* they do or that you similarly *need* to love what *you* do to become an achiever. One characteristic shared by many real top performers is that they *often* love what they do and derive enjoyment from fulfilling their task. However, *often* they feel a sense of obligation, a sense of duty, and an awareness of the call of duty.

Conducting an orchestra may at first sight seem to be the kind of profession that anyone exercising it must surely love, a profession predestined to be a source of enjoyment. Let us take a closer look at this assumption and find out whether *loving* your profession and *deriving enjoyment* from it are essential for excellent performance and also how we may be able to influence both.

Leonard Bernstein (1918–1990) had no easy introduction to music. His father, the wealthy businessman Samuel Bernstein, fought very hard to bring his son's artistic career to a halt, for his dearest wish was to see his eldest son relinquish the path of a starving artist and finally look to his father's lucrative cosmetics business to make a living. But the boy persisted, and, after studying at the Curtis Institute of Music, in 1943 Leonard Bernstein was given his big break when the new director of the New York Philharmonic, Artur Rodzinski, appointed him as assistant conductor.

Leonard Bernstein's big breakthrough came on November 14 that same year, when he had to step in as a last-minute replacement for the star conductor Bruno Walter, who had been taken ill. The performance was a sensational success, and the review of the concert, which was broadcast live over the radio throughout the United States was printed on the front page of the *New York Times*. Bernstein's meteoric rise as a conductor had begun. After his son's success, Samuel Bernstein apologetically explained his previous opposition by saying, *"After all, you don't expect your child to be a Moses, a Maimonides, a Leonard Bernstein."*[1]

Bernstein became world-famous as a conductor and composer and made a substantial contribution to bolstering America's musical self-confidence. In 1958 he became the first American-born-and-trained musician to lead the New York Philharmonic. His crowd-pleasing style of conducting went down very well with concert-goers from all social strata, and he successfully challenged the traditional clear distinction between serious music and music for entertainment. His musical *West Side Story*, first performed in New York in 1957, is still a solid favorite, being regularly staged around the world. Bernstein also made a major contribution to Gustav Mahler's global renaissance, as well as gaining extensive plaudits as a music educator by commentating music programs on television and publishing popular books about music that reached a broad readership.

We can safely assume that Leonard Bernstein loved his work and derived enjoyment from it. For as he once said, *"There is no aspect of music that doesn't totally fascinate me or capture my interest one hundred percent, whether performing, talking about, or writing music."*[2] In spite of the enthusiasm underlying that statement, we should not forget that Leonard Bernstein's view of his own work is rather one-sided.

Let us now take a look at what all this means with respect to your professional activities as a manager.

1. Enhance the likelihood of deriving enjoyment from your profession by taking pleasure in results

It is a conspicuous fact that people who achieve something extraordinary often derive enjoyment from their work. However, this is by no means *always* the case, and it is *not* a prerequisite for achieving greatness. Every professional activity entails numerous routine tasks. Nobody can honestly say that he or she always enjoys fulfilling these tasks—and Leonard Bernstein was no exception. Think of his endless rehearsals, running through the same passage time and time again, the many nights he spent in hotels, and the endless travel. Even concerts themselves can lose their appeal, because anyone who has already performed the same symphony a hundred times would have to be quite an extraordinary person to regard yet another one as a pure pleasure, even if—as with Bernstein's three symphonies, *Jeremiah*, *The Age of Anxiety*, and *Kaddish*—the compositions in question were his own.

Assume, then, that a proven top performance is more an indication of *true professionalism* than a reflection of pure enjoyment. When you hear Simon Rattle conducting the Berlin Philharmonic, you can *expect* a top performance—regardless of whether Rattle himself derived particular enjoyment from the concert given that evening. That is something you will not even notice, because this ability to constantly produce top performances is the mark of a true professional and definitely merits admiration.

You should also bear in mind that some tasks, taken as a whole, are inherently *anything but enjoyable*, examples being work that is monotonous, hard, boring, or physically exacting. Nonetheless, this kind of work still gets done, sometimes necessitating almost superhuman performances. *Deriving enjoyment from your work*—should you be fortunate enough to do so—is a wonderful thing, but be warned: any belief in an *entitlement* to such enjoyment from your professional life will almost invariably be misplaced. Nonetheless, you *can* learn to derive enjoyment from the *results* of your work—which is a different thing altogether. Results are always a ready source of enjoyment, or at least satisfaction, even if the work associated with achieving them generates no positive feelings.

2. Enhance the likelihood of deriving enjoyment from your profession by concentrating on what you contribute

Most managers busy themselves with their *input*, that is, what they themselves do and their own efforts, rather than focusing on results and their personal *contribution* to a broader objective. You can make deriving enjoyment from your profession more likely by asking yourself this question: *"How can I contribute toward making this organization successful?" Assume responsibility*. Remember, there is a big difference between feeling that you are breaking stones and feeling that you are shaping stones to build a cathedral. So *focus on the bigger picture*. Doing so is not just a key to success, but a great potential source of enjoyment.

3. Enhance the likelihood of deriving enjoyment from your profession by placing high demands on yourself

How you go about your work can also be a source of enjoyment. If you *set challenges* for yourself and *place high demands* on yourself, you will find the quality of your activities enhanced. All good musicians know that playing monotonous scales can be almost indescribably fulfilling, provided that they concentrate intently on performing them perfectly. In fact, the enjoyment derived from doing so goes beyond the actual outcome (the degree of virtuosity attained). The task itself becomes more interesting by focusing so intently on it and *placing higher demands on its execution*.

4. Doing one's duty can also be a source of enjoyment

In principle this point is covered in the previous paragraph, especially with respect to deriving pleasure from results. It is also akin to the perceived importance of serving a cause noted by Viktor Frankl. All the same, it is worthwhile once again acknowledging the fulfillment of a duty as a *source of strength and meaning*, even though the notion that *doing one's duty* is a positive thing seems less widespread now than it once was. Doing one's duty is not merely useful to the individual, it is also absolutely vital if organizations and societies are to function properly. Especially in connection with the arduous toil referred to above, which can prove extremely exacting, individuals can always earn respect and take pride in doing their duty and thus derive enjoyment, or at least satisfaction, from their work in spite of the heavy physical toll it takes on them.

If, after reading all this, you conclude that your profession is a source of *enjoyment* or that you even *love* what you do, you should feel highly privileged, one of the fortunate few. Of course, love of your job or the ability to derive enjoyment from exercising your profession can never actually *guarantee* top performance or turn you into a great achiever, but one thing is certain. These elusive, yet powerful sentiments can give any career a definite lift, and—as with Bernstein—unquestionably serve to inspire others.

ACTION POINTS AND FOOD FOR THOUGHT

- In which of the four domains covered above—deriving enjoyment from results, concentrating on your own contribution, placing high demands on yourself, or finding satisfaction and pride in doing your duty—can you take steps to eke more enjoyment out of your profession?
- How will you make a concerted effort over the next six months to try to derive greater enjoyment from exercising your profession?

CHAPTER **51**

Think Constructively

LEARNING FROM

Niki Lauda

The Austrian *Niki Lauda* (born in 1949) has repeatedly made headlines by turning his life around in spectacular fashion. Not only in Formula 1 racing, but also as an entrepreneur he has proved, time and time again, that something that seemed impossible *can* be accomplished. His personal mixture of individualism, an uncompromising attitude, pragmatism, and sheer force of will have earned him plenty of successes and gained him many admirers. But another equally remarkable facet of his character is his undeniable ability to *think constructively*. This attitude can be summed up in just two points:

1. Concentrate on *opportunities rather than problems*.
2. Cultivate a *constructive and positive basic outlook,* even if your setbacks seem serious and problems seem insurmountable.

In 1975, Niki Lauda won the Formula 1 World Championship. The next season he was seriously injured in a terrible accident on the Nürburgring when his Ferrari swerved off the track at a speed of over 135 miles per hour and then bounced back into the path of oncoming cars and caught fire. Lauda's colleagues pulled him out of the blazing wreck of his car, and for five days his life hung in the balance. Then, just six weeks after surviving that inferno, he drove his next race, taking fourth place in the Italian Grand Prix in Monza. If Niki Lauda was not already world famous by then, this feat clinched his reputation. And he went on to gain the status of a true legend by winning another World Championship title in 1977. The reason he cited for his surprise retirement from motor racing in September 1979 has already almost achieved cult status: *"I've had enough of driving round in circles."*[1]

That same year he started his first airline, *Lauda Air*. Setting the objective of using his own airline to break Austrian Airlines' state monopoly, he embarked on a seemingly hopeless venture. But in spite of receiving support from Bruno Kreisky, who was the Austrian chancellor at the time, Lauda's company failed to obtain the licenses it needed. So without altogether abandoning his dream of running his own airline, Lauda put the endeavor on hold and turned back to Formula 1, incredibly becoming world champion for the third time in 1984.

He still lacked the concession he needed from the Austrian government to offer scheduled long-haul flights, but in the end sheer persistence paid off, and he secured it. Later on he also acquired a stake in Austrian Airlines, though he subsequently described that investment as the biggest mistake he had ever made, and it caused him mounting difficulties over subsequent years. At the end of 2000, because of major differences between the corporate cultures of the two companies, he stepped down as chairman of Lauda Air. Two years later he sold his remaining shares in the company, and many people saw his dream of being an airline entrepreneur in tatters.

Richard Branson, the billionaire founder of the Virgin Group, when asked, *"How do you become a millionaire, Mr. Branson?"* is said to have replied that it is quite easy: you should start off as a billionaire and set up an airline. Flying in the face of this, Niki Lauda once again proved, by establishing his airline NIKI, that he knows how to exploit opportunities. The company took off in 2003 and in 2008 reported its fifth consecutive year in profit. The airline's fleet of Airbuses is steadily growing, as is the number of destinations it serves, and in surveys NIKI regularly rates as the top low-cost airline in terms of its performance.[2]

But that is not the only opportunity that Lauda has efficiently exploited. He also set up another mobility operator, a car rental company called LaudaMotion that rented cult vehicles like Smarts and Minis at spectacularly low prices: "*1 Smart, 1 day, 1 euro*." The clever idea was this: instead of earning its money from the car rental customer, it derived its income from advertising customers whose messages are emblazoned on the vehicles they drive. In October 2009, Lauda sold his 51 percent stake in the company to his business partner, Stefan Miklauz.

Although Niki Lauda last passed the checkered flag in a Formula 1 race around 25 years ago, today his media presence is stronger than that of most active Formula 1 drivers. Very few former professional sports stars have succeeded in maintaining such a high profile as he has.

If you want another example of clever exploitation of *opportunities and constructive thinking*, look no further than Niki Lauda's trademark red cap. Having suffered severe burns to his scalp in the crash on the Nürburgring, Lauda took to wearing a cap to prevent people from staring at his injuries. So why not simultaneously turn it into a lucrative advertising space? In a recent interview given to the German weekly newspaper *Die Zeit*, he said, "*Originally I received €100,000 a year; now I get €1.2 million.*"[3]

Unlike almost anyone else, Niki Lauda has proved more than once that there *is* a way back from even the greatest setbacks: his terrible motor-racing accident; years of struggling to obtain a concession for scheduled long-haul flights; remedying the serious damage to the image of Lauda Air after one of its scheduled flights crashed in 1991, through no fault of his company. Not only that, but by setting up his low-cost airline NIKI and his car rental company, LaudaMotion, he proved that success is possible, even under the toughest competitive conditions. Such examples of successful entrepreneurship are invaluable, especially for the young people in society.

So how can constructive thinking and the systematic exploitation of opportunities be achieved? Most people who are successful have simply *made a habit* of thinking constructively. There may be some natural talents out there, who manage to hold onto a basic positive attitude for years at a time, even in the face of adversity, but most people tend to make a conscious choice to think constructively and positively after suffering a few setbacks, and they will then endeavor to maintain such an outlook thereafter.

To succeed in the long run, it would be rather risky to rely on one's "temperament," because you never know what pressure you might one day find yourself under or which limits you may be driven to. Even the most optimistic sports stars would never dispense with a methodical approach and training designed to improve their mental attitude. Some use autogenic training or other forms of relaxation; others resort to mental training or leave themselves notes to remember to adopt the right mind-set. *How* you make a habit of thinking constructively and positively is not important. What counts is that you *do it* and embrace this attitude with such discipline that you never stray from it.

A similar situation applies to *systematically exploiting opportunities.* Managers need to force themselves to focus their attention and that of the other members of their organization on opportunities, because *that is where results can be achieved.* Naturally, important problems cannot be ignored, but organizations that concentrate primarily on problems instead of seeking opportunities will always be on the defensive.

From Niki Lauda's track record, it is obvious that even when he was really up against formidable competition, he must have asked himself what opportunity such a situation might present. If you want to direct your own gaze or focus your organization on opportunities, the exploitation of such openings must be a high priority, and you must demand the corresponding basic positive attitude from the members of your organization. The rough questions to ask are: *"Where do particular opportunities lie at the moment? And which opportunities in my area of responsibility would have the biggest impact on our performance and results if they were exploited?"* As time goes by, seeking out opportunities this way will become second nature to you and your organization. So take the following basic rule as your guideline: *Think constructively and be opportunity-driven, not problem-oriented.*

ACTION POINTS AND FOOD FOR THOUGHT

- ■ What can you do to adopt or shore up a constructive, positive attitude?
- ■ Where do your particular opportunities lie at the moment? Which opportunities in your area of responsibility would make the greatest contribution to the success of your organization if you exploited them?

CHAPTER **52**

Act

Responsibly

LEARNING FROM

Hippocrates

The now almost 2,400-year-old *Hippocratic Oath,* named after *Hippocrates of Kos* (circa 460–370 BC), established physicians' fundamental obligation to exercise their profession responsibly and to the best of their ability. In essence, the key maxim derived from Hippocrates' teachings *"primum non nocere"* (*First, do no harm*) applies to anyone seeking to exercise their profession responsibly, including management. No doctors, managers, or legal experts can actually promise to do *only* good, but they *can* promise *not to knowingly do harm.* This was what Peter F. Drucker considered to be the fundamental rule of professional ethics and public responsibility.

Bearing in mind management's noble obligation to practice corporate social responsibility and discuss business ethics and responsibility, the requirement to act responsibly seems precious little to ask. But it is essential to start off with something really simple, yet totally fundamental: *a personal decision.* One such personal decision is to exercise your profession responsibly.

The main thing people need to do to honor their commitment to professional responsibility is to be responsible for what they do—and occasionally for what they fail to do.[1] As Peter F. Drucker pointed out, many discussions about business ethics have nothing to do with business and little to do with ethics. His impression was that the core issue actually boiled down to straightforward, everyday *honesty*. Accordingly, Drucker's response to solemn declarations that managers should not steal, lie, cheat, bribe, or be corrupt was that such an outlook had nothing to do with specific business ethics. Moreover, against this backdrop there was no need for such business ethics anyway, because the values in question were of a moral nature, the key factor being basic honesty, which should naturally apply to *everyone*, not merely managers.

In this connection, senior managers have to assume a special responsibility. As individuals, on the one hand, managers are employees of their organization, and set an example within it, but on the other hand top executives, especially in public, are also representatives of *professional managers in general*. The problem here is that immoral conduct, especially in senior management, affects the general public's view of "business." The portrayal of some top executives in the media and their apparent scope of influence leads people to believe that misconduct by managers is the norm and that "business" itself is equally immoral, corrupt, and dishonest. Consequently, the damage caused by immoral behavior, especially in senior management, extends way beyond the individual's respective organization. Public debate totally ignores the fact that the vast majority of top managers are honest, responsible, and decent in how they go about their work. In other words, irresponsible behavior by managers divides society, projecting a false picture to the public and eliciting hostility to business—the very last thing a modern society needs! In short, *managers serve as role models* whether they like it or not. How they behave affects the "bigger picture" in people's minds and thus also impacts on social cohesion.

Plenty of aspects of management *can* be learned, but the willingness to assume responsibility for what one does or fails to do is not among them. Occasionally, responsibility can be forced onto people, imposed as a requirement; and individuals can also appeal to another human being's sense of responsibility, though ultimately the positive decision to act responsibly remains a personal one.

While starting out with the simple principle to, *"Above all not knowingly do harm"* may not be much—and arguably just represents a modest first step, as doctors following the traditional Hippocratic doctrine have always known—living up to this maxim is no easy matter.

ACTION POINTS AND FOOD FOR THOUGHT

- Consider the issue of responsible management in depth and discuss it with others. Have your say!
- Take responsibility both for what you have done and for what you have failed to do.
- Above all, do no harm.

CHAPTER 53

Foster Creativity All Life Long

LEARNING FROM

Pablo Picasso

Pablo Picasso (1881–1973) was 56 years old when he created his monumental masterpiece *Guernica*. In many industrialized countries, had he been an employee, he would have been sent into retirement just a few years later. Just stop and think for a moment how *fundamentally misguided* that practice is.

To many art lovers Picasso was *the* outstanding genius of the twentieth century, producing large quantities of paintings, sculptures, drawings, etchings, ceramics, and other works of art. Yet it was only when he was age 66 that Pablo Picasso even *began* working with ceramics. At age 70 he created the powerful painting *Massacre in Korea*. And at age 76 in the Las Meninas series he once again showed in 58 paintings (44 of which were interpretations of Diego Velázquez's masterpiece *Las Meninas*) what an astounding mix of playful virtuosity he could bring to handling different styles, topics, and techniques, while always maintaining his characteristic touch. At the ripe old age of 87, Picasso produced a series of 347 etchings titled *The Artist and His Models*. Undeniably, Picasso's tremendous inventiveness and seemingly endless creativity, right up to his death at the ripe old age of 91 years, made him one of the most important modern artists.

We are living at a time and in a society in which people are growing old in good health. Bearing in mind how important demographic development is to the economy, as a manager you, too, need to consider this issue. As an individual, you may prefer to consider the personal contribution you envisage making even at an advanced age; but as a manager you must also consider how you can best exploit the opportunities that a generation mix opens up for your organization. Is there any good reason why your organization should *not* have staff covering an age range of, say, 25 to 75? After all, some of Picasso's most outstanding works were produced when he was way past 50, yet even at that age many people already have a tough time finding a new job if they lose their old one. Even though they are still full of mental creativity and have a real wealth of experience, they are deprived of the opportunity of making a worthwhile contribution to their organization. By exhibiting such a naive fixation on employing young people—a trend that thankfully now appears to be waning—organizations fritter away some of their most valuable resources: *specialist knowledge, management know-how, general knowledge, business relations, and experience.* As a manager you need to think about how you can create ways of harnessing such precious assets. Bear in mind, too, that it is usually older people in particular who can be expected to exhibit such positive traits as *discipline, diligence, modesty, conscientiousness, and a sense of responsibility.* Unfortunately, nowadays the importance of such character traits is sometimes overlooked.

Being prejudiced against the over-50 population positively undermines the effectiveness of an organization. Institutions need to devise new employment concepts in which both young and older people can pull together. In practice, this means doing the following: looking for possible ways in which the potential of older workers can be maintained and continue to be harnessed for the good of the organization. Why not consider steadily reducing their working time while simultaneously adapting their duties? Arrange things so that older employees *want* to stay in the organization because they are being deployed in areas where they can perform well and thus remain productive. Think about concepts that enable people to work in mixed groups, so that young and old can make *joint* contributions, drawing more effectively on the strengths of different age groups.

It is a major and very frequent mistake not to fully integrate older staff members into continuing training programs, because not only are they often expensive employees, but intelligence research has ascertained that human beings start exploiting their full mental capacity only when 50 years old and remain capable of learning up to a high age. Naturally, decisions about who embarks when on what kind of training need to be made carefully, on a case-by-case basis. But if you expect employees to remain in your organization for several more years, sending them to a training course will always pay off. It will also show them that you value them, which they are likely to appreciate. So bear in mind that if you create opportunities here, you will be sending out an important signal regarding your corporate culture. And do not underestimate the value of the trust such an approach will generate.

The next time you think about how to design continuing training programs or sending staff to undergo training, remember that the German statesman Konrad Adenauer was elected federal chancellor for the fourth time at the age of 85 and only finally relinquished the leadership of his party, the Christian Democratic Union (CDU), at the age of 90. Alexander von Humboldt concluded his five-volume *Cosmos* when he was 88 years old, an age at which Michelangelo was still working on his *Pietà Rondanini* sculpture. Of course, you may rightly point out that not everybody working for your organization is such a genius. And no organization is likely to envision continuing training programs for people who are over 85 years old.

Maybe you will choose to follow the personal advice given by the German writer *Paul Heyse,* winner of the Nobel Prize for Literature in

1910: *"If your short time here on Earth is to yield a life of worth, when young your elders heed, and when old from younger feed!"*[1]

ACTION POINTS AND FOOD FOR THOUGHT

- ■ What do you need to do in your organization to establish an effective generation mix? What specific use can you make of it?
- ■ Review your training and continuing training programs to see whether all age categories are adequately integrated. Think where you personally would like to take part in these programs.
- ■ Find out about demographic change and its anticipated consequences. There is hardly any other area in which the future can be so accurately predicted. Try to "recognize the future that has already happened" and foresee the impact on your organization, as discussed in Chapter 24 on Ray Kroc.

CHAPTER 54

Assume Responsibility

LEARNING FROM
Harry Truman

In 1944, *Harry Truman* (1884–1972) became vice president under Franklin D. Roosevelt. When President Roosevelt died suddenly on April 12, 1945, Truman was duly sworn in as president, in keeping with the U.S. Constitution. One of the reasons Truman was chosen to run for the office of vice president was his exceptional grasp of domestic policy issues. In addition, as World War II appeared to be nearing its end, it was assumed that in the aftermath the United States would increasingly focus on domestic affairs, so Truman's dearth of foreign policy experience would not matter.

Things turned out differently, however, and Truman was quick to realize that foreign policy would remain the dominant theme and that consequently the main thrust of his contribution as president would lie in that domain. At the same time, he was aware that in the past he had not been terribly interested in that area, and he was also mindful that he knew precious little about it. All the same, he had no choice but to assume the responsibility of representing his country in the foreign policy arena and thus of playing a central role in determining the post-war geopolitical situation.

Truman did *not* ask himself what he would *like* to do (the answer would have been work in the domestic policy area, which was what he was most passionate about); instead he asked, *"What contribution am I called upon to make in this situation?"*

What ensued is one of the most remarkable acquisitions of competence by a politician and an almost matchless example of a realigned political career. After taking office as president, over several months Truman had General George Marshall and Dean Acheson, later a U.S. secretary of state, give him a thorough grounding in foreign policy. As a result, it was Truman—rather than Churchill or Stalin—who played a decisive role in reshaping world order during the postwar years. Prime examples of this are his rejection of the Soviet Union's pretensions to power in Eastern, Southeastern, and Central Europe and the limitation of the spread of Communism through a policy of containment. Others include the establishment of NATO, the Marshall Plan for the reconstruction of Western Europe, support for the reconstruction of Japan, and Truman's efforts to stabilize the "free world" by implementing a globally oriented military and economic policy.

This development began with Truman's *assumption of responsibility* for the central issue of his time, or as Truman rather casually put it himself, *"The buck stops here." Leadership means responsibility,* not rank, status, or privileges. All effective managers know that ultimately the responsibility lies with them, not with anybody else. Assuming such responsibility is a precondition for effective, credible management.

Set out below are the main practical points to bear in mind when aiming to competently exercise your responsibility for managing an organization.

1. Management is responsibility

This basic premise has to be accepted and fulfilled. You occupy a management position so that you can carry out your responsibility. Rank, status, money, or privileges are *not* what management is all about.

2. It is the task—not you—that matters

Subordinate yourself to the task at hand. What really matters are the requirements imposed by the task, not your own personal wishes, needs, or leanings. True greats in history have always been committed to their work.

3. What counts are the results you achieve, not how popular you are

Management is not a popularity contest. You are responsible for achieving results, not aiming to be universally liked.

4. Stand by your responsibility

Admit to errors. Stand up and be counted especially if things do not go as planned. *Both outwardly and in the eyes of your superiors*, mistakes made by employees are errors committed by their boss. Internally, employees must remedy any errors they commit, but they must also be able to count on support from their boss.

5. Listen and learn in order to competently discharge your responsibilities

You will never become an excellent manager if you do not listen. The *ability to listen* is a voluntary decision that requires self-discipline and openness. If you are not firmly in control of an issue for which you are responsible, improve your know-how in that domain. Truman was exemplary in this connection. Competence is a basic prerequisite for credible management.

6. Make yourself understood by communicating effectively

To become an effective manager, you must *be readily understandable.* You need the support of large numbers of staff, superiors, and colleagues. *Be patient;* it can take time for your message to get across.

7. Recognize that assuming responsibility will further your own development

The main responsibility for your own development lies with you. If *you* do not strive for excellence, it will not come about of its own accord. Take responsibility for your own performance. This is crucial for your success.

8. Set an example

As a manager you are very exposed. The example you set sets a standard for your area of responsibility, and if you are high up in the hierarchy, it will extend well beyond that. Be aware of this responsibility and also of its potential impact on others.

ACTION POINTS AND FOOD FOR THOUGHT

- What do you need to do to implement the eight points set out above? Decide which measures to take and then work through them.
- What contribution can you make to your organization to ensure that the prevailing corporate culture is characterized by achievement and a willingness by people to take responsibility?

CHAPTER 55

Look After Yourself

LEARNING FROM
Jamie Oliver

Do not let anybody tell you that, to be a successful manager, you need to be as good an athlete as LeBron James, as forceful a leader as Larry Ellison, as entertaining as Robbie Williams, preferably as intelligent as Albert Einstein, and as good-looking as George Clooney. So totally forget all the conventional wisdom about how managers should be and all the claims about what they are actually like in real life. Management is about *results*, and the individuals who deliver them are as different as people happen to be in any other domain. Consequently, you can find every conceivable type of manager. Yet there is one common denominator that is crucial to the *long-term performance and achievements* of any manager, or for that matter of any human being, and that is *good health.*

Not everyone has good health, and some of the individuals mentioned in this book achieved great things despite health problems. But all of us make choices that can positively or adversely affect our health and thus determine our performance and the potential scope of our achievement.

This chapter is *not* about management in the narrow sense. Rather it *is* about a personal decision that may not make you a better manager *per se* but that *will* affect your ability to perform over the long term, namely the decision to try and *be and remain healthy*. Moreover, it is a decision that you do not necessarily make only for yourself, but to a certain extent, for others as well, both at work and at home.

Star chef *Jamie Oliver* (born in 1975) has set himself the task of arousing people's interest in healthy eating. After concluding a deal with ABC, in early 2010 he presented a prime time reality show on TV in which the inhabitants of a small town in the United States were introduced to the *art of healthy eating*. The program, titled *Jamie's Food Revolution*, won an Emmy Award, though the second series proved less successful. But Jamie Oliver is nothing if not tenacious, and in a bid to fulfill his dream of a healthier population on a broader scale, his next book, *30-Minute Meals*, again drew attention to the subject and became an international bestseller and the fastest-selling nonfiction title of all time in the United Kingdom.

The cult status Jamie Oliver has earned down the years fuels expectations that his plan really *will* ultimately succeed in making a difference in the United States. After all, he learned a tremendous amount from his experience in the United Kingdom, where he strove to improve the quality of the food dished up at British schools, and he is perfectly aware of just how difficult, exacting, and in some respects impossible it can be to *reform people's eating habits*.

And the problems he experienced in the United Kingdom arose despite backing from Prime Minister Tony Blair for the *Feed Me Better* campaign launched in 2004, through which Jamie Oliver planned to change the food served at model schools. Indeed, the government said it was willing to spend an additional £280 million on healthier school meals.

Jamie Oliver has become as famous as a pop star in more than 50 different countries thanks to the 14 million books he has sold, the fact that over 20,000 guests have appeared on his cooking show (making it the most successful of its genre), and his own innumerable TV appearances. He has also received countless awards and honors for his out-of-the-ordinary cooking skills and for his commitment to boosting health awareness. On top of that, he has won the *GQ* "Man of the Year Award," in 2003 was made a *Member of the Order of the British Empire*, and in 2010 became the recipient of a prestigious TED award for exceptional individuals active in the areas of technology, entertainment, or design. But success has not gone to Jamie Oliver's head, and he has never lost sight of the need for healthy—as well as hearty—eating.

Organizations in Western societies and Japan are characterized by aging workforces. This development will force these societies to abandon the idea of a fixed retirement age. Knowledge workers in particular will be physically able to work up to an advanced age, way beyond the traditional age of retirement. Increasingly, it will become the norm to speak about a working life lasting 50 years. Creating circumstances that support the health and well-being of people in an organization will certainly contribute to productivity and effectiveness, but will also show that the organization in question takes responsibility for what it can contribute to individuals' health.

Against this backdrop it is worthwhile—for every individual, every organization, and for society as a whole—to think critically about how the issue of health needs to be tackled.

ACTION POINTS AND FOOD FOR THOUGHT

- Make your own personal decision to try and age healthily and then take active steps to implement that decision.
- What exactly do you plan to do and by when?

CHAPTER **56**

Commit Yourself to More Than Just Your Own Well-Being

LEARNING FROM
Muhammad Yunus

"Poverty is the absence of all human rights. The frustrations, hostility and anger generated by abject poverty cannot sustain peace in any society. For building stable peace we must find ways to provide opportunities for people to live decent lives."[1]

Who would ever have imagined the founder of a bank receiving a Nobel Peace Prize? Yet the awarding of the 2006 prize, shared equally between *Muhammad Yunus* (born in 1940) and the *Grameen Bank* did not come as a complete surprise, for the Grameen Bank Yunus founded had set a shining example for the entire global microfinance sector. Yunus was a pioneer in awarding loans to poor people, and it was he who first brought the issue to the public's attention. In the presentation speech justifying the award, the *Norwegian Nobel Committee* said, *"Lasting peace can not be achieved unless large population groups find ways in which to break out of poverty. Micro-credit is one such means. Development from below also serves to advance democracy and human rights."*[2]

255

In the meantime, microcredit has become a widespread instrument for combating poverty in developing countries. Poor people usually have no access to loans because they have no collateral to offer. Yet in many cases tiny loans are all it takes to turn a business idea into an activity. For instance, sums as modest as $5 or $50 can be used to purchase a pottery wheel, a millstone, a plow, or a rickshaw to form the basis for somebody's subsistence. As *Yunus* has tirelessly reiterated, in the absence of such loans poor people are effectively denied their potential. *"People don't want charity, they need opportunities."*[3] Awarding them microloans gives them just such an opportunity, enabling them to gradually free themselves from misery and ultimately repay their loan to the Grameen Bank.

The size of these loans is tailored to the poor recipients' ability to make payments so that they do not fall into the trap of overindebtedness. A typical sum paid out by the Grameen Bank is around $30. Naturally, interest is charged on the borrowed amounts, because the loan is not meant to constitute alms for the poor, but should rather pay for itself. Microcredits differ from conventional commercial loans in that no collateral at all is offered by the borrower.

The loans in question are associated with a series of fairly unusual principles. For example, the Grameen Bank awards credit almost exclusively to women because *"they simply deal more diligently with money,"*[4] as Yunus put it. And since women are put in charge of finances, they become irreplaceable for the family business, which in practice invariably helps them compensate for their gender's disadvantaged status within their family. In the Islamic society of Bangladesh, this is tantamount to a revolution. A second principle is that individual would-be creditors must form a group of five female borrowers. Within that group they hold regular discussions and monitor each other's repayment of the individual loans. Instead of paying out money to all five women at the same time, the bank starts off by awarding just one member of the group the sum that one particular individual requires. The remaining women in the group are awarded their loans only when the first recipient's repayment record has been monitored over a certain period and deemed dependable. If one member defaults on her loan repayments, the entire group will automatically be affected. From a management point of view, this is a striking example of effective self-management.

Many further rules apply, which Yunus stresses arose from daily experience with the fight against poverty. For example, the women pledge to limit the number of children they have, to drink only boiled water, and to grow as many vegetables as possible.

These and numerous other examples show pragmatic ways in which an organization can be rendered more effective by *applying lessons it has learned from experience.* When Yunus awarded his first loans, he was astonished at how swiftly they were repaid, and today he is proud that his bank's loan default rate is so very low—at just over 2 percent.

"When I started I had no idea," Yunus said. *"We professors were all so intelligent, but we knew absolutely nothing about the poverty surrounding us."*[5] Yunus was not always committed to combating poverty, having originated from a respected family in Bangladesh and having been sent to the best schools by his father, who was a jeweler. Thus his career trajectory began, rather typically for a son from a good home, by studying economics. Having secured a Fulbright scholarship, he then went on to complete a Ph.D. at Vanderbilt University in Tennessee. In 1972 he was appointed professor at the university in his home town of Chittagong and, by his own estimation, he had perfectly isolated himself from poverty. In 1974, when Bangladesh gained its independence from Pakistan, a famine tore through the country, claiming hundreds of thousands of lives. That proved a turning point in his life: *"I started hating myself, the arrogance with which I acted, as though my elegant economic theories gave me the answer."*[6]

Yunus started taking his students into villages, and in 1976 he launched the *Grameen Bank Project*, which in 1983 led to his founding *Grameen Bank*, of which he served as the managing director until

March 2011. Today, Grameen Bank has some 8 million borrowers, 97 percent of whom are women. Meanwhile, Yunus has received the Nobel Peace Prize, the Presidential Medal of Freedom (the highest U.S. honor for civilians), and countless other awards worldwide.

At the same time, Yunus also has his critics. Some reproach him for charging excessive interest and maintain that he is not doing enough for the poorest of the poor, like those individuals who are too sick to continue working. Fortunately, Yunus does not allow himself to be upset by this, because he is probably aware that every successful human being in history always had critics. It would be interesting to know how many of his detractors make their claims from the comfort of their cozy studies and on which *real results* they can base their comments in comparison to those achieved by Yunus.

The work done by Muhammad Yunus shows in impressive fashion the extensive power of effective management applied to the *individual*, the *organization*, and *society as a whole*.

Yunus's system *benefits society* by *benefiting its customers*. The really noteworthy fact is that by offering his *customers* outstanding benefits, Yunus is developing a strong, healthy *organization*, which is in turn in a position to contribute toward a stable, healthy *society*. The sequence is important here and cannot be randomly shuffled: customer benefit *must* come first. And the organization's obligations to society are *not* fulfilled through special social responsibilities, but by creating satisfied customers.

Naturally, any organization has to take responsibility for the influence it exerts either directly or indirectly over individuals, its impact on the environment, and the consequences of its actions. However, it can assume more extensive responsibility for social tasks only if the organization, in so doing, does not jeopardize the attainment of its actual purpose, *its business mission*. The organization must also be competent in the first place in the domain in which it is supposed to assume responsibility; otherwise, the organization itself could encounter difficulties or cause damage. Consequently, it is essential to resist the temptation to palm off onto large, strong businesses and nonprofit organizations tasks for which they are unable to assume responsibility because doing so is simply not within their capability. After all, good intentions are not always socially responsible.

Even where Grameen Bank's overall objective—the fight against poverty—is concerned, only if the company has customers can it take on other social tasks. The clear consonance between *satisfied customers* and the *creation of benefits for society*, which in this instance are even going so far as to make a contribution toward world peace, is extremely clear, thanks to Grameen Bank's specific business mission and its special business model. The really great thing about the project is that it shows how good management *can* be used to realize business models that used to be regarded as impossible. Nobody before Yunus had believed that poor people could be integrated into the economic cycle so effectively and with such lasting effect.

Yunus provides us with countless examples of effective management, including his innovative approach, which on numerous occasions took him into uncharted territory: the calculating—never rash or hasty—way he takes risks, the way he harnesses the power of self-organization, and his clever involvement of powerful partners to attain shared objectives. But one aspect of his approach merits particular attention: he displays *true leadership*, above and beyond what is normally understood as professional management.

Grameen Bank's website presents a statement by Yunus which is one of the most remarkable statements ever made about management. Yunus and Grameen Bank had won the Nobel Peace Prize, yet *what* and *how* he writes about this goes way beyond what can even be expected from professional management, because it displays *leadership* in its purest form. In fact, his statement encapsulates what *leadership* is all about, standing in very stark contrast to the otherwise totally inflationary use of the term. What Yunus wrote about the Nobel Prize awarded to him and Grameen Bank was this:

> *"October 13, 2006 was the happiest day for Bangladesh. It was a great moment for the whole nation. Announcement came on that day that Grameen Bank and I received the Nobel Peace Prize, 2006. It was a sudden explosion of pride and joy for every Bangladeshi. All Bangladesh felt as if each of them received the Nobel Peace Prize. We were happy that the world has given recognition through this prize, that poverty is a threat to peace. Grameen Bank, and the concept and methodology of micro-credit that it has elaborated through its 30 years of work, have contributed to enhancing the chances of peace by reducing poverty. Bangladesh is happy that it could contribute to the world a concept and an institution which can help bring peace to the world."[7]*

Finally, let us read what *Peter F. Drucker* wrote about *leadership*: *"The last basic competence [of four that a genuine leader needs] is the willingness to realize how unimportant you are compared to the task. . . ."*[8] *"The most important [thing to] do, I have said again and again already: Keep your eye on the task, not on yourself. The task matters, and you are its servant."*[9]

Could Yunus have expressed the mental attitude of a true leader any better than by saying what he did about the Nobel Prize awarded to him?

ACTION POINTS AND FOOD FOR THOUGHT

- Commit yourself to more than just your own well-being.
- Focus on the task, not on yourself. The task matters, and you are its servant.

EPILOGUE

By now you should have gained some valuable insights into *effective management*. The most important question at this point is this:

What will you do differently starting tomorrow?
The truly interesting part of effective management lies in its implementation, so if you *really* want to make the most of what you have read, you should now concentrate on applying what you have learned.

The issues raised in this book are all time-honored questions from the *practical application of effective management*. I would advise you to start with those that are of greatest use to you personally and then take it from there. It is not very important where you begin, as long as you ultimately end up running through all the questions. The three parts of the book cover the essentials of management, and each chapter presents an important module for effective management. All the modules are compatible with each other.

With very few exceptions, *all* organizations can be made both more *effective* and more *efficient*. Often it is the best-performing organizations and managers that steadily endeavor to boost their achievement potential even further.

What do you need to bear in mind at the implementation stage?
1. Make sure your objective is clear
Make certain you know exactly *why* you want to acquire the know-how

in question. The reasons should be *yours,* reasons that make sense to *you,* and only *you* can define them. So be honest with yourself about what motivates you to learn how to manage *effectively, efficiently, and responsibly.* If you have a compelling reason, you will be able to draw strength and stamina from it when the going gets tough. Practicing effective management *competently* is a tall order, as is applying expertise in any of the various disciplines that exist. However, management *can be learned* and is *extremely rewarding.* If the examples and achievements presented in this book have inspired you, know that *management know-how* is the *knowledge of how to succeed.*

There are no real secrets in management. As already stated in the Preface, if you apply this know-how, you will become exceedingly *effective,* highly *efficient,* and probably also extremely *successful.*

2. Focus on one thing at a time

If there *was* a secret in management, it would be to *focus on one thing at a time.* In this respect you should be *uncompromising* in your implementation of effective management, taking up only a *single* issue and then really seeing it through. The more you concentrate on one topic, the sooner it will become a habit; and you will then build on it by concentrating on the next issue. There simply is no faster way of becoming effective and efficient in the long run.

If you choose a different path, you will run a major risk of gaining some mastery in different domains, but of never becoming truly competent in any of them: and the greatest danger then will be that you will break off your implementation because it does not yield results or bring you success. You are better off concentrating on *one* thing, for therein lies the key to success.

3. Make entries on your own schedule

Enter on your schedule the issues on which you intend to focus. Everything takes time, and only if you *systematically allocate yourself the time* to work on an issue will you achieve results. Otherwise you will be left with nothing but good intentions. Since many of the issues in question will need to be discussed with your colleagues, workers, or boss, and perhaps even with customers or other people outside your organization, you will also need to schedule appointments for such discussions. Entries on a manager's schedule stand a good chance of being attended to, whereas anything not allotted any time will simply not get done. Take enough time to really think issues through to their logical conclusion. This may not be difficult, but you must ensure that you actually do it and invest the necessary effort. Otherwise you will be "found out" at the implementation stage.

4. Make sure that any measures are clearly defined

One key question asked by organizations that are good at implementation is this: *who will do what by when?*

If the decision about *what* needs to be done is made by one manager or a group of managers, a *specific person* must be designated to take responsibility for implementing that decision. The individual in question will need to ensure that the decision *is indeed carried out*, but the responsibility for the decision will remain with the person or group that made it. All experience indicates that strength of implementation results from *individual responsibility*, so do not make a team, group, or body responsible.

Next, make sure that each measure has a *specific deadline* for its completion. It is better to set tight, as opposed to generous, deadlines, because you will mostly find it easier to allow yourself a little more time than to bring a deadline forward.

When decisions are made in your organization, be aware that you can never win *everyone*'s support. If you are interested in becoming a strong implementer, concentrate on convincing the *key people* to back a decision. The number of such people will often be rather small but their word will carry clout, being the best minds in your organization. Experienced senior managers go to great lengths to promote *consensus* among such top people and secure their *commitment* because they know that implementing something *against the will* of such powerful individuals will almost inevitably end in failure. Indeed, this is only logical, because they are the best, most highly respected managers. And if they disagree among themselves about what needs to be done, how can the other members of the organization in question be expected to know?

5. Make certain that decisions are actually implemented

Once a decision has been made, organizations that are strong on implementation do not lose sight of it until it has either been implemented or postponed with good reason. But no decision ever gets forgotten. Everything gets *followed up*. So make sure that you have an absolutely watertight system for implementing decisions. Note *in writing* any matters you intend to deal with yourself or have delegated to others and *always set a deadline* for following up on them. This is not difficult, but it does take *discipline*. Above all, take a look at the results yourself; do not merely rely on reports by others. Strength of implementation is achieved by doggedly following up until the desired result has been achieved. This might not always make life comfortable for the people around you, but it *will* make you effective and respected. Managers' performance is convincing when they achieve important results for their organization. It is by doing this that they display their competence and show what an impact they can have.

Management is one of the most fascinating topics there is. If you apply management know-how, there is almost no limit to what you can achieve.

So what will you start doing tomorrow?

The introduction to this book began with the sentence: "*Management know-how is the key to success for individuals, organizations, and societies.*" Now it is up to you to seize the opportunities such know-how opens up to you.

BIBLIOGRAPHY

Allen, David: *Getting Things Done: The Art of Stress-Free Productivity*, New York: Penguin Books, 2001.

Beatty, Jack: *The World According to Peter Drucker*, New York: Broadway Books, 1998.

Beaujean, Alfred, Beer, Monika, et al.: *Harenberg Opernführer: Der Schlüssel zu 500 Opern, ihrer Handlung und Geschichte*, 3rd revised and expanded edition, Dortmund, Germany: Harenberg Verlag, 2002.

Beaujean, Alfred, Brembeck, Reinhard, et al.: *Harenberg Konzertführer: Der Schlüssel zu 600 Werken von 200 Komponisten*, 6th edition, Dortmund, Germany: Harenberg Verlag, 2001.

Beer, Stafford: *The Heart of Enterprise*, 4th edition, Chichester, UK: John Wiley & Sons, 2000.

Bennis, Warren: *On Becoming a Leader*, Reading, MA: Perseus Books, 1994.

Biden, Joe: *Promises to Keep: On Life and Politics*, New York: Random House, 2007.

Bossidy, Larry, and Charan, Ram: *Execution: The Discipline of Getting Things Done*, New York: Crown Business, 2002.

Braun, Richard: *Harenberg Komponistenlexikon: 760 Komponisten und 1060 Meilensteine der Musik*, Mannheim, Germany: Meyers Lexikonverlag, 2004.

Buzan, Tony, and Buzan, Barry: *The Mind Map Book,* 4th edition, Harlow, UK: BBC Active, 2006.

Clausewitz, Carl von: *On War,* Oxford, UK: Oxford University Press, 2007 (first published in Berlin, Germany by Dümmlers Verlag, 1832).

Clinton, Hillary Rodham: *Living History,* New York: Scribner Publisher, 2004.

Cohen, William A.: *A Class with Drucker: The Lost Lessons of the World's Greatest Management Teacher*, New York: AMACOM, 2008.

Cohen, William A.: *Drucker on Leadership: New Lessons from the Father of Modern Management*, San Francisco: Jossey-Bass, 2010.

Collins, Jim, and Lazier, William: *Beyond Entrepreneurship: Turning Your Business into an Enduring Great Company*, New York: Prentice Hall, 1992.

Collins, Jim, and Porras, Jerry I.: *Built to Last: Successful Habits of Visionary Companies*, 2nd edition, New York: HarperCollins Publishers, 1997.

Collins, Jim: *Good to Great: Why Some Companies Make the Leap And Others Don't*, New York: HarperCollins Publishers, 2001.

Collins, Jim: *Good to Great and the Social Sectors: A Monograph to Accompany Good to Great*, New York: HarperCollins Publishers, 2005.

Collins, Jim: *How the Mighty Fall: Why Some Companies Never Give In*, New York: HarperCollins Publishers, 2009.

Covey, Stephen R.: *The 7 Habits of Highly Effective People*, revised edition, New York: Free Press, 2004.

Crainer, Stuart: *The 75 Greatest Management Decisions Ever Made . . . and 21 of the Worst*, New York: AMACOM, 1999.

Cray, Ed: *General of the Army: George C. Marshall, Soldier and Statesman*, New York: Cooper Square Press, 2000.

Csikszentmihalyi, Mihaly: *Flow: The Psychology of Optimal Experience*, New York: Harper Perennial Modern Classics, 2008.

Cunningham, Lawrence: *The Essays of Warren Buffett: Lessons for Investors and Managers*, 3rd edition, Singapore: John Wiley & Sons, 2002.

Dell, Michael, and Fredman, Catherine: *Direct from Dell: Strategies That Revolutionized an Industry*, 2nd edition, New York: HarperCollins Publishers, 2006.

Dietz, Wolfgang et al.: *Der Brockhaus Geschichte: Personen, Daten, Hintergründe*, Mannheim, Germany: Brockhaus Verlag, 2003.

Drucker, Peter F.: *Adventures of a Bystander*, 5th edition (Harper & Row Publishers, 1978), New Brunswick, London: Transaction Publishers, 2005.

Drucker, Peter F.: *The Age of Discontinuity: Guidelines to Our Changing Society*, reprinted edition (Harper & Row Publishers, 1969) New Brunswick/London: Transaction Publishers, 1992.

Drucker, Peter F.: *Concept of the Corporation*, 5th edition (John Day Company 1946), New Brunswick, London: Transaction Publishers, 2005.

Drucker, Peter F.: *The Effective Executive: The Definitive Guide to Getting the Right Things Done*, reprinted edition (Harper & Row Publishers, 1967), New York: HarperCollins Publishers, 2006.

Drucker, Peter F.: *The End of Economic Man: The Origins of Totalitarianism*, 4th edition (John Day Company, 1939), New Brunswick/London: Transaction Publishers, 2005.

Drucker, Peter F.: *The Essential Drucker*, reprint edition, Burlington, MA, Oxford: Butterworth-Heinemann, 2006.

Drucker, Peter F.: *Innovation and Entrepreneurship: Practice and Principles*, reprint edition (Harper & Row Publishers, 1985), New York: HarperCollins Publishers, 1993.

Drucker, Peter F.: *Management Challenges for the 21st Century*, reprint edition (HarperCollins Publishers, 1999), Oxford: Butterworth-Heinemann, 2005.

Drucker, Peter F.: *Management: Tasks, Responsibilities, Practices*, reprint edition (Harper & Row Publishers, 1973), New York: HarperCollins Publishers, 1993. (This original source was later thoroughly updated and published as *Management: Revised Edition.*)

Drucker, Peter F.: *Managing for the Future: The 1990s and Beyond*, Oxford: BCA by arrangement with Butterworth-Heinemann, 1992.

Drucker, Peter F.: *Managing the Non-Profit Organization: Principles and Practices*, New York: HarperCollins Publishers, 1990.

Drucker, Peter F.: *Managing for Results*, reprint edition (Harper & Row Publishers, 1964), Oxford: Butterworth-Heinemann, 1999.

Drucker, Peter F.: *The New Realities*, reprint edition (Heinemann Professional Publishing, 1989), New Brunswick: Transaction Publishers, 2003.

Drucker, Peter F.: *The Practice of Management*, reprint edition (Harper & Row Publishers, 1954), New York: HarperCollins Publishers, 2006.

Drucker, Peter F., and Maciariello, Joseph A.: *Management*, revised edition; edition of *Management: Tasks, Responsibilities, Practices*, Harper & Row, 1973 (New York: HarperCollins Publisher, 2008).

Drucker, Peter F., and Maciariello, Joseph A.: *Management Cases*, revised edition, New York: HarperCollins Publishers, 2009.

Drucker, Peter F., and Nakauchi, Isao: *Drucker on Asia: A Dialogue between Peter Drucker and Isao Nakauchi*, reprint edition (Diamond Inc. Tokyo, 1995), Oxford: Butterworth-Heinemann, 1997.

Drucker, Peter F., and Wartzman, Rick: *The Drucker Lectures: Essential Lessons on Management, Society and Economy*, New York: McGraw-Hill, 2010.

Ebert, Johannes, and Schmid, Andreas: *Chronik des 20. Jahrhunderts*, Gütersloh, Germany: Chronik Verlag, 2000.

Ellis, Joseph J.: *Founding Brothers—The Revolutionary Generation*, New York: Alfred A. Knopf, 2000.

Fassmann, Kurt (ed.): *Die Großen: Leben und Leistung der 600 bedeutendsten Persönlichkeiten unserer Welt*, 24 volumes, Zurich, Switzerland: Haus Coron, Kindler Verlag, 1976.

Fölsing Albrecht: *Albert Einstein: A Biography*, London/New York: Penguin Books, 1997.

Forcellino, Antonio: *Michelangelo: A Tormented Life*, Cambridge, UK: Polity Press, 2009.

Förster, Stig, Pöhlmann, Markus, and Walter, Dierk (ed.): *Kriegsherren der Weltgeschichte: 22 historische Portraits* (Warlords in World History: 22 Historical Portraits), Munich, Germany: C.H. Beck Verlag, 2006.

Frankl, Viktor E.: *Man's Search For Meaning*, 6th edition (first published in 1946 as *From Death-Camp to Existentialism: A Psychiatrist's Path to a New Therapy*), Boston: Beacon Press, 2006.

Frankl, Viktor E.: *The Will to Meaning: Foundations and Applications of Logotherapy*, New York, Plume Books, 1988.

Franklin, Benjamin: *The Autobiography of Benjamin Franklin*, New York: Dover Publications, 1996.

Franklin, Peter: *The Life of Mahler (Musical Lives)*, Cambridge, UK: Cambridge University Press, 1997.

Freiberg, Kevin, and Freiberg, Jackie: *Nuts! Southwest Airlines' Crazy Recipe for Business and Personal Success*, New York: Broadway Books, 1998.

Gates, Bill: *Business @The Speed of Thought: Using a Digital Nervous System*, New York: Warner Books, 1999.

Gerstner, Louis V., Jr.: *Who Says Elephants Can't Dance?: Inside IBM's Historic Turnaround*, London: HarperCollins Publishers, 2002.

Gibbon, Edward: *The History of the Decline and Fall of the Roman Empire*, abridged edition (first published in six volumes in 1776), London/New York: Penguin Books, 2000.

Gladwell, Malcolm: *Outliers: The Story of Success*, New York: Little Brown and Company, 2008.

Gladwell, Malcolm: *The Tipping Point: How Little Things Can Make a Big Difference*, New York: Back Bay Books, 2002.

Goldratt, Eliyahu M., and Cox, Jeff: *The Goal: A Process of Ongoing Improvement*, 3rd revised edition, Great Barrington, MA: North River Press, 2004.

Gracián, Baltasar: *The Art of Worldly Wisdom*, (first published in Spanish as *Oráculo manual y arte de prudencia*, Huesca 1647), Radford, VA: Wilder Publications, 2009.

Gradenwitz, Peter: *Leonard Bernstein: The Infinite Variety of a Musician*, Oxford, UK: Berg Publishers, 1987.

Grove, Andrew S.: *Only the Paranoid Survive: How to Exploit the Crisis Points that Challenge Every Company*, New York: Currency NS Doubleday, 1999.

Harriss, Joseph: *The Tallest Tower: Eiffel and the Belle Epoque,* 2nd edition, Bloomington, IN: Unlimited Publishing, 2004.

Hollister, Geoff: *Out of Nowhere: The Inside Story of How Nike Marketed the Culture of Running,* Aachen, Germany: Meyer & Meyer Sport, 2008.

Honour, Hugh, and Flemming, John: *A World History of Art,* 7th edition, London: Laurence King, 2009.

Jenkins, Roy: *Churchill,* 2nd edition, London/Oxford: Pan Books, 2002.

Kaiser, Joachim: *Harenberg Das Buch der 1000 Bücher: Werke, die die Welt bewegten, Autoren und Entstehung, Inhalt und Wirkung,* 3rd expanded and updated edition, Mannheim, Germany: Meyers Lexikonverlag, 2005.

Kim, W. Chan, and Mauborgne, Renée: *Blue Ocean Strategy: How to Create Uncontested Market Space and Make the Competition Irrelevant,* Cambridge, MA: Harvard Business School Press, 2005.

Klein, Stefan: *The Science of Happiness: How Our Brains Make Us Happy—and What We Can Do to Get Happier,* New York: Marlowe & Company, 2006.

Klein, Stefan: *The Secret Pulse of Time: Making Sense of Life's Scarcest Commodity,* reprint edition, Cambridge, MA: Da Capo Lifelong Books, 2009.

Krames, Jeffrey A.: *Inside Drucker's Brain,* New York: Portfolio, 2008.

Krames, Jeffrey A.: *What the Best CEOs Know: 7 Exceptional Leaders and Their Lessons for Transforming Any Business,* New York: McGraw-Hill, 2003.

Kroc, Ray: *Grinding It Out: The Making of McDonald's,* New York: St. Martin's Press, 1987.

Krockow, Christian von: *Churchill: Man of the Century,* London: London House, 2000.

Kurz, Joachim: *Bugatti: Der Mythos: Die Familie: Das Unternehmen,* Berlin, Germany: Econ Verlag, 2005.

Kurzke, Hermann: *Thomas Mann: Life as a Work of Art: A Biography,* Princeton, NJ: Princeton University Press, 2002.

Kustenmacher, Werner Tiki, and Seiwert, Lothar J.: *How to Simplify Your Life: Seven Practical Steps to Letting Go of Your Burdens and Living a Happier Life,* New York: McGraw-Hill Professional, 2004.

Landes, David: *Dynasties: Fortunes and Misfortunes of the World's Great Family Businesses,* New York: Viking, 2006.

Larsen, Kristine: *Stephen Hawking: A Biography,* New York: Prometheus Books, 2007.

Laue-Bothen, Christine; Issel, Ulrike; and Reuter, Ingrid (eds.): *Harenberg Das Buch der 1000 Frauen: Ideen, Ideale und Errungenschaften in Biografien,*

Bildern, und Dokumenten, Mannheim, Germany: Meyers Lexikonverlag, 2004.

Levinson, Jay Conrad: *Guerrilla Marketing: Easy and Inexpensive Strategies for Making Big Profits from Your Small Business*, 4th updated and expanded edition, Boston: Houghton Mifflin, 2007.

Locher, J. L.: *The Magic of M. C. Escher,* New York: Harry N. Abrams, 2000.

Machiavelli, Niccolo: *The Prince*, reprint edition, London: Penguin Books, 2003.

Malik, Fredmund: *Management: Das A und O des Handwerks*, updated edition, Frankfurt am Main/New York: Campus Verlag, 2007.

Malik, Fredmund: *Managing, Performing, Living: Effective Management for a New Era*, Frankfurt am Main, Germany/New York: Campus Verlag, 2006.

Malik, Fredmund: *Unternehmenspolitik und Corporate Governance: Wie Organisationen sich selbst organisieren*, Frankfurt am Main, Germany/New York: Campus Verlag, 2008.

Maucher, Helmut: *Management Breviary: A Guideline to Corporate Success*, Frankfurt am Main, Germany/New York: Campus Verlag, 2007.

McCullough, David: *Truman*, New York: Simon & Schuster, 1993.

McGregor, Douglas: *The Human Side of Enterprise*, 25th anniversary printing, New York/Chicago/San Francisco, et al.: McGraw-Hill, 1985.

McLynn, Frank: *Napoleon—A Biography*, reprint edition, New York: Arcade Publishing, 2011.

Menard, Pierre, and Vassal, Jacques: *Formula 1 Legends: Niki Lauda: The Rebel*, St. Sulpice, Switzerland: Chronosports, 2004.

Mintzberg, Henry: *Managers Not MBAs: A Hard Look at the Soft Practice of Managing and Management Development*, San Francisco: Berrett-Koehler Publishers, 2004.

Mintzberg, Henry: *Managing*, San Francisco: Berrett-Koehler Publishers, 2009

Mooney, Brian, and Simpson, Barry: *Breaking News: How the Wheels Came Off at Reuters*, Chichester, UK: Capstone Publishing Ltd, 2003.

Morand, Paul, with illustrations by Lagerfeld, Karl: *The Allure of Chanel*, London: Pushkin Press, 2010.

N.a.: *Brockhaus-Enzyklopädie* in 30 volumes, volume 21, fully revised edition, Mannheim, Germany: Brockhaus, 2006.

N.a.: *Business: The Ultimate Resource*, with an introduction by Goleman, Daniel, London: Bloomsbury Publishing Plc, 2002.

N.a.: *Die Großen der Moderne: Menschen, die unsere Welt prägten und veränderten*, authorized special edition, Cologne, Germany: Serges Verlag, 2001.

N.a.: *Michelin: Paris*, Clermont-Ferrand, France: Michelin et Cie, 1990.

N.a.: *Weltgeschichte*, volumes 1–36, authorized edition by Fischer-Taschen-buch-Verlag, Augsburg, Germany: Weltbild Verlag, 2000.

Obama, Barack: *The Audacity of Hope: Thoughts on Reclaiming the American Dream*, New York: Crown Publishers, 2006.

Obama, Barack: *Dreams from My Father*, reprint edition, New York: Crown Publishers, 2007.

O'Brian, Patrick: *Picasso: A Biography*, 2nd edition, New York and London: W. W. Norton & Company, 1994.

Osborne, Richard: *Herbert von Karajan: A Life in Music*, Boston: Northeastern University Press, 2000.

Packard, David: *The HP Way: How Bill Hewlett and I Built Our Company*, New York: HarperCollins Publisher, 2006.

Peters, Thomas J: *The Little Big Things—163 Ways to Pursue Excellence*, New York: Harper Business, 2010.

Peters, Thomas J., and Waterman, Robert H.: *In Search of Excellence: Lessons from America's Best-Run Companies*, New York: HarperBusiness Essentials, 2004.

Philipps-Matz, Mary Jane: *Verdi: A Biography*, New York: Oxford University Press, 1993.

Porter, Michael E.: *On Competition*, revised edition, Boston: Harvard Business Review Book, 1998.

Puryear, Edgar F., Jr.: *Nineteen Stars: A Study in Military Character and Leadership*, 2nd edition, New York: Presidio Press, 1981.

Rewald, John: *Cezanne—A Biography*, New York: Harry N. Abrams, 1996.

Rueger, Christoph (ed.): *Harenberg Klaviermusikführer*, 2nd revised edition, Dortmund, Germany: Harenberg Verlag, 1998.

Rupke, Nicolaas A.: *Alexander von Humboldt: A Metabiography*, Chicago/London: University of Chicago Press, 2008.

Schmied, Wieland, et al. (eds.): *Harenberg Malerlexikon: 1000 Künstler-Bio-grafien aus sieben Jahrhunderten*, 3rd reviewed edition, Mannheim, Germany: Meyers Lexikonverlag, 2007.

Schmied, Wieland, et al. (eds.): *Harenberg Museum der Malerei: 525 Meister-werke aus sieben Jahrhunderten*, Dortmund, Germany: Harenberg Lexikon Verlag, 1999.

Schneider, Wolf: *Die Sieger: Wodurch Genies, Phantasten und Verbrecher be-rühmt geworden sind*, 3rd edition, Zurich, Switzerland/Munich, Germany: Piper Verlag, 2001.

Schroeder, Alice: *The Snowball: Warren Buffett and the Business of Life*, updated and condensed edition, New York: Bantam Books, 2009.

Schumacher, Michael: *Schumacher: The Official Inside Story of the Formula One Icon*, London: Ebury Press, 2003.

Schumpeter, Joseph A.: *Capitalism, Socialism, and Democracy*, 6th edition (first published 1942), London: Routledge Chapman & Hall, 1994.

Seiwert, Lothar J.: *Wenn Du es eilig hast, gehe langsam: Das neue Zeitmanagement in einer beschleunigten Welt*, Frankfurt am Main, Germany/New York: Campus Verlag, 1998.

Senge, Peter M.: *The Fifth Discipline: The Art and Practice of the Learning Organization*, New York: Doubleday, 1990.

Simon, Hermann: *Beat the Crisis—33 Quick Solutions for Your Company*, New York: Springer, 2009.

Simon, Hermann: *Hidden Champions of the Twenty-First Century: The Success Strategies of Unknown World Market Leaders*, New York: Springer, 2009.

Sloan, Alfred P., Jr.: *My Years with General Motors*, McDonald, John, and Stevens, Catherine (eds.), New York/London/Toronto/Sydney/Auckland: Currency Doubleday, 1990.

Sprenger, Reinhard K.: *Trust: The Best Way to Manage*, Frankfurt am Main, Germany: Campus Verlag, 2007.

Stanley, Thomas, J., and Danko, William, D.: *The Millionaire Next Door: The Surprising Secrets of America's Wealthy*, New York: Pocket Books of Simon & Schuster, 1996.

Stauffer, René: *The Roger Federer Story: Quest for Perfection*, Washington, DC: New Chapter Press, 2007.

Stross, Randall E.: *The Wizard of Menlo Park: How Thomas Alva Edison Invented the Modern World*, New York: Three Rivers Press, 2007.

Surowiecki, James: *The Wisdom of the Crowds: Why the Many Are Smarter Than the Few and How Collective Wisdom Shapes Business, Economies, Societies, and Nations*, New York: Doubleday, 2004.

Taylor, Frederick Winslow: *The Principles of Scientific Management*, reprint edition, Mineola, NY: Dover Publications, 2003.

Tzu, Sun: *The Art of War*, reprint edition, Oxford/London/New York: Oxford University Press, 1971.

Vasari, Giorgio: *The Lives of The Artists*, (the Italian original dates from 1550–1568), reprint edition, New York: Oxford University Press, 1998.

Vise, David A.: *The Google Story: Inside the Hottest Business, Media and Technology Success of Our Time*, Basingstoke/Oxford: Pan Books, 2008.

Walton, Sam, and Huey, John: *Made in America: My Story*, reprint edition, New York: Doubleday, 2003.

Watson, Thomas J., Jr.: *A Business and Its Beliefs,* New York: McGraw-Hill, 2003.

Welch, Jack, and Byrne, John: *Jack: Straight from the Gut,* New York: Business Plus, 2003.

Welch, Jack, and Welch, Suzy: *Winning,* New York: HarperCollins Publishers, 2005.

Welch, Jack, and Welch, Suzy: *Winning: The Answers: Confronting 74 of the Toughest Questions in Business Today,* New York: HarperCollins Publishers, 2006.

Whiting, Jim: *The Life and Times of Leonard Bernstein* (Masters of Music: The World's Greatest Composers series), Hockessin, DE: Mitchell Lane Publishers, 2005.

Witzel, Morgen: *Builders and Dreamers: The Making and Meaning of Management,* London/New York: Financial Times Prentice Hall, 2002.

Young, Jeffrey S., and Simon, William L.: *iCon Steve Jobs: The Greatest Second Act in the History of Business,* revised edition, Hoboken, NJ/Chichester, UK: Wiley 2005.

Yunus, Muhammad, with Weber, Karl: *Creating a World without Poverty: Social Business and the Future of Capitalism,* New York: Public Affairs, 2007.

NOTES

Chapter 1: Harness the power of a business mission

1. See http:// http://www.microsoft.com/about/en/us/default.aspx, Our Mission and Our Values, as consulted on May 13, 2011.

2. See http://www.microsoft.com/about/companyinformation/ourbusinesses/profile.mspx, Microsoft's Tradition of Innovation: from Revolution to Evolution, as consulted on May 13, 2011.

3. See also Drucker, Peter F. and Maciariello, Joseph A.: *Management*, revised edition, New York, HarperCollins Publishers, 2008 (revised edition of *Management: Tasks, Responsibilities, Practices*, Harper & Row, 1973), p. 85 ff., Chapter 8 "The Theory of the Business," and Malik, Fredmund: *Management: Das A und O des Handwerks*, updated edition, Frankfurt am Main, Germany/New York: Campus Verlag, 2007, p. 170 ff.

Chapter 2: Create customer value

1. Krames, Jeffrey: *What the Best CEOs Know: 7 Exceptional Leaders and Their Lessons for Transforming Any Business*, New York: McGraw-Hill, 2003, p. 110.

2. Ibid., p. 115.

3. Drucker, Peter F.: *The Practice of Management*, reprint edition (Harper & Row Publishers, 1954), New York: HarperCollins, 2006, p. 37.

4. Venohr, Bernd: Wachsen wie Würth: Das Geheimnis des Welterfolgs, Frankfurt am Main, Germany: Campus Verlag, 2006, p. 55; translation by Frank Arnold.

5. Krames, Jeffrey: *What the Best CEOs Know: 7 Exceptional Leaders and Their Lessons for Transforming Any Business*, New York: McGraw-Hill 2003, p. 120.

6. Ibid., p. 107.

Chapter 3: Make effective decisions

1. Drucker, Peter F.: *Management: Tasks, Responsibilities, Practices*, reprint

edition (Harper & Row Publishers, 1973), New York: HarperCollins Publishers, 1993, p. 472; see also Drucker, Peter F.: *Adventures of a Bystander*, 5th edition (Harper & Row Publishers, 1978), New Brunswick, London: Transaction Publishers, 2005, p. 287.

2. Based on Drucker, Peter F.: *The Effective Executive: The Definitive Guide to Getting the Right Things Done*, reprint edition (Harper & Row Publishers, 1967), New York: HarperCollins Publishers, 2006, pp. 122–140. Complemented based on Malik, who follows lines similar to those of Drucker; see: Malik, Fredmund: *Managing, Performing, Living: Effective Management for a New Era*, Frankfurt am Main, Germany/New York: Campus Verlag, 2006, pp. 188–189.

3. Sloan, Alfred P., Jr.: *My Years with General Motors*, McDonald, John, and Stevens, Catherine (eds.), New York/London/Toronto, Sydney/Auckland: Currency Doubleday, 1990.

Chapter 5: Make the right compromise

1. New American Standard Bible: 1 Kings 3:16–28, Anaheim, CA: Foundation Publications, Inc., 1998.

2. Drucker, Peter F.: *The Effective Executive: The Definitive Guide to Getting the Right Things Done*, (Harper & Row Publishers, 1967), New York: HarperCollins Publishers, 2006, p. 135.

Chapter 6: Just do it! Keep fine-tuning the right strategy

1. Drucker, Peter F.: *Managing the Non-Profit Organization: Principles and Practices*, New York: HarperCollins Publishers, 1990, p. 59.

2. Transcript of J. B. Bird's interview with Herb Kelleher on July 9, 2002, at Southwest Airlines headquarters in Dallas, reproduced on the Web site of the University of Texas at Austin's McCombs School of Business, see http://www.mccombs.utexas.edu/news/pressreleases/kelleher_into3.asp.

Chapter 7: Structure your organization around the customer

1. Dell, Michael, and Fredman, Catherine: *Direct from Dell: Strategies That Revolutionized an Industry*, 2nd edition, New York: HarperCollins Publishers, 2006, p. 22.

2. See Malik, Fredmund: *Management: Das A und O des Handwerks*, updated edition, Frankfurt am Main, Germany/New York: Campus Verlag, 2007, p. 218; translation by Frank Arnold.

3. Dell, Michael, and Fredman, Catherine: *Direct from Dell: Strategies That*

Revolutionized an Industry, 2nd edition, New York: HarperCollins Publishers, 2006, p. 39.

4. See Malik, Fredmund: *Die richtige Corporate Governance: Mit wirksamer Unter¬nehmensaufsicht Komplexität meistern,* Frankfurt am Main, Germany/New York: Campus Verlag, 2008, p. 221; translation by Frank Arnold, based on Drucker, Peter F.: *Management: Tasks, Responsibilities, Practices,* reprinted edition (Harper & Row Publishers, 1973), New York: HarperCollins Publishers, 1993, pp. 611 ff.

Chapter 8: Be productive

1. Krames, Jeffrey: *What the Best CEOs Know: 7 Exceptional Leaders and Their Lessons for Transforming Any Business,* New York: McGraw-Hill, 2003, p. 153.
2. Ibid., p. 162.

Chapter 9: Demand effective management

1. See Drucker, Peter F.: *The Essential Drucker,* reprint edition, Burlington, MA, Oxford: Butterworth-Heinemann, 2006. p. 8, and Drucker, Peter F.: *The New Realities,* reprint edition (Heinemann Professional Publishing, 1989), New Brunswick, NJ: Transaction Publishers, 2003, p. 220.
2. Berkshire Hathaway Inc.: "Annual Report 2008," Omaha, NB, 2009, p. 93.
3. *Fortune,* online edition: "A Conversation with Warren Buffett," June 25, 2006, cited in http://money.cnn.com/2006/06/25/magazines/fortune/charity2 .fortune/index.htm.

Chapter 10: Understand profit; strive for independence

1. N.a.: *Die Großen der Moderne: Menschen, die unsere Welt prägten und veränderten,* authorized special edition, Cologne, Germany: Serges Verlag, 2001, p. 92; translation by Frank Arnold.
2. Sichtermann, Barbara: *50 Klassiker Frauen: Die berühmtesten Frauengestalten der Geschichte,* 2nd edition, Hildesheim, Germany: Gerstenberg-Verlag, 2001, p. 202; translation by Frank Arnold.

Chapter 12: Understand your sphere of action

1. *The Economist,* see the contents section of every current edition, p. 3.
2. *The Economist,* online edition, "About Us" section, May 10, 2011.
3. Peter F. Drucker in a lecture on innovation; from lecture notes taken by Frank Arnold.

Chapter 13: Recognize inflection points and utilize performance indicators

1. Krames, Jeffrey: *What the Best CEOs Know: 7 Exceptional Leaders and Their Lessons for Transforming Any Business,* New York: McGraw-Hill, 2003, p. 136.
2. Grove, Andrew S.: *Only the Paranoid Survive: How to Exploit the Crisis Points that Challenge Every Company,* New York: Currency NS Doubleday, 1999, p. 89.
3. Ibid., p. 118.
4. Ibid., p. 20.
5. Ibid., back cover.
6. For more information, see Drucker, Peter F.: *The Practice of Management,* reprint edition (Harper & Row Publishers, 1954), New York: HarperCollins, 2006, p. 62ff. Drucker also described the first five objectives of performance in (among other places) *Managing for the Future,* specifying the fourth point in terms of "liquidity and cash flow"; see Drucker, Peter F.: *Managing for the Future: The 1990s and Beyond,* Oxford: BCA by arrangement with Butterworth-Heinemann, 1992, pp. 210–214.

Chapter 14: Secure feedback

1. Gracián, Baltasar: *The Art of Worldly Wisdom,* (first published in Spanish as Oráculo manual Y arte de prudencia, Huesca, 1647), Radford, VA: Wilder Publications, 2009.
2. Cray, Ed: *General of the Army: George C. Marshall, Soldier and Statesman,* New York: Cooper Square Press, 2000, p. 530.

Chapter 16: Remember, innovations are rarely welcomed with open arms

1. Yee, Roger: *Jean-Pierre Heim, Architect,* New York, Visual Reference Publications, 2003, p. 121.
2. Davidson, Frank P., and Lusk Brooke, Kathleen: *Building the World: An Encyclopaedia of the Great Engineering Projects in History,* two volumes (Greenwood Publishing Group, Oxford, 2006), Volume 1, Chapter 20, cited at http://buildingtheworld.com/book/featured/, as consulted on January 24, 2011.

Chapter 18: Innovate systematically

1. Pacher, Maurus: *Harenberg Anekdotenlexikon: 3 868 pointierte Kurzgeschichten über mehr als 1 150 Persönlichkeiten aus Politik, Kultur und Gesellschaft,* Dortmund, Germany: Harenberg Lexikon Verlag, 2000, p. 304; translation by Frank Arnold.

2. Schneider, Wolf: *Die Sieger: Wodurch Genies, Phantasten und Verbrecher berühmt geworden sind,* 3rd edition, Zurich, Switzerland/Munich, Germany: Piper Verlag, 2001, p. 170; translation by Frank Arnold.

3. Ibid.

4. Based on Drucker, Peter F.: *Innovation and Entrepreneurship: Practice and Principles,* reprint edition (Perennial Library, 1986), New York: HarperCollins Publishers, 1993, p. 35.

5. Pacher, Maurus: *Harenberg Anekdotenlexikon,* Dortmund, Germany: Harenberg Lexikon Verlag, 2000, p. 304; translation by Frank Arnold.

Chapter 19: Exploit success

1. Frankfurter Allgemeine Sonntagszeitung, "Der Milliardär mit der Dose," April 7, 2002; translation by Frank Arnold.

2. *Forbes Special Issue Billionaires,* "The World's Richest People, the Soda with Buzz," March 28, 2005.

3. Frankfurter Allgemeine Sonntagszeitung, "Der Milliardär mit der Dose," April 7, 2002; translation by Frank Arnold.

Chapter 20: Practice purposeful abandonment

1. Drucker, Peter F.: *Managing for Results,* reprint edition (Harper & Row Publishers, 1964), Oxford: Butterworth-Heinemann, 1999, pp. 134–136, 204–207; Drucker, Peter F.: *The Effective Executive: The Definitive Guide to Getting the Right Things Done,* reprint edition (Harper & Row Publishers, 1967), New York: HarperCollins Publishers, 2006, pp. 104–108.

2. Vasari, Giorgio: *Lebensläufe der berühmtesten Maler, Bildhauer und Architekten,* Zurich, Switzerland: Manesse Verlag, 1974, 2005, (originally published in Italy in 1550 and partly rewritten and enlarged in 1568), p. 317; translated by Frank Arnold.

3. Welch, Jack, and Byrne, John: *Jack: Straight from the Gut,* New York: Business Plus, 2003, p. 132.

Chapter 21: Practice creative destruction

1. Schumpeter, Joseph A.: *Capitalism, Socialism, and Democracy,* 6th edition (first published in 1942), London: Routledge Chapman & Hall, 1994, p. 83.

2. Frankfurter Allgemeine Zeitung, online edition, "Walkman des 21. Jahrhunderts: 100 Millionen iPods verkauft," April 9, 2007, Spiegel, online edition, "iTunes wird immer dominanter," August 19, 2009.

3. Stein, Leonard (ed.) with translations by Leo Black: *Style and Idea: Selected Writings of Arnold Schönberg,* University of California Press, 1984, p. 226.

Chapter 23: Exploit opportunities arising from new technologies

1. *Fortune*, "The best advice I ever got," http://money.cnn.com/galleries/2008/fortune/0804/gallery.bestadvice.fortune/2.html, consulted on April 13, 2011.
2. Bill Gates, September 11, 2000, Sidney, Australia in: Krames, Jeffrey: *What the Best CEOs Know: 7 Exceptional Leaders and Their Lessons for Transforming Any Business*, New York: McGraw-Hill, 2003, p. 154.
3. See http://investor.google.com/conduct.html, September 22, 2010.

Chapter 24: Recognize the future that has already happened

1. Brown, Tom; Davis, Stan; Meyer, Christopher; et al.: *Business: The Ultimate Resource,* with an introduction by Daniel Goleman, London: Bloomsbury Publishing Plc, 2002, p. 1104.

Chapter 25: Focus on a single objective

1. Rapelli, Paola: *Symbols of Power in Art: A Guide to Imagery*, Los Angeles: J. Paul Getty Museum, 2011, p. 344.
2. Rüdiger, Wilhelm: "Michelangelo" in: Fassmann, Kurt (ed.): *Die Großen: Leben und Leistung der 600 bedeutendsten Persönlichkeiten unserer Welt,* 24 volumes, Zurich, Switzerland: Haus Coron, Kindler Verlag, 1976, Volume IV/2, p. 720; translated by Frank Arnold.
3. Ibid., p. 724.
4. Drucker, Peter F.: *Adventures of a Bystander,* 5th edition (Harper & Row Publishers, 1978), New Brunswick, London: Transaction Publishers, 2005, p. 255.
5. Vasari, Giorgio: *The Lives of the Artists*, (the Italian original dates from 1550–1568), reprint edition, New York: Oxford University Press, 1998, p. 297.
6. Ibid., p. 460.

Chapter 26: Create a perfect whole

1. Welch, Jack, and Welch, Suzy: *Winning*, New York: HarperCollins Publishers, 2005, p. 63.
2. Ibid, p. 68.

Chapter 27: Be results driven

1. See Der Spiegel, online edition, "Michael Schumachers F1-Rekorde," July 30, 2009.

Chapter 28: Draw on your strengths

1. Calaprice, Alice. (ed.): *The Expanded Quotable Einstein*. Princeton, N J: Princeton University Press, 2000, p. 155, cited in Root-Bernstein, Michele and Robert: "Einstein on Creative Thinking: Music and the Intuitive Art of Scientific Imagination," *Psychology Today*, March 31, 2010 at http://www.psychologytoday.com/blog/imagine/201003/einstein-creative-thinking-music-and-the-intuitive-art-scientific-imagination.
2. Letter to Paul Plaut, October 23, 1928: Einstein Archive 28-065; quoted in Dukas and Hoffmann, *Albert Einstein, the Human Side*, p. 78, cited at http://www.asl-associates.com/einsteinquotes.htm.
3. Einstein, A.: "On My Participation in the Atom Bomb Project," short essay cited at http://www.atomicarchive.com/Docs/Hiroshima/EinsteinResponse.shtml, August 15, 2010.
4. Drucker, Peter F.: *The Practice of Management*, reprint edition (Harper & Row Publishers, 1954), New York: HarperCollins, 2006, p. 144.
5. Drucker, Peter F.: *Managing the Non-Profit Organization: Principles and Practices*, New York: HarperCollins Publishers, 1990, p. 148.
6. Pacher, Maurus: *Harenberg Anekdotenlexikon: 3868 pointierte Kurzgeschichten über mehr als 1150 Persönlichkeiten aus Politik, Kultur und Gesellschaft*, Dortmund, Germany: Harenberg Lexikon Verlag, 2000, p. 311; translated by Frank Arnold.

Chapter 29: Manage by objectives

1. Persché, Gerhard: "Gustav Mahler," in: *Harenberg Konzertführer: Der Schlüssel zu 600 Werken von 200 Komponisten*, 6th edition, Dortmund, Germany: Harenberg Verlag, 2001, p. 498; translated by Frank Arnold.

Chapter 30: Plan meticulously

1. Clausewitz, Carl von: *On War*, Oxford: Oxford University Press, 2007 (first published in Berlin, Germany; by Dümmlers Verlag 1832), p. 134.
2. Ibid., p. 65.

Chapter 31: Be true to your own values

1. Jenkins, Roy: *Churchill*, 2nd edition, London/Oxford: Pan Books 2002, p. 591.
2. Mendelssohn, Peter de: "Winston Churchill," in: Fassmann, Kurt (ed.): *Die Großen: Leben und Leistung der 600 bedeutendsten Persönlichkeiten unserer Welt*, vol. IX/2 Zurich. Switzerland: Haus Coron, Kindler Verlag, p. 882; translated by Frank Arnold.
3. Ibid., p. 894.

Chapter 32: Surround yourself with good people

1. Drucker, Peter F.: *Adventures of a Bystander*, 5th edition (Harper & Row Publishers, 1978), New Brunswick, London: Transaction Publishers, 2005, p. 280–281.
2. Welch, Jack, and Welch, Suzy: *Winning*, New York: HarperCollins Publishers, 2005, p. 89.
3. Ibid., p.90.
4. Braun, Richard: *Harenberg Komponistenlexikon: 760 Komponisten und 1060 Meilensteine der Musik*, Mannheim, Germany: Meyers Lexikonverlag, 2004, p. 743; translated by Frank Arnold.

Chapter 33: Create a culture of effectiveness

1. Donlan, J. P.: "Air Herb's Secret Weapon, Chief Executive," July-August 1999, p. 32 in: Krames, Jeffrey: *What the Best CEOs Know: 7 Exceptional Leaders and Their Lessons for Transforming Any Business*, New York: McGraw-Hill, 2003, p. 181.
2. Maucher, Helmut: *Management Breviary: A Guideline to Corporate Success*, Frankfurt am Main, Germany/New York: Campus Verlag, 2007, p. 49.

Chapter 34: Nurture and develop people

1. N.a.: *Management*, vol. 2, Frankfurt am Main, Germany/New York: Campus Verlag, 2003, p. 1383; translated by Frank Arnold.
2. Drucker, Peter F.: *Managing the Non-Profit Organization: Principles and Practices*, New York: HarperCollins Publishers, 1990, p. 151.

Chapter 35: Invest in training

1. Knopp, Guido, and Arens, Peter: *Unsere Besten: Die 100 größten Deutschen*, Munich, Germany: Econ Verlag, 2003, p. 162; translated by Frank Arnold.
2. Meyer-Abich, Adolf: "Alexander von Humboldt," p. 201, in: Fassmann, Kurt (ed.): *Die Großen: Leben und Leistung der 600 bedeutendsten Persönlichkeiten unserer Welt*, 24 volumes, Zurich, Switzerland: Haus Coron, Kindler Verlag, 1976, vol. VII/1, pp. 194–219; translated by Frank Arnold.
3. First published in Paris in 1814 and titled *Relation du voyage aux régions équinoxiales du nouveau continent*.
4. Knopp, Guido, and Arens, Peter: *Unsere Besten: Die 100 größten Deutschen*, Munich, Germany: Econ Verlag, 2003, p. 161; translated by Frank Arnold.
5. Zimmermann, Martin (ed.): *Allgemeinbildung: Große Persönlichkeiten,*

Würzburg, Germany: Arena Verlag, 2004, p. 208; translated by Frank Arnold.

6. Maucher, Helmut: *Management Breviary: A Guideline to Corporate Success*, Frankfurt am Main, Germany/New York: Campus Verlag, 2007, p. 164.

Chapter 36: Seek wise dialogue partners

1. Musée d'Orsay Web site archive: "Cézanne & Pissarro 1865–1885;" translated by Frank Arnold.
2. Welch, Jack, and Welch, Suzy: *Winning*, New York: HarperCollins Publishers, 2005, p. 291.
3. *Fortune*, "The Best Advice I Ever Got," interviews conducted by Julia Boorstin, March 21, 2005, consulted on July 2, 2009, http://money.cnn.com/magazines/fortune/fortune_archive/2005/03/21/8254830/index.htm

Chapter 38: Establish effective cooperation

1. Tagesschau, online edition: "Obamas 'Running Mate' Joe Biden im Porträt," September 23, 2008; translated by Frank Arnold.
2. *Financial Times* Deutschland online edition: "Joe Biden: Der heimliche Außenminister," November 11, 2008; translated by Frank Arnold.
3. Welch, Jack, and Welch, Suzy: *Winning*, New York: HarperCollins Publishers, 2005, p 302.

Chapter 40: Embody integrity

1. Cray, Ed: *General of the Army: George C. Marshall, Soldier and Statesman*, New York: Cooper Square Press. 2000, p. xi.
2. Ibid., p. xiii.

Chapter 41: Harness the potential of women

1. Simon, Hermann: *Hidden Champions of the 21st Century: Success Strategies of Unknown World Market Leaders*, New York: Springer, 2009, p. 294.

Chapter 42: Make intelligent use of your time

1. See http://www.hawking.org.uk, Disability, June 22, 2011.
2. Jenkins, Roy: *Churchill*, 2nd edition, London, Oxford: Pan Books, 2002, p. 647.
3. On the Web site www.arnoldmanagement.com you will find plenty of more useful information on the topic of time management

Chapter 43: Perfect your own working methods

1. See Drucker, Peter F., and Maciariello, Joseph A.: *Management:* revised edition, New York: HarperCollins Publishers, 2008; revised edition of: *Management: Tasks, Responsibilities, Practices,* Harper & Row, 1973, pp. 484–488; and Malik, Fredmund: *Managing, Performing, Living: Effective Management for a New Era,* Frankfurt am Main, Germany/New York: Campus Verlag, 2006, pp. 283–299.
2. Drucker, Peter F., and Maciariello, Joseph A.: *Management,* revised edition, New York: HarperCollins Publishers, 2008; revised edition of *Management: Tasks, Responsibilities, Practices,* Harper & Row, 1973, p. 487.

Chapter 45: Make a life plan: What will your most important contribution be?

1. Krames, Jeffrey A.: *Inside Drucker's Brain,* London: Portfolio, 2008, p. 73.
2. Krames, Jeffrey A.: *Inside Drucker's Brain,* London: Portfolio 2008.
3. Beatty, Jack: *The World According to Peter Drucker,* New York: Broadway Books, 1998.
4. Drucker, Peter F., and Maciariello, Joseph A.: *Management:* revised edition, New York: HarperCollins Publishers, 2008 p. v.

Chapter 46: Be demanding of yourself and strive for perfection

1. Drucker, Peter F., and Nakauchi, Isao: *Drucker on Asia: A Dialogue between Peter Drucker and Isao Nakauchi,* reprint edition (Diamond Inc., Tokyo 1995), Oxford: Butterworth-Heinemann, 1997, p. 103.
2. Ibid., p. 103–104.

Chapter 47: Find meaning; then use it!

1. For further details, see Frankl, Victor: *Der Mensch vor der Frage nach dem Sinn,* 16th edition, Munich, Germany/Zurich, Switzerland: Piper Verlag, 2003, p. 47; translated by Frank Arnold.
2. Ibid.
3. Frankl, Viktor E.: *Man's Search for Meaning,* 6th edition (first published in 1946 as *From Death-Camp to Existentialism: A Psychiatrist's Path to a New Therapy*), Boston: Beacon Press, 2006, p. 104.

Chapter 48: Harness the power of discipline

1. Schneider, Wolf: *Die Sieger: Wodurch Genies, Phantasten und Verbrecher berühmt geworden sind,* 3rd edition, Zurich, Switzerland/Munich, Germany: Piper Verlag, 2001, p. 168; translated by Frank Arnold.

2. Ibid., p. 169.
3. Ibid., p. 175.

Chapter 49: Motivate yourself
1. Frankfurter Allgemeine Zeitung, online edition, Hahn, Jörg: "Erfrischung ersehnt," July 6, 2009.
2. Ibid.

Chapter 50: Derive enjoyment from your profession
1. Schneider, Wolf: *Die Sieger: Wodurch Genies, Phantasten und Verbrecher berühmt geworden sind,* 3rd edition, Zurich, Switzerland/Munich, Germany: Piper Verlag, 2001, p. 334; translated by Frank Arnold.
2. Various authors: "Leonard Bernstein," in: *Die Großen der Moderne: Menschen, die unsere Welt prägten und veränderten,* approved special edition, Cologne, Germany: Serges Verlag, 2001, p. 52; translated by Frank Arnold.

Chapter 51: Think constructively
1. Frankfurter Allgemeine Zeitung: "Einzelkämpfer am Limit," April 4–5, 2009; translated by Frank Arnold.
2. FlyNiki corporate information, survey by Reise & Preise, consulted on February 12, 2011 http://www.flyniki.com/niki/about_us.php?LANG=eng&name=aboutus.
3. Die Zeit, online edition: "Es ist ein Glück, dass ich schon so viel Unglück erlebt habe," June 9, 2009; translated by Frank Arnold.

Chapter 52: Act responsibly
1. Malik, Fredmund: *Managing, Performing, Living: Effective Management for a New Era,* Frankfurt am Main/New York: Campus Verlag, 2006, p. 59.

Chapter 53: Foster creativity all life long
1. Siegert, Werner: "Alte Fahrensmänner dringend gesucht," in: M.o.M., volume 2, St. Gallen, Switzerland, 2005, p. 33; translated by Frank Arnold.

Chapter 56: Commit yourself to more than just your own well-being
1. Yunus, Muhammad, with Weber, Karl: *Creating a World without Poverty: Social Business and the Future of Capitalism,* New York: Public Affairs, 2007, "Poverty Is a Threat to Peace," the Nobel Prize acceptance speech given in Oslo, Norway, on December 10, 2006, pp. 237–248.
2. The Norwegian Nobel Committee: Award Ceremony Speech, December

10, 2006, http://nobelprize.org/nobel_prizes/peace/laureates/2006/presentation-speech.html.

3. Frankfurter Allgemeine Zeitung, online edition, "Muhammad Yunus, Banglade¬schs bekanntester Bürger," October 13, 2006; translated by Frank Arnold.

4. Der Spiegel, online edition, "Business statt Almosen," October 13, 2006; translated by Frank Arnold.

5. Frankfurter Allgemeine Zeitung, online edition, "Muhammad Yunus, Bangladeschs bekanntester Bürger," October 13, 2006; translated by Frank Arnold.

6. Der Spiegel, online edition, "Business statt Almosen," October 13, 2006; translated by Frank Arnold.

7. See http://www.grameen.com, About us, At a glance; http://www.grameen.com/index.php?option=com_content&task=view&id=26&Itemid=175, July 20, 2010.

8. Drucker, Peter F.: *Managing the Non-Profit Organization: Principles and Practices,* New York: HarperCollins Publishers. 1990, p. 20.

9. Ibid., p. 27.

INDEX

ABOUT THE AUTHOR

Frank Arnold is a leading consultant, best-selling author, and keynote speaker on management issues. His award-winning books are published worldwide. He continues to write and speak about the practice of effective management. Join him at www.frankarnold.com.

Frank Arnold is CEO of ARNOLD Management, a management consultancy specializing in activating corporate intelligence. Today he is one of the most sought-after international experts on managing change: see www.arnoldmanagement.com.

He is also a columnist, blogger, and regular contributor to leading German-language business magazines and newspapers.

Born in 1973, Frank Arnold earned a Ph.D. in economics and is an associate lecturer at the Department of Strategy, Organization, and Leadership at the European Business School (EBS). He has lived and worked in the United States, France, Spain, and China.